FRANCIS PATRICK KENRICK'S
OPINION ON SLAVERY

This dissertation was conducted under the direction of Very Reverend Francis J. Connell, C.SS.R., as major professor, and was approved by Reverend Dr. Joseph B. Collins, S.S., and Reverend Alfred C. Rush, C.SS.R., as Readers.

THE CATHOLIC UNIVERSITY OF AMERICA
STUDIES IN SACRED THEOLOGY
(Second Series)
No. 85

FRANCIS PATRICK KENRICK'S OPINION ON SLAVERY

A DISSERTATION

*Submitted to the Faculty of the School of Sacred Theology
of the Catholic University of America in Partial
Fulfillment of the Requirements for the Degree
of Sacred Theology*

by the

REVEREND JOSEPH D. BROKHAGE, S.T.L.

THE CATHOLIC UNIVERSITY OF AMERICA PRESS
WASHINGTON, D. C.
1955

NIHIL OBSTAT:
  FRANCIS J. CONNELL, C.SS.R.
    Censor Deputatus

IMPRIMATUR:
  ✠ PAUL C. SCHULTE, D.D.
    Archbishop of Indianapolis

March 7, 1955

TABLE OF CONTENTS

CHAPTER VI
KENRICK'S TEACHING CONCERNING THE OBLIGA-
TIONS OF SLAVES TOWARD THEIR MASTERS

CHAPTER VII
SUMMARY AND CONCLUSIONS

BIBLIOGRAPHY

PREFACE

The completion of this work makes the author humbly grateful to many benefactors for their various kindnesses and favors that have combined to make it possible for him to complete the study.

The first acknowledgment in the point of time must be extended to His Excellency, the Most Reverend Joseph E. Ritter, Archbishop of St. Louis, who directed the author to the North American College in Rome for what was to be the remote preparation for this work. He it was, also, who directed the author to the Catholic University of America for graduate study connected with this undertaking. The author acknowledges with gratitude the patient encouragement of His Excellency, the Most Reverend Paul C. Schulte, Archbishop of Indianapolis, who, having the understanding of the problems of scholarship, allowed the added time required for the completion of the study. Adequate thanks can be expressed only with greatest difficulty to the Very Reverend Francis J. Connell, C.SS.R., whose direction and constant encouragement have been a prominent factor in the completion of the study. Grateful acknowledgment is made to the readers, the Reverend Joseph Collins, S.S., and the Reverend Alfred Rush, C.SS.R., for their trouble and for the correction they have offered to the author in finishing the manuscript. The historical data for this study have originated after many hours at the Mooreland Room of Howard University's Library and after uncounted kindnesses and assistance from the scholarly staff there. The competent staff of the law library of the Library of Congress was most helpful in assisting the author to find the old codes of laws of the various states. The library staff of the Catholic University of America has been competently helpful in all the demands that have been made on it for books and technical helps. Dr. Joseph Kempf of the faculty of St. Mary-of-the-Woods has rendered invaluable help to the author in preparing the work for printing. To many other friends the author owes a debt of thanks for the many kindnesses shown him.

CHAPTER I

THE STUDY AND THE LITERATURE

During the past several years much interest has been shown in the race question. One interested in understanding the injustices of race prejudice naturally turns back to the situation that caused it—slavery. The moral theologian is interested in viewing the facts of that early situation and evaluating the solutions given by the theologians of that day.

I. THE STUDY

Scope of the Study. This dissertation deals with the morality of slavery existing in the United States prior to the passing of the fourteenth amendment. The work will be based on the theological opinions expressed by the American theologian Francis Patrick Kenrick.[1] In this work an attempt will be made to summarize the background of the slavery issue, then to give Kenrick's definition of slavery as well as his opinions of the moral obligations that slavery imposed upon the master. Kenrick's opinion will be compared with that of other reputable theologians and then with the laws and customs prevalent in the United States in the middle of the nineteenth century. No attempt will be made to quote the laws of all the states on each point. Some samples will merely be given to show the contrast that existed between Kenrick's teaching and the laws and customs prevailing. Then Kenrick's opinion regarding the morality of slavery in general and his opinion of the morality of domestic slavery will be given and discussed. Two final chapters will conclude the work. In the one, Kenrick's teaching concerning the slave and religious practices will be

[1] Francis Patrick Kenrick, *Theologia moralis*, (2 vols. Mechlin: H. Dessain, 1860-1861).

1

given, and in the other the obligations that slaves have toward their masters will be indicated.

Reason for choosing Kenrick. Kenrick's work has been chosen as the basis for this study because he was a capable theologian, who attempted to solve American problems.[2] That he was quite a thorough student is evidenced by his many works not only in the field of moral theology but in dogmatic theology, liturgy, apologetics and Sacred Scripture as well.

Moreover, his various places of residence fitted him well for the task of discussing slavery. Kenrick was born in Dublin on December 3, 1797,[3] the son of Thomas Kenrick. He received his early education in his native land and later studied theology at the Collegio Urbano de Propaganda Fide in Rome, where he was ordained in 1821. Shortly after his ordination he came to this country to labor in the diocese of Bardstown in Kentucky. Besides caring for souls as pastor of a small parish in this mission land, he also taught Greek and history at St. Joseph's College and theology in the Seminary of St. Thomas, founded by Bishop Flaget. He accompanied Bishop Flaget to the provincial Council of Baltimore in 1828, where he acted as theologian. On June 6, 1831 he was consecrated Bishop of Arath *in partibus* and was sent by the Holy See to Philadelphia as coadjutor to the bishop and administrator of the diocese. He continued in this difficult work of ruling the diocese amidst its problems of trusteeism and nativist uprising until he was named Archbishop of Baltimore by the Holy See in 1851. This post he held until his death on July 8, 1863.

[2] Francis J. Connell, "The Theological School in America," *Essays on Catholic Education in the United States*, Roy J. Deferrari, editor. (Washington, D.C.: The Catholic University of America Press, 1942), pp. 221 f.

[3] Some writers give 1796 as the year of his birth. cf. Hugh Nolan, *The Most Reverend Francis Patrick Kenrick Third Bishop of Philadelphia 1830-1851* (Washington, D.C.: The Catholic University of America Press, 1948), p. 1.

Thus having lived in the South—in Kentucky as a young priest and later in Baltimore as archbishop—and in the North—as bishop of Philadelphia—he was eminently qualified to understand both sides of the problem of slavery.

Importance of the study. It is difficult for human beings to dissociate themselves from the pressure of current prejudices in solving a problem. It is well for the moral theologian to look at the solutions to problems given in the past to ascertain how correct and objective the solutions were. This work attempts to do just that. Evidently the problem of slavery was uppermost in the mind of Kenrick for it appears very frequently through his two volumes. All the references to slavery have been taken from the various parts and will be presented and discussed in a systematic way.

II. LITERATURE

Literature on Catholic attitudes toward slavery. Already a study has been made of the Catholic social thought in the United States in which slavery is considered.[4] This study stops before the period when the slavery issue became quite violent because of the movements for abolition.

Another dissertation has been written precisely on the subject of the Catholic viewpoint of slavery.[5] However, this study while demonstrating much research, is based principally on writings in the press and public pronouncements of some of the leaders of the Church, and as a result fails to give the more thorough theological view. It fails to point out that when Catholic theologians teach that slavery is not contrary to the natural law they speak of a completely different type of slavery than was practiced in the United States. Hence, investigation indicates that

[4] Celestine Joseph Nuesse, *The Social Thought of American Catholics 1634-1829* (Washington, D.C.: The Catholic University of America Press, 1945).

[5] Madeline Hooke Rice, *American Catholic Opinion in the Slavery Controversy,* (New York: Columbia University Press, 1944).

nothing has been done in the way of studying the theological opinion of domestic slavery itself and the solutions given to the various cases that arose in connection with this complicated problem. That is the purpose of this dissertation.

Literature used. The literature on slavery is enormous. In discussing the theological matters, Kenrick's views will be compared with some of the reputable theologians who considered slavery in their works. In presenting the laws, legal sources were used when they were available. In discussing the customs, an attempt was made to use works of trustworthy historians. At times, works written by persons devoted to abolition were of necessity used.

CHAPTER II

THE BACKGROUND OF SLAVERY AND ITS CONTROVERSY

A discussion of slavery in the United States must necessarily include a resume of its background. This discussion will be helpful and interesting insofar as it will show us how the Negroes got to this country and it will be necessary in the discussion of the morality of the titles by which they were held. In this chapter the slave trade will be discussed, then briefly the attitude of other nations toward slavery. The greater part of the chapter will be devoted to the attitude toward slavery in the United States.

I. THE SLAVE TRADE

The scene in Africa. A discussion of the background of slavery must necessarily begin with the scene in Africa. While it seems that there was much superstition in Africa, at the time when the slave trade flourished and much cruelty was practiced, since the natives placed little value on human life,[1] there still was considerable order, civiliza-

---

[1] Sir Thomas F. Buxton, *The Slave-Trade and Remedy* (London: John Murray, 1840), pp. 226-267; W. D. Weatherford, *The Negro from Africa to America* (New York: George H. Doran Co., 1924), chap. "The African Background of the Negro" and "Religious and Social Life in Africa"—C. G. Woodson, *JNH*, 9 (1924), p. 574 says that these chapters contain many interesting facts on geography, ethnology, and enthnography, but that the author draws some unwarranted conclusions from them; Carter G. Woodson, *The African Background Outlined* (Washington, D.C.: Association for the Study of Negro Life and History, 1936); Leo Frobenius, *Im Schatten des Kongostaates* (Berlin: G. Reiner, 1907); *Der Schwarze Dekameron* (Berlin: Deutches Verlaghaus, 1910); *Kulturgeschichte Afrikas* (Zurich): Phaedonverlag, 1933).

5

tion and government found there.[2] English seamen in the sixteenth century when visiting the west coast of Africa found

> ... a quiet, peaceable and contented people, basking in the sunshine of harmless idleness and receiving strangers with the unsuspecting trustfulness, which is observed in the birds and animals of new countries when for the first time they come in contact with a man.—The Europeans first converted the Negro into a savage, and then made use of his brutality as an excuse for plunging him into slavery.[3]

True, slavery was quite general among these people themselves. In fact it is said that there were three times as many slaves as free men.[4] Natives became slaves by capture, debt, malfeasance or inheritance of status.[5]

Molina,[6] in his treatment on justice, claimed to have made a thorough study of the situation in Africa and found that persons were reduced to slavery for very slight reasons. A typical incident of this is the following: Two leaders argue. The dispute is taken to the king, and whoever is judged wrong is either killed or enslaved together with all the men who accompany him, and at times with their whole families.[7] He listed several other examples to show how the natives were enslaved for crimes both great and small; at times for only the suspicion of a fault, a person and all his relatives were enslaved. In one case cited, the King of Angola held peacocks in high regard,

---

[2] L. P. Jackson, "The Elizabeth Seamen and the African Slave-Trade," *JNH*, 9 (1924), 2 ff.

[3] *Ibid.*, 10 f.

[4] William O. Blake, *The History of Slavery and the Slave-Trade* (Columbus, Ohio: H. Miller, 1860), p. 94.

[5] Ulrich B. Phillips, *American Negro Slavery* (New York: D. Appleton & Co., 1918) p. 6; for environmental causes that let to slavery cf. Jerome Dowd, "Slavery and the African Slave Trade," *JNH*, 2 (1917), pp. 1-5.

[6] Ludovicus Molina, *De justitia et jure*, (6 vols. Fratres de Tournes: Coloniae Allogrogum, 1759), tr. II, disp. 34.

[7] Paul Allard, "Esclavage," *DAFC*, 1 (1911) pp. 1511-17.

and made a law that anyone who plucked a feather from one of these birds would be killed or enslaved together with his entire family.[8]

In another region if a man died leaving debts, all his sons were enslaved, even if the debts were very small. In times of peace one person would send the slaves of another to a place where plots were laid to capture them. Fathers would sell their wives and children because of a little fault. At times they would sell them for a trinket such as a little bell or mirror. There were cases where the human flesh-eaters, who sold slaves in the public market would offer them for a certain price, but if the price asked were not given, the cannibals prepared to slaughter and eat the slaves rather than sell them at a lower price. Molina says that he could relate many other similar incidents to show that slavery was full of cruelty and injustice.[9]

In concluding this topic, Molina noted that the Portuguese had no scruples about the justice of the title of slavery when they bought a slave. He censured the bishops and the clergy for seemingly not being worried about these sales.[10]

When white men first went to Africa to procure slaves, they would generally establish themselves in a base on an island, and go ashore to capture the inhabitants by burning and destroying their towns.[11] Later the natives themselves became eager traders, and would utilize raids, wars and robberies to obtain slaves.[12] The seamen then built "factories" on the coast where they would keep the merchandize used in the trades, and the slaves, once they had contracted for them. The native traders would go into the interior

[8] Molina, *loc. cit.*
[9] *Ibid.*
[10] *Ibid.*
[11] Jackson, *JNH*, 9 (1924), 10; cf. T. D. Jervey *The Slave-Trade* (Columbia, S.C.: The State Co., 1925).
[12] Jackson, *loc. cit.* Ulrich B. Phillips, *American Negro Slavery* (New York: D. Appleton & Co. 1918), p. 6.

and procure the slaves in various ways.[13] At times they bought them from masters, leaders, or kings, who would sell their superfluous slaves. A father would sell a son, or a son his old father, or the creditor would sell the debtor. Starving families would surrender themselves to slavery, particularly when there was great scarcity of food. Again, a savage would sell a boy or girl kidnapped for that purpose.[14] In some towns persons guilty of some infraction were brought before a tribunal, which would judge them guilty and sell them.[15] But the most frequent source was war. A petty chief or king would make an expedition into the territory of another leader, taking prisoners as he went. If the natives took a stand, a battle ensued, the invader usually being victorious. He would kill as many as he thought necessary, and captives by the thousands would be taken to be sold. In 1794, the King of the southern Foulaks, a powerful tribe in Nigritia, was known to have an army of 16,000 employed in slave-hunting expeditions. The slaves procured made the largest item in his revenue.[16] These raids were continued until towns by the hundreds were swept from the earth, and great zones lay void of their teeming populations.[17]

Buxton says that on the authority of published documents of the English Parliament and from the works of travellers in Africa, there is evidence to the fact that the only cause of wars in Africa was to procure slaves for the market.[18]

[13] Blake, *op. cit.*, p. 99; Phillips, *American Negro Slavery*, p. 12; Ulrich B. Phillips, *Life and Labor in the Old South* (Boston: Little, Brown & Co., reprint, 1941), p. 160.

[14] Blake, *op. cit.*, pp. 102-105; Phillips, *American Negro Slavery*, p. 45, notes that these kidnappings became so frequent that hardly a man or woman, much less a child, was safe outside the village.

[15] Jackson, *JNH*, 9 (1924), 10.

[16] Blake, *op. cit.*, p. 102; Jerome Dowd "Slavery and the African Slave-Trade" *JNH*, 2, (1917), 11; William Paley, *Principles of Moral and Political Philosophy* (London: F. Davis, 5th ed., 1788), 1: 237.

[17] Phillips, *American Negro Slavery*, p. 45.

[18] Buxton, *op. cit.*, p. 74.

In most of these cases the Negroes strongly resisted capture,[19] making the mortality rate very high.[20] Once the native agents procured the slaves, they were placed in caravans and brought to the "factories."[21] Here the mortality rate was also quite high.[22]

It is evident that the trade was quite extensive. Buxton calculates that yearly the Christian slave-trade took 150,000 natives, and the Mohammedan trade 50,000.[23] Of these, it is estimated that three-fourths were slaves, not from the existing slave-status of Africa, but rather because they were taken by wars, kidnapping and the like.[24]

The white man begins the trade. This slave trade referred to began in Europe in the fifteenth century. For after having become extinct in Europe through the influence of the Church, it began again in the fifteenth century when some Moors from Africa offered Negroes in exchange for some Moors whom the Portuguese held as prisoners of war. From this incident the Portuguese conceived the idea to go to Africa themselves to acquire slaves. Thus, on August 8, 1444, Captain Lanzarate landed at Lagan, in the kingdom of Algrave, with two hundred and thirty-five slaves whom he sold. This commerce continued so that in the course of the year 1539 the sale in Lisbon amounted to 12,000 heads. The Spanish soon followed the example of their neighbor and Seville became a slave-selling center. Then England followed Spain into the slave trade.[25]

Once the white man had come to the New World, there was a tendency to enslave the native Indians. The Spanish

---

[19] Jackson, *JNH*, 9 (1924), 12.

[20] Buxton, *op. cit.*, pp. 97-113.

[21] Dowd, *JNH*, 2 (1917), 7-16.

[22] Buxton, *op. cit.*, pp. 113-122.

[23] *Ibid.*, pp. 15-72.

[24] Jackson, *JNH*, 9 (1924), 11; for cruelties in the "middle passage," cf. Blake, *op. cit.*, pp. 126-141 and Buxton, *op. cit.*, pp. 122-174.

[25] Augustin Cochin, *The Results of Slavery*, Trans. Mary L. Booth (Boston: Wise & Co., 1863), p. 348; Jackson *JNH*, 9 (1924), 2 ff; Winfield H. Collins, *The Domestic Slave Trade of the Southern States.* (New York: Broadway Pub. Co., 1904), p. 2 f.

Crown at the insistence of the missionaries attempted to protect the natives. Before long, in the second decade of the sixteenth century, the King of Spain granted permission to ship some Negroes as slaves to the American colonies. As a result of this, there followed the *asiento* system under which the colonies received slaves for several centuries.[26]

In like manner in Brazil, the Portuguese needed workers. The colonists argued that there was an economic need, and that it was right and fitting that the Indians work in return for the blessings of the Faith. The native population declined. Portugal had a supply of Negroes in its colony in Africa, and hence began to ship them to the colonies in America.[27]

The missionaries who accompanied the conquistadores took an active part in attempting to protect the Indians.[28]

The Roman Pontiffs from the very beginning of this upsurge condemned the slave trade and attempted to protect the natives who were being enslaved.[29]

Slave trade in the American Colonies. In like manner when the Englishmen came to the great spaces of the new world, they employed every source of labor available. At first they captured Indians in sporadic wars, but had to transfer them to places beyond the reach of their kinsmen.

[26] Sir Arthur Helps, *Spanish Conquest of America* (4 Vols. London: John W. Parker & Son, 1855), 2: 5 ff.; Phillips *American Negro Slavery*, pp. 1-13; Rice, *American Catholic Opinion in the Slave Controversy*, pp. 17-19; Sir Arthur Helps, *The Conquest of the New World and their Bondsmen* (2 vols. London: W. Pickering, 1848-1852)—treats of the events leading to Negro slavery in the West Indies and America.

[27] Madeleine Hooke Rice, *American Catholic Opinion in the Slavery Controversy* (New York: Columbia University Press, 1944), pp. 18-19.

[28] Helps, *op. cit.*, 1: 247 ff; 4: 370. This author treats of the work of Las Casas throughout his 4 Vol. work. Jackson, "The Elizabethan Seamen and the African Slave Trade," *JNH*, 9 (1924), 2 f.

[29] Leo XIII, "In Plurimis," *Acta Leonis*, 8: 185-187.

It was soon found that it was much safer to use Negroes who were far removed from their kinsmen.[30]

The first Negroes reached our shores in 1619 when twenty Negroes were transported.[31] Only a few more were imported in the next thirty years, due to the reluctance of the planters to receive them.[32]

Some of the early laws enacted by the colonies completely prohibited life-long slavery,[33] but so far as practice was concerned, these enactments were dead letters, for slaves were imported, sold, and their offspring born in slavery.[34] Slavery existed by custom long before any laws were enacted to uphold it. Slaves were brought here as slaves and held as such.[35] Gradually it made its way into the thirteen colonies and received sanction by legislation.[36]

The first American-built slave ship of which there are

[30] Phillips, *Life and Labor in the Old South*, p. 160.

[31] Joseph Butsch, S.S.J., "Negro Catholics in the United States," *CHR*, 3 (1917), 34-35; Phillips, *Life and Labor in the Old South*, p. 25; *The Negro in Virginia*, compiled by workers of the Writer's program of the Works Project Administration in the State of Virginia (New York: Hastings House, 1940), p. 1.

[32] *The Negro in Virginia*, p. 10; Winfield Hazlitt Collins, *The Domestic Slave Trade of the Southern States*, (New York: Broadway Publishing Co., 1904), p. 4.

[33] Law adopted by the General Court of Mass., 1641, and Gen. Court of Rhode Island, 1652; cf. *Report of the Committee on Slavery to the Convention of the Congregationalist Ministers of Mass.*, presented May 30, 1849 (Boston: T. R. Marvin, 1849), p. 57; Va. under Patrick Henry in 1778 forbade importation of slaves, cf. *The Negro in Virginia*, p. 25; Mass., on March 26, 1788 passed a law to prevent slave-trade and for granting relief to the families of such unhappy families, as may be kidnapped. cf. Thomas Gray, *Sermon Delivered in Boston before the African Society* (Boston: Parmenter and Norton, 1818), pp. 39 f.

[34] Albert Bushnell Hart, *Slavery and Abolition* (New York and London: Harper & Bros., 1906), p. 51.

[35] William Goodell, *Our National Charters* (New York: American Aboltion Society, 1857), pp. 18 ff.

[36] John W. Cromwell, *The Negro in American History* (Washington, D.C.: the American Negro Academ., 1914), pp. 3-5; dates and enactments are here given.

definite records, was the "Desire" which was built at
Marblehead in 1636.[37] The trade advanced and by 1671,
Governor Berkeley of Virginia reported some two thousand
Negro slaves, and six thousand white servants in a total of
forty thousand souls. He commented that only about two
or three ships of Negroes had come in during the past
seven years.[38] The slave trade increased tremendously
after 1688, to such an extent in fact, that, in the eight
months preceding July 12, 1753, there were five hundred
and eleven slaves imported into South Carolina alone, and
one thousand four hundred and eighty-two into Georgia.[39]

By the middle of the eighteenth century, shipyards of
Massachusetts and Rhode Island turned out special vessels
for slaving. The holds were partitioned into racks, about
2 x 6, fitted with leg-irons and bars.[40]

By 1770, Rhode Island had one hundred and fifty vessels
in the trade.[41] Slaves were packed in like fish, so that
hundreds could be carried on each voyage. In the wet or
blowing weather the hatches had to be fastened down; the
tortured blacks would faint or die in droves. To one ob-
server, a slave-deck was "so covered with blood and mucous
that it resembled a slaughter house." The stench of a slave
ship could be perceived for miles. The greater part of the
"middle passage" was across the torrid zone, and the between deck space of the vessels was so extremely hot as to
be bearable to crew members for a short time only. Lack
of food and water also led to sickness and to great loss
of life.[42]

A contradiction between the colonial custom and the Eng-

[37] John Randolf Spears, *The American Slave Trade* (New York
C. Scribner's Sons, 1900), p. 7; *The Negro in Virginia*, p. 7.

[38] Phillips, *Life and Labor in the Old South*, p. 25.

[39] Henry Carey, *The Slave-Trade Domestic and Foreign* (Philadelphia: A. Hart, 1853), p. 15.

[40] *The Negro in Virginia*, p. 7.

[41] Spears, *op. cit.*, p. 20.

[42] Spears, *op. cit.*, *passim*; *The Negro in Virginia*, p. 7; Cochin,
op. cit., p. 349.

lish law was brought out in 1772 by the celebrated case of James Sommerset, a Negro brought from Boston by his master to England. When his master attempted to bring him back, he sued for a writ of habeas corpus, which Lord Mansfield allowed on the ground that "the state of slavery is of such a nature that it is incapable of being introduced on any reasons, moral or political. It is so odious that nothing can be suffered to support it but positive law."[43]

In 1790 the Quakers sent a memorial to Congress, asking for action against slave-trade. The resolution passed was that: (1) importation of slaves could not cease by virtue of the Constitution until 1808; (2) that Congress has no power to emancipate or legislate concerning domestic slavery, this belonging to the individual States; (3) that Congress does have the power to restrict citizens of this country from carrying on trade to supply foreigners, and to provide for humane treatment on the voyage of slaves to the States which wish to receive them; (4) that Congress does have the authority to prohibit foreigners from fitting out vessels in any of the ports of the United States for transporting persons from Africa to any foreign port. A penalty was to be placed on citizens engaging in slave-trade to foreign markets.[44] The many violations of this act led to another, of May 10, 1801, which amplified the former act and made the penalties a little more stringent.[45]

In 1803 a ship carrying some free Negroes from Guadeloupe came to this country. The citizens were apprehensive about their own safety. A law was passed providing for forfeiture of a ship bringing persons to a State which pro-

---

[43] John Codman Hurd, *The Law of Freedom and Bondage in the United States*, (2 Vols.; Boston: Little, Brown & Co., 1858), 1: 189-191.

[44] Bassett, *op. cit.*, p. 188; Rowland Calhoun McConnell, "The Reopening of the Slave-Trade in the United States of America, 1850-1860" (unpublished Master's thesis, Howard University, Washington, D.C., 1933), p. 5.

[45] McConnell, *op. cit.*, p. 6.

hibited their entrance.[46] As this year 1808 approached, Jefferson recommended that Congress take action to stop the slave-trade. As a result the law of March 2, 1807 was passed which put an end to the importation of slaves into the United States after January 1, 1808, and placed penalties of fines and imprisonment for the offenders.[47]

Nevertheless, after the suppression of the slave-trade in 1808, the needs of the South continued to be met by vessels loaded with human cargo which passed along the coasts and into the Mississippi and its tributaries. It seems that the Federal Government was rather apathetic toward enforcing the law.[48] These violations let to the supplementary acts of 1818, 1819 and 1820.[49] A great help toward eliminating this illegal traffic was given by the signing of the treaty of Washington in 1842 between the United States and England. The eighth article of this treaty provided for the proposed mutual right of search; and of the maintenance of a squadron off the coast of Africa, to enforce separately and respectively the laws, rights, and obligations of the two countries for the suppression of the slave-trade.[50]

Still, despite all these provisions, between 1850 and 1854, there was agitation to re-open the slave-trade in order to supply the demand for slaves in the South. One proposal was to abolish all the laws prohibiting the slave-trade, but

[46] Edward Channing, *The Jeffersonian System*, Vol. 12 of The American Nation: A History. (New York and London: Harper and Bros., 1906), p. 102; McConnell, *op. cit.*, p. 5.

[47] "Act to Prohibit the Importation of Slaves," Henry Steele Commanger, (ed.) *Documents of American History* (New York: F. S. Crofts Co., 3rd ed., 1943), pp. 197-198; Channing, *The Jeffersonian System*, pp. 105-110; McConnell, *op. cit.*, pp. 7-8.

[48] William Edward Burghardt DuBois, *The Suppression of the African Slave-Trade, 1638-1870* (New York: Longmans, Green & Co., 1896), pp. 108-130; Collins, *The Domestic Slave-Trade of the Southern States*, pp. 12-16.

[49] McConnell, *op. cit.*, p. 8.

[50] "The Webster-Ashburton Treaty," August 9, 1842, Art. VIII, Commanger, *Documents of American History*, p. 300; cf. McConnell, *op. cit.*, p. 8; DuBois, *op. cit.*, pp. 131-158.

it failed. The other alternative was to make the methods of smuggling more effective. This was done.[51]

On the other hand, however, by the time Kenrick wrote his text some northern States had already freed their slaves and others were in the process of doing so. These gradual emancipations effected by the various States began with Pennsylvania and Massachusetts in 1780 and continued little by little until in 1861 there were eighteen free States out of a total of thirty-three.[52]

II. Attitudes Towards Slavery Outside the United States

More and more the Catholics in Europe began to realize that the laws enacted for the regulating of slavery were impractical and were not being observed. They felt that radical action was needed. Daniel O'Connell was sponsoring emancipation in various places, and even addressed a message to the members of his race in this country concerning the abolition of slavery.[53] In France, while Montalembert and Cochin were petitioning for freedom in the colonies,[54] Bishop Felix R. P. Doupanloup of Orleans issued a pastoral in which he condemned slavery and its evils, asking prayers for the Negroes in the United States.[55]

In England, the British and Foreign Anti-Slavery Society was established in April, 1839. The purpose of this society was the universal extinction of slavery and the slave-trade, the protection of the rights and interests of the enfranchised populations of the British possessions, and all persons cap-

[51] McConnell, *op. cit.*, 11 ff.

[52] George M. Stroud, *A Sketch of Laws Relating to Slavery in the Several States of the United States of America* (Phila.: Kimbler and Sharpless, 1827), pp. 129-137; John Spencer Bassett, *The Federalist System.* American Nation Series, 11 (New York: Harper and Sons, 1905), pp. 184 ff; Cochin, *op. cit.*, pp. 10-11.

[53] Daniel O'Connell, *Letter to the Irish Repeal Society of Cincinnati, Oct. 11, 1843* (New York, no date).

[54] Cf. Cochin, *The Results of Slavery.*

[55] *RACHS*, 25 (1914), 18-29.

tured as slaves. The members strove to circulate information about the atrocities of slavery and the slave-trade, and about the good results of emancipation. They recommended the use of free-grown produce in the place of slave-grown. They tried to get the principle recognized, that any person, regardless of color, entering the British Isles would be free. They desired to show the slaveholders that slavery was abhorrent and contrary to Christianity.[56] Likewise, it is well to remember that all the while various countries were gradually taking action in the form of treaties and agreements to stop the inhuman traffic.[57] These culminated in the treaty between England and the United States.[58] England, by means of twenty-three treaties in less than thirty years had succeeded in causing nearly all nations to consider the injustice of the slave-trade.[59]

As a sequel to abolition of the slave-trade came abolition of slavery itself, in the various countries and colonies.[60]

Amidst the world-wide agitation for the abolition of slavery and the slave-trade, the Vicar of Christ, Gregory XVI, lifted his voice to condemn severely the enslaving of men and shipping them far from their homes like cattle.

[56] The British and Foreign Anti-Slavery Society, *Internal Slave-Trade in the United States of America*, (London: Thomas Ward, & Co., 1841), pp. 1 f.

[57] Du Bois, *op. cit.*, pp. 131-158.

[58] Webster-Ashburton Treaty, Art. VIII.

[59] Cochin, *op. cit.*, p. 238.

[60] DuBois, *op. cit.*, p. 144; Cromwell, *The Negro in American History*, p. 18; *The Report to the Congregational Ministers*, pp. 65-67; Cochin, op. cit., pp. 236 f; cf. LaRoy Suderland, *Anti-Slavery Manual* (New York: Peercy & Read, 2nd ed., 1837), pp. 79-82; Henry Charles Carey, *The Slave-Trade Domestic and Foreign* (Philadelphia: A. Hart, 1853), pp. 21-35; William I. Mathieson, *British Slavery and Its Abolition, 1823-1838* (London and New York: Longmans, Green & Co., 1926); William I. Mathieson, *British Slave Emancipation 1838-1849* (London and New Yrok: Longsman, Green & Co., 1932); Eduardo Posada, *La esclavitud en Columbia* (Bogota: Imprenta Nacional, 1933); Edward Derbyshire Seeber, *Anti-Slavery Opinion in France during the Second Half of the Eighteenth Century* (Baltimore: Johns Hopkins Press, 1937).

The Constitution which is entitled "In Supremo Apostola-tus Fastigio" was issued on December 3, 1839.[61] Later Pope Pius IX conferred knighthood on M. Augustin Cochin expressly for his work "L'abolition de l'esclavage."[62]

In the Spanish and Portuguese colonies, legislation gave governmental sanctions to the requirements of the Church for religious instructions of slaves, privileges such as no work on Sundays and Holydays, and at least a minimum of decent food and clothing.[63] Manumissions were easier and more frequent in the Catholic countries. In the Spanish colonies the slave had the right of self purchase at a set price.[64] In Brazil, freedom might be given as a privilege for many reasons, such as to an infant at Baptism, to a faithful nurse, to the mother of a large family and the like.[65]

III. THE SLAVERY CONTROVERSY IN THE UNITED STATES

Colonization. The idea of colonization of the slave arose at a rather early date in American history. At least as early as 1777, Thomas Jefferson proposed to the legislature of Virginia that they incorporate in the revised code a plan for the colonization of the free colored of the United States. He thought this probably could be done in the western lands.[66] Another attempt was made in 1787 by Dr. Thorn-

[61] *Collectanea S. Cong. de Prop. Fide*, 1: pp. 503-505, no. 891.

[62] Orestes Brownson, *Works*, edited by Henry Brownson, 20 Vols. (Detroit: Thornike, Nours, Pub., 1884), 17: 343. This article was written by Brownson in 1862. He said that the Pope "has just conferred a knightship...."

[63] Sir Arthur Help, *Spanish Conquest of America* (4 Vols.: London: J. W. Parker & Sons, 1855-1861), 4: 350 ff; Mary W. Williams, "The Treatment of Negro Slaves in the Brazilian Empire," *JNH*, 25 (1930), 315-336.

[64] Rice, *American Catholic Opinion in the Slavery Controversey*, p. 23.

[65] Mary W. Williams, "Modern Slavery," *Ency. of Soc. Sciences*, 14: 82 f; Mary W. William, *art. cit. JNH*, 25 (1930), 315-336.

[66] Matthew Carey, *Letters on the Colonization Society and its Probable Results Addressed to the Honorable C. F. Mercer*, M. H. R.

ton of Washington who formed a project to establish a
colony on the west coast of Africa. Sufficient numbers
agreed to go, but the project failed because of lack of
funds.[67]

In the South, it was felt that if the time came when two
distinct races, one black and the other white, were to oc-
cupy the same territory and were numerically nearly equal,
a war of extermination would be inevitable. It further was
reasoned, especially in the border States, early in the nineteenth century, that (1) abolition of slavery, if practicable
with the safety of the whites and the welfare of the blacks,
was desirable; (2) that any scheme of immediate and
unconditional emancipation was impracticable; (3) that
there was a tendency among newly emancipated slaves to
incite the other slaves to revolt; (4) that emancipated
Negroes, as a class, were not benefited by emancipation, but
rather passed to a worse condition. In fact up until 1830
the opinion prevailed in all the States, except Georgia and
South Carolina, that for the sake of the free and un-
hampered development of his possibilities, and for the purpose of stimulating more frequent emancipation, the free
Negro must be sent to a home outside the limits of the
United States.[68]

Carey[69] says that actual organization was begun when
the Rev. Robert Finley of New Jersey wrote a letter on
February 14, 1815, depicting the wretched condition of free
Negroes and urging that they be colonized in Africa. Finley
met in Washington on December 16, 1816, with many men
of prominence, such as Bushrod Washington, Henry Clay,
John Randolf of Roanoke, Colonel Mercer, Elias B. Caldwell, Francis Scott Key and others.[70] The Society, to be

U. S. (Phila.: stereotyped by L. Johnson, 1832), p. 6.

[67] *Ibid.*, p. 6; Early Lee Fox, *The American Colonization Society,
1817-1840* (Baltimore: Johns Hopkins University Press, 1919), pp.
13-45.

[68] Fox, *op. cit.*, pp. 27-37.

[69] Carey, *Letters to Mercer*, p. 7.

[70] Carey, *Letters to Mercer*, p. 7; Fox, *op. cit.*, p. 46.

known as the American Colonization Society, was finally
organized during the last days of the year 1816, and on
January 1, 1817 the officers were elected. Judge Bushrod
Washington was elected the first president.[71] The Society
continued under the constitution established at this time
until the early part of 1834, when an effort was made to
reorganize it.[72]

The American Colonization Society was a reflection of
the attitude that slavery was a great national problem that
pressed for a solution.[73] It was "essentially a moderate
middle-states movement, counting among its supporters the
moderate men of every part of the Union."[74] It strove to
establish itself on a national and local basis.[75] An official
paper, "The African Repository" was published by the
Society.[76]

From the very beginning, but especially during the
Garrisonian epoch, the American Colonization Society met
opposition from two quarters, that is from New England,
where it was accused of riveting the chains of servitude,
and from South Carolina, where it was blamed for invading
the rights of private property, which were secured by the
Constitution and the laws of the slave-holding States.[77]

The objective of the American Colonization Society was
"To promote and execute a plan for colonization (with their
consent)—of the free People of Color residing in our
Country, in Africa, or such other place. The society hopes

[71] Fox, *op. cit.*, pp. 50 f gives the names of the other officers;
Henry Noble Sherwood, "Formation of the American Colonization
Society," *JNH*, 2 (1917), 209-229.

[72] Fox, *op. cit.*, pp. 113 ff.

[73] Celestine Joseph Nuesse, *The Social Thought of American Catholics*, p. 262.

[74] Fox, *op. cit.*, p. 49.

[75] *Ibid.*, p. 60

[76] *The African Respository*, vols, 1-67, Mar. 1825- Jan. 1892 (Washington, D.C.: American Colonization Society, 1826-1892); cf. American Col. Soc., *Annual Report*, 1st-91st (Washington, 1818-1910).

[77] Fox, *op. cit.*, p. 49.

to effect this plan, in cooperation, with the Federal Government and the individual States."[78]

The society believed that immediate and unconditional emancipation was impractical and undesirable, since (1) the federal government had no constitutional right to effect general emancipation; (2) The State alone having the right to emancipate, would be affected only when the public sentiment would become favorable to emancipation; (3) public opinion was not yet favorable.[79]

Further, it was undesirable, they felt, since (1) 3,000,000 slaves set free at one time would not be able to care for themselves, and would as a result be more wretched than before; (2) free Negroes were not really, free, they would be so only in their native country under sympathetic governors, who would instruct and educate them; (3) there would be great danger of a race war in the South.[80]

The members of the Society recognized slavery as an evil, but an evil that could be remedied only by gradual emancipation, which would be accomplished by (1) cooperation between members of the different sections of the Union; (2) education of the slave holders; and (3) transportation of the emancipated.[81]

Several Catholics of prominence were interested in the work of the society. Among whom Matthew Carey, Luke Tiernan of Baltimore and Charles Carroll of Carrolton were numbered.[82] Bishop England apparently hoped that the hierarchy would take cognizance of the movement and that the Council of 1829 would provide missionaries for the movement.[83]

Kenrick, too, must have favored the work of colonization,

[78] *Ibid.*, p. 47.

[79] *Ibid.*, p. 142.

[80] *Ibid.*, p. 143; Carey; *Letters to Mercer*, pp. 5, 8, 13; Brownson, *Works*, 17: 260.

[81] Fox, *op. cit.*, p. 143.

[82] Nuesse, *op. cit.*, p. 262.

[83] Peter Guilday, *The Life and Times of John England* (2 vols.; New York: The American Press, 1927) 2: 275.

for in his early edition, he said that masters were to be praised if for the sake of religion and humanity, they would manumit their slaves, when there was an opportunity of sending them to the colony of Liberia.[84]

Likewise, between 1818 and 1820 the assemblies of several Protestants groups approved of the work of the society.[85] Among them can be named the Presbyterians, the Episcopalians, the Congregationalists, the Baptists, the Methodists, the Lutherans, and the Dutch Reformed.[86]

Moreover, prior to 1832 several State legislatures in the North and border States apparently approved of the colonization project carried on by the society.[87] And even in the South, where abolition was condemned, the American Colonization Society had a large clientele among the State and local branches of government.[88] Carey names Georgia and Tennessee as well as the border States and Maryland, Virginia, Kentucky, Ohio and Indiana among the states proposing legislation in favor of colonization and the society.[89]

But while the American Colonization Society was quite generally acclaimed by moderate men throughout the country, its work was hindered by difficulties in raising money, by opposition of the Abolitionists of Garrison's school[90] as well as by difficulties suffered in founding the colony.[91]

Although relatively small numbers of freed slaves were colonized, the accomplishments of the Society must not be measured solely by the boat loads of persons that were shipped to Liberia. It had some effect on national unity; it did secure emancipation for thousands of slaves; it

[84] Kenrick, *Theologia moralis* (3 vols.; Philadelphia: Eugene Cummiskey, 1840-1843), tr. V, cap. VI, no. 39.
[85] Fox, *The American Colonization Society*, pp. 78 f.
[86] Carey, *Letters to Mercer*, pp. 18 f.
[87] Fox, *op. cit.*, pp. 79 f; Carey, *Letter to Mercer*, p. 17.
[88] Hart, *Slavery and Abolition*, p. 237.
[89] Carey, *Letter to Mercer*, pp. 17, 6, 9.
[90] Carey, *Letter to Mercer*, p. 6; Fox, op. cit., p. 125.
[91] Cf. *infra*, pp. 152-155.

definitely had an influence on the slave-trade in Africa itself.[92]

Slavery and the national charters. There was a tendency on the part of the early leaders to prohibit the slave-trade. The Articles of Association, signed on October 20, 1774, agreed that the colonies would neither import nor purchase any slave imported after the first of December of that year (1774), when the slave-trade would be wholly discontinued.[93] This agreement was made in order to damage the slave-trade of England. This attitude was maintained throughout the Revolutionary War, most States prohibiting the trade by law with the result that after the war was over there was no importation of slaves for a while.[94]

The Articles of the Confederation were agreed to by Congress on November 15, 1777, and ratified and in force March 1, 1781. The articles make no direct mention of slavery in the colonies, although in referring to the States furnishing men for the armed forces, it is stated that the quota is to be assigned in proportion to the number of "white" inhabitants.[95]

In the Declaration of Independence there seems to be no distinction made between free and slave, white and black. "We hold these truth to be self evident—that all men are created equal, that they are endowed by their Creator with certain unalienable rights; that among these are life, liberty and the pursuit of happiness."

The word "slave" does not appear in the Constitution but slavery is recognized and safeguarded.[96] A reference is made to the institution in the following article:

[92] Fox, *op. cit.*, p. 11.

[93] The Association, art. 2; John Spencer Bassett, *The Federalist System*, American Nation Series (New York; Harper & Bros., 1906), p. 179; Melvin Banks, "The Coastwise Slave-Trade," (unpublished Master's thesis, Howard University, Washington, D.C., 1922), p. 2.

[94] A. B. Hart, "Slavery," *Encyclopedia Americana*, 27: 393; Bassett, *op. cit.*, p. 179; Banks, *op. cit.*, pp. 2-4.

[95] Art. IX, Sec. 5.

[96] Mary W. Williams, "Modern Slavery" *ESS*, 14: 85.

Representatives and direct taxes shall be appor-
tioned among the several States, which may be
included within the Union, according to their re-
spective numbers, which shall be determined by
adding to the whole number of free persons including those, bound to service for a term of years,
and excluding Indians not taxed, three-fifths of
all other persons.[97]

The argument about adding three-fifths of all other
persons was an economic measure. The South wanted
taxes for the expense of the government to be limited by
the percentage of white inhabitants. It was a distinction
based on finances, not on moral rights.[98]

An article more definitely affecting the slavery issue is
the following one that permits slave-trade, at least until
1808.

The Migration or Importation of such Persons as
any of the States now existing shall think proper
to admit, shall not be prohibited by the Congress
prior to the year one thousand eight hundred and
eight, but a Tax or duty may be imposed on such
Importations, not exceeding ten dollars for each
Person.[99]

The following clause of the Constitution is the basis for
the fugitive slave laws, which will be discussed later.

No Person held to Service or Labour in one State,
under the Laws thereof, escaping into another,
shall, in Consequence of any Law or Regulation

[97] Art. I, Sec. II. Cf. Andrew McLaughlin Cunningham, *The Confederation and the Constitution*. Vol. 10 of *The American Nation:
A History*. (New York and London: Harper Bros., 1905), pp. 252,
257, 265; Henry Wilson, *History of the Rise and Fall of Slave Power
in America* (3 vols.; Boston: Houghton, Mifflin & Co., 1872), 1:
39-68.

[98] *Report to the Congregational Ministers*, pp. 68-72; Cochin, *op.
cit.*, p. 9, A. B. Hart, *EA*, 27: 393.

[99] Art. I, Sec. IX; cf. Goodell, *National Charters*, pp. 36-41; *Report to the Congregational Ministers*, p. 71, shows how Madison was
opposed to the measure permitting the trade for twenty years; Gray,
Sermon, p. 11; Cochin, *op. cit.*, p. 9; McLaughlin, *op. cit.*, pp. 262-
264, 304.

therein, be discharged from such Service or Labour, but shall be delivered up on Claim of the
Party to whom such Service or Labour may be
due.[100]

The Ordinance of 1778—the charter for the government of the Northwest Territory explicitly prohibited slavery and involuntary servitude except as punishment for
crime, but recognized that fugitives escaping into this territory from another State could be restored to the person
claiming the fugitive's labor or services.[101]

The majority of the Founding Fathers of our country—
the men who wrote the documents mentioned—men like
Washington, Franklin, Jefferson, and Madison, were all
opposed to the institution of slavery in principle, even
though they themselves belonged to the slave-holding families and States.[102] Although they believed the Negro to be
inferior to the white man still they proposed various sug-
gestions for the solution of the problem and hoped for legislation designed to abolish slavery in the United States.[103]

The anti-slavery movement. While at times anti-slavery
and abolition were used as interchangeable terms, nevertheless a distinction can be made between them. Anti-
slavery was a negative force, an attempt to wall in an ob-

[100] Art. IV, Sec. II.
[101] Art. VI.
[102] Concerning Washington, cf. Matthew Mellon, *The Early American Views on Negro Slavery* (Boston: Meader Pub. Co., 1934),
pp. 28-85; George Livermore, *An Historical Research Respecting the
Opinions of the Founders of the Republic, on Negroes as Slaves,
Citizens and Soldiers* (Boston: John Wilson & Son, 1862), pp. 36-
44; concerning Franklin cf. Mellon, *op. cit.*, pp. 17-37; concerning
John Adams cf. Mellon, *op. cit.*, pp. 85-88; Livermore, *op. cit.*, pp.
24-52; concerning Jefferson, cf. Mellon, *op. cit.*, pp. 89-115, 120-122;
Livermore, *op. cit.*, pp. 21-24; concerningMadison, cf. Mellon, *op. cit.*,
pp. 123-158; concerning Hamilton, Patrick Henry, Monroe, the
Randolfs, cf. John Elliott Cairnes, *The Slave Power* (London: Macmillan & Co., 1863), p. 166.
[103] Mary Stroughton Locke, *Anti-slavery in America from the Introduction of African Slaves to the Prohibition of Slave Trade* (Boston:
Ginn & Co., 1901), p. 47.

noxious system of labor, so that it might die of itself. On the other hand, abolition was a positive force, founded on moral considerations, staunchly denying that slavery could ever be lawful, and perfectly willing to see the social and economic system of the South disrupted. At first there was a marked distinction between the two ideas, but later on they became identified.[104] The anti-slavery movements in the colonies and the United States might be divided into periods.

The earliest protest against slavery was the resolution of the Germantown Menonnites issued on February 18, 1688.[105] However, the first Abolition Society was not organized until April 14, 1775 in Pennsylvania. The original object of this society was the relief of free Negroes unlawfully held in bondage. Most of the members of this organization were Quakers. Three years later the group reorganized, calling itself "The Pennsylvania Society for Promoting Abolition of Slavery, the Relief of Free Negroes Unlawfully Held in Bondage, and for Improving the Condition of the African race." This group spread copies of its constitution, the emancipation act of Pennsylvania and other tracts. It corresponded with other societies at home and abroad, with governors and State legislatures.[106]

Originally the Abolition Society was formed to meet local conditions, but very early it was found necessary to have united action on the matter throughout the country. Accordingly delegates from the various groups came together to form the "American Convention of Delegates from Abolition Societies." After 1818 this name was changed to "The American Convention for the Promotion of Abolition of Slavery and the Improving the Condition of the African Race."[107] In the early period, prior to 1808, the philosophy

---

[104] Hart, *Slavery and Abolition*, pp. 174 f.
[105] Commanger, *Documents of American History*, pp. 37 f.
[106] Locke, *op. cit.*, pp. 97 f; Hart, *Slavery and Abolition*, p. 160.
[107] Hart, *Slavery and Abolition*, p. 162; Locke, *op. cit.*, p. 101.

of the revolutionary period had much to do in awakening
sentiment for the oppressed Negro. The matter was reasoned out by arguments.[108] But later public opinion was
aroused in behalf of the Negro by individual ministers, edu-
cators, lawyers, members of Congress, and other profes-
sional men.[109] There was an abundance of anti-slavery literature in this period, which was directed principally toward
the arousing of public opinion. With few exceptions, it was
not directed toward political movements.[110]

However, eventually there were some political movements, directed toward emancipation by State legislatures,
by a gradual process, and State liberty laws;[111] attempts
to prevent slavery from entering the territories;[112] suppression of the African slave trade by State and national
action, memorials to this effect being sent to Congress and
legislatures by the Convention.[113]

The efforts of this period bore some fruit for, of the six-
teen States admitted to the Union before 1800, eight became free.[114] But toward the turn of the century the abolition societies began to decline.[115]

The second period began in 1808. The period of 1808-
1815 was one of relative inactivity. However, after 1815
there was gradual revival. Anti-slavery pamphlets were
published, and new vigor came from the formation of the
American Colonization Society.[116]

In general this period had many of the features of the
first period. Meeting were still held, gradual emancipation

[108] Locke, *op. cit.*, pp. 46-65.
[109] *Ibid.*, pp. 88-97.
[110] *Ibid.*, pp. 166-197.
[111] *Ibid.*, pp. 112-134.
[112] *Ibid.*, pp. 157-165.
[113] *Ibid.*, pp. 134-156.
[114] Hart, *EA*, 27: 393.
[115] Locke, *op. cit.*, pp. 109-111.
[116] Locke, *Anti-Slavery in America*, pp. 4-8; Louise Paulette Alexander, "Slavery Sentiments as Expressed Through Newspapers and
Periodicals," (unpublished Master's thesis, Howard University, Washington, D.C., 1934), p. 6, cf. *supra*, pp. 23-28.

was advocated, but the political issue was slowly becoming more apparent.[117]

The third period began in 1831. That year 1831 was an important one in the history of abolition for it was then that the abolition movement really got under way. Previous to that date attempts were sporadic and spontaneous.[118]

Several reasons can be given for the upsurge of fierceness in the program. (1) The last vestige of serfdom was disappearing from Central Europe, and the same spirit was extended to the European colonies in America. (2) There was a change in the public attitude toward the weak and helpless—reform in the treatment of paupers, convicts, and public provisions were made for the training of the blind, deaf, and other unfortunate persons. (3) There was a sudden springing up of new fields of activity, manufacturing, growth of large cities, exchange of products far and wide, which called for a kind of labor unsuited for slavery, and the laborer himself felt that the slave was a competitor. (4) The South with its cry of State rights showed its hostility towards anti-slavery, fanning it to a flame.[119] Sympathy was engendered for the abolitionists as a result of riotous attempts to break up their meetings all over the country.[120]

The period may be said to have begun when William Lloyd Garrison published his "Liberator" in 1831, which continued until 1866, and which contained fierce denunciations not only of the system of slavery but of all persons connected with it.[121] In 1833 it was planned to edit four periodicals: "Human Rights," a small paper, "The Anti-slavery Record," a magazine with illustrations, "The Eman-

[117] Locke, *op. cit.*, p. 6; cf. Alice Adams, *The Neglected Period of Anti-Slavery in America, 1808-1831* (Boston: Ginn & Co., 1908).

[118] Nuesse, *The Social Thought of American Catholics*, p. 261.

[119] Hart, *Slavery and Abolition*, pp. 170-172.

[120] Hart, *Slavery and Abolition*, pp. 245-251; Octavius Brooks Frothingham, *Gerrit Smith* (New York: G. P. Putnams's Sons, 1909), pp. 164-166.

[121] Unsigned Article "Slavery" *EA*, 1: 24.

cipator," and "Slaves Freed," a magazine for the young people.[122]

Another great step came, about 1835, when the abolitionists, encouraged by the English acts abolishing slavery in the West Indies (1830-1835), began to send petitions to Congress, asking for the prohibition of slavery in the District of Columbia. The southerners tried to stop the rising discussion in Congress, but John Quincy Adams arose as a champion of free speech and, aided by others like Josua Giddings of Ohio, would not be silenced. Soon the issue began to be highly discussed because of the prevalence of slavery in the Teritories.[123]

In general, the third period followed the lines of the earlier period and used most of the same methods. But it was particularly characterized by strong efforts for total, universal and immediate emancipation.[124]

From the beginning of this period local societies rapidly increased through the East. In 1835 there were 200 of them, in 1836 over 500, and by 1840, there were about 2,000 local societies with a membership of nearly 200,000. The income of the society in 1834 was about $1,000 while in 1840 it was $47,000.[125]

In the earlier periods the South and the border States were the leaders in anti-slavery. After 1831, however, the movement was confined to the middle and northern States.[126] Hence we might say that the distinctive effect of the Garrisonian period was the alienation of New England and the West from the spirit of cooperation with the South.[127] Several reasons contributed to this difference of opinion in the two sections of the country. In the South, there was the rapid growth of the cotton industry, with its need for slaver labor, the Nat Turner insurrection in 1831, the de-

---

[122] Guilday, *The Life and Times of John England*, 2: 151.
[123] Hart, *EA*, 27: 396.
[124] Alexander, *op. cit.*, p. 6 *et passim*.
[125] Hart, *Slavery and Abolition*, p. 184.
[126] Alexander, *op. cit.*, pp. 73 f.
[127] Fox, *op. cit.*, p. 138.

bates in the legislature of Virginia, attempting to plan for total or partial abolition; while on the part of the Northern members, there was the opposition of Garrison and his followers to the Colonization plan, which most southerners advocated.[128]

The abolitionists of Garrison's type maintained that slavery is intrinsically evil, and therefore always wrong. No man can be the property of another, they said, since property in man is impossible for all come from the same Creator, all men have equal rights.[129] From a consideration of the ltierature of the times it can be seen that some writers attempted to prove this from Sacred Scripture, or by reasoning that men had natural rights to equality. It was asserted that the knowledge of this equaltiy came from the consciousness of man's soul, which was claimed to be the highest test of moral truth. They attempted to prove this by maintaining that each man feels that it would be wrong for any one to enslave him for he would reason that he has a God-given right to freedom. Now, that same thing should apply to all other men.[130] The abolitionists attempted to deflate the idea that slavery was an economic necessity, arising from the contention that the work on the plantation could not be carried on without slave labor. They further tried to prove that slave labor was unprofitable to the slave holder, as well as to the community.[131] They also tried to show that restriction on the intellectual improvement of the Negro was unwholesome for the good of the individual

---

[128] Alexander, *op. cit.*, p. 74.

[129] Church Anti-Slavery Society, *Proceedings of the Convention met at Worcester, Mass. March 1, 1859* (New York: F. Trow, 1859), p. 28; Locke, *op. cit.*, 178 ff; Hart, *Slavery and Abolition*, p. 153 ff.

[130] William Bowditch, *The Anti-Slavery Reform* (Boston: Robert Walcut, 1850), pp. 1-14; Arthur Young Lloyd, *The Slavery Controversy*, Chapel Hill, N.C.: The University of North Carolina Press, 1939, pp. 71-101.

[131] Locke, *Anti-Slavery in America*, pp. 178-185; James Buckingham, *Slave States of America* (London, Paris: Fischer Son and Co., 1842), 1: 201-214, 399-404.

as well as the nation. And in general they pointed out the
political weaknesses and dangers of the system.[132]

The different turns which their arguments took can be
gleaned from the literature of the various periods. In the
period ending 1830, the literature shows that the arguments were based on moral, religious, social, economic, and
sentimental grounds. Most of the plans in this period were
for gradual emancipation.[133]

The rapid increase of abolition societies after 1831 made
the amount of published material of that period enormous.
The literature is marked with bitterness between the abolitionists and the slaveholders. Frequent references are
made to the assistance of fugitive slaves. Arguments based
on sentimental reasons were frequently used. Immediate
and unconditional emancipation was vigorously advocated
and much opposition was offered to the American Colonization Society.[134]

After 1850 the literature is still more copious and more
effective. The Fugitive Slave Act of September 18, 1850,
and attempts to enforce it gave rise to many literary pro-
ductions. The novel was used extensively in this period,
Harriet Beecher Stowe's "Uncle Tom's Cabin" being the
most famous of them. In general, there is a bitter spirit
of defiance in the literature.[135]

The leaders of abolition had two main plans in mind.
First they attempted to unify the movement by combining
the various societies on a national basis, collecting reports
and actions of the various societies. Secondly, they en-
deavored to arouse public sentiment by working through
the churches, legislatures, and other existing bodies, against

---

[132] Hart, *Slavery and Abolition*, p. 168; Locke, *op. cit.*, p. 9.

[133] Lorenzo Dow Turner, *Anti-slavery Sentiment in American Literature Prior to 1865* (Washington, D.C.: The Association for the
Study of Negro Life and History, Inc., 1929), pp. 3-49, 120 f.

[134] *Ibid.*, pp. 47-67, 121.

[135] *Ibid.*, pp. 70-100, 122.

the evils of slavery, with a view to emancipation and the improvement of the Negro race.[136]

In naming some of the more prominent leaders in this active period of abolitionism, the first to be mentioned should be William Lloyd Garison, who, as has been noted, resurrected the anti-slavery movement by the publication of the "Liberator."[137] Another prominent man resembling Garrison in fierceness and merciless attitude was Wendell Phillips.[138] Another was James Russell Lowell, who first wrote for the "Pennsylvania Freeman" at Philadelphia and later became editor of the "National Anti-slavery Standard," and who was the author of the unrelenting satire "The Bigelow Papers."[139] Another author was Theodore Weld.[140] This list would be incomplete if the fiery ministers, Theodore Parker[141] and George Bourne[142] were not mentioned.

[136] William Bowditch, *The Anti-Slavery Reform* (Boston: Robert F. Walcut, 1850), pp. 4-19; LaRoy Sunderland, *Anti-Slavery Manual*, 120 f; Locke, *op. cit.*, pp. 101-109; Hart, *Slavery and Abolition*, p. 158.

[137] Cf. Oliver Johnson, *William Lloyd Garrison and his Times* (Boston: B. B. Russell, 1880); Archibald Henry Grimpke, *William Lloyd Garrison, Abolitionist* (New York: Funk and Wagnalls, 1891); William Lloyd Garrison, *Selections from Writing and Speeches* (Boston: R. F. Walcut, 1852).

[138] Lowell George Austin, *The Life and Times of Wendell Phillips* (Boston: Lee and Shephard, 1888); Wendell Phillips, *The Philosophy of the Abolition Movement* (New York: American Anti-Slavery Society, 1860).

[139] Francis Henry Underwood, *James Russell Lowell* (Boston: J. R. Osgood and Co., 1882); Ferris Greenslet, *James Russell Lowell* (Boston and New York: Mifflin & Co., 1912).

[140] Arthur Young Lloyd, *The Slavery Controversy* (Chapel Hill: The University of North Carolina Press, 1939), pp. 88 ff.

[141] Octavius Frothingham, *Theodore Parker: a Biography* (Boston: J. R. Osgood & Co., 1874); James Freeman Clarke, *Theodore Parker and his Theology* (Boston: Walker, Wise and Co., 2nd ed., 1859); Theodore Parker, *A Letter to the People of the United States Touching on the Matter of Slavery* (Boston: J. Monroe & Co., 1848).

[142] Lloyd, *op. cit.*, 88 ff.

It should be noted, however, that besides the radical group just mentioned, there were three milder groups of abolitionists. (1) In New England Dr. William Ellery Channing, the Unitarian minister of Boston, was the great moral force. He sympathized with the movement, but disliked the Garrisonian severity of tone and methods. He set forth the evil of slavery but suggested remedies other than immediate emancipation. (2) The Middle States group was particularly strong in New York and Pennsylvania. In this group there were many wealthy and generous members. (3) The western group, began its discussions at Lane Theological Seminary in Cincinnati in 1832, Dr. Lyman Beecher was the president. Because of these discussions many students left the Seminary and settled at Oberlin.[143]

Attitude of the Protestant groups toward the movement. The earlier period of anti-slavery that was based on colonization was well received in the South. But since most of the advocates were slaveholders themselves, it was impossible for them to take a very staunch stand against slavery. They formed protection or colonization societies, advocating the amelioration of the conditions of the Negro. However, they resembled greatly the societies in the North of the same period. They were very conservative and advocated only gradual emancipation. Although their numerical strength was not great, the character of the men associated with the movement caused the undertaking to be seriously considered,[144] But the movement of the Garrisonian period was violently opposed by the South. Laws were tightened against printing and circulating anything that would tend to produce dissatisfaction among the slaves.[145] The South claimed that it was a federal responsibility to stop the northerners from the odious movement that was not satisfied with legislative movement or enlight-

[143] Hart, *Slavery and Abolition,* pp. 188-201.
[144] Alexander, "Anti-Slavery Sentiment as Expressed through Newspapers and Periodicals," pp. 71-73.
[145] Hart, *Slavery and Abolition,* p. 234.

enment of the public, but which eventually took on the form of mob violence.[146] Threats of dire punishment were made if the abolitionists showed themselves in the South.[147] The Protestant Church was quite divided over the issue. During the slavery controversy many books were published and many speeches given by ministers and men of high standing in the Protestant Church. In the North many held that slavery was in itself sinful and contrary to the natural law.[148] On the other hand in the South the leaders equally vehemently maintained that slavery does not trample on the natural rights, and not only can be justified but is good, because of the inequality of the races.[149] Inevitably this controversy entered the meetings of the various Protestant sects.

The churches affected most by this controversy were those that were distributed throughout the North and South, namely, the Baptists, the Methodists and the Presbyterians.[150] The Congregationalists were generally anti-slavery, but were confined to the northern states, with practically no slave-holding membership. Hence there was no occasion for divisions in their ranks.[151] While there was

[146] Hart, *Slavery and Abolition*, p. 236; William Goodell, *Slavery and Anti-slavery* (New York: W. Harned, 1852), p. 413.

[147] Hart, *Slavery and Abolition*, p. 235; Goodell, *Slavery and Anti-slavery*, p. 411, 437, 441-443; Buckingham, *Slave States*, 1: 531.

[148] Cf. Theodore Parker, *A Letter to the People of the United States Touching the Matter of Slavery* (Boston: James Munroe, & Co., 1848), pp. 104-111; Charles Elliott, *Sinfulness of Slavery* (Cincinnati: L. Swormstedt & Co., J. H. Power, 1850); LaRoy Sunderland, *Anti-Slavery Manual* (2nd ed.; New York: Peercy and Read, 1837).

[149] Benjamin Fletcher Wright, Jr., *American Interpretations of the Natural Law* (Cambridge, Mass.: Harvard University Press, 1931), pp. 231-241. Cf. Harper "Memoir on Slavery" *Pro-slavery Argument;* William Gilmore Simms, "The Morals of Slavery" *Pro-slavery Argument.*

[150] William Warren Sweet, *The Story of Religion in America* (New York and London: Harper & Bros., 1939), p. 427.

[151] William Goodell, *Slavery and Anti-slavery* (New York: W. Harned, 1852), pp. 163 f; Sweet, *op. cit.*, p. 427.

much anti-slavery discussion among the Presbyterians, Methodists and the Baptists before the close of the eighteenth century, it was not until after the rise of the abolition leaders in 1830 that the issue became a factor of importance among them, eventually leading to radical divisions.[152]

The Presbyterians were divided into the New School and the Old School in 1837-1838.[153] Slavery was much discussed in the General Assemblies of the New School. The General Assembly of 1846 adopted a resolution by an overwhelming majority condemning slavery as wrong and urging churches to dispel the evil. The abolition movement continued to grow. The General Assembly of 1853 ordered a census to be taken to determine the number of slaveholders in the Church and to what extent slaves were held by unavoidable necessity, and what provision was being made for their religious well-being. In defiance the Presbyterians of Lexington, Kentucky, reported that a number of their ministers and elders held slaves from principle, believing it to be just and right. In the General Assembly of 1857 twenty-seven anti-slavery memorials were presented and after days of discussion a resolution was adopted exhorting "all our people to eschew the doctrine that slavery is an ordinance of God" and is "Scriptural and right." The Southerners protested. They placed a call for a General Assembly where slavery would not be discussed. This resulted in the United Synod of the South. Thus the Presbyterian Church was divided.[154] While there was considerable anti-slavery sentiment in the Old School Presbyterians[155] they generally held a very reasonable middle road

---

[152] Sweet, *op. cit.*, pp. 425 f.

[153] Goodell, *Slavery and Anti-slavery*, p. 154 f.

[154] Sweet, *op. cit.*, pp. 440 f; Rev. John Robinson, *The Testimony of the Presbyterian Church in Reference to American Slavery* (Cincinnati: John D. Thorpe, 1852), pp. 225-251, gives the teachings of the various branches of the Presbyterian Church on slavery.

[155] Sweet, op. cit., p. 444.

view on slavery. The view is summarized by one of the ministers of this group.

> In short, the mere legal relations they hold to be not necessarily sinful; they condemn the system. The wrongs authorized by it they forbid under the penalty of church discipline; they enjoin the duties which men standing in this relation to others owe them.[156]

The fundamental principle of the Baptists is their independence of congregations, yet they do unite in voluntary organizations. The most prominent of these voluntary organizations are the "General Convention of Baptist Denominations in the United States for Foreign Missions," which was founded in 1814 with headquarters in Boston and the "Baptist Home Missionary Society," founded in 1832. Both societies meets triennially, known as the "Triennial Convention." Between 1841 and 1844 anti-slavery was being pressed in the North and protests against anti-slavery were voiced in the South. There were occasions that nearly led to a break but they were averted by cooperation. In the Fall of 1844 a member of the Alabama Baptist Convention raised the question about slaveholders having equal privileges with non-slaveholders. On December 17, 1844 the board answered that in thirty years no slaveholder had applied to be a missionary, but if one did, they could not appoint him if he insisted on holding slaves, for that would imply approbation of slavery. Steps were soon taken for separation. The Virginia Baptist Foreign Missionary Society led the way, breaking with the Boston Board. On May 9, 1845 a constitution was presented for the "Southern Baptist Convention." Thus the rupture was made in the Baptist Church.[157]

Amongst the Methodists there were many anti-slavery movements,[158] although in the early period the General

---

[156] Robinson, *op. cit.*, p. 76.

[157] Sweet, *op. cit.*, pp. 428-433; Robinson, *op. cit.*, pp. 251-252, summarizes their opinions on slavery.

[158] Lucius C. Matlack, *The History of American Slavery and Methodism, from 1780-1849* (New York: the author, 1849), pp. 98 ff.

Conferences appeared to have been in the form of anti-
abolitionism.[159] While the moderate men were in control
the bishops went from conference to conference attempting to restrain the discussion on slavery.[160] Eventually several attempts were made to induce the conferences to prohibit slavery. The crisis came in the General Conference
of 1844, where slavery was the burning issue. The question
arose as to what was to be done about a slaveholding minister, who had been suspended by the Baltimore Conference for refusing to free his slaves. The majority upheld
the decision of the Baltimore Conference. This merely indicated the more important decision that was later made
concerning Bishop James O. Andrews of Georgia, who had
come into possession of slaves by marriage. After debate
the bishop was asked to desist from episcopal labors until
he disposed of his slaves. The closing session of this conference was occupied with drawing up a "Plan of Separation," if the southern churches found such action necessary.
After the Conference the southern members met at Louis-
ville, on May 1, 1845. Using the "Plan of Separation" as
their *Magna Carta* they set up the Methodist Episcopal
Church, South. In 1848 the Methodist Episcopal Church
(the branch in the North) repudiated the "Plan of Separation' offered in 1844, which led to a period of bitterness
between the two branches of Methodism. There were several lawsuits over property in the border States.[161]

Attitude of Catholics toward the abolition movement.
Upon reading of the social movements going on in the country concerning slavery, one may wonder what the Catholics were doing all the while. In answer it must be remembered that the Church in colonial life was a proscribed
and negligible force. Outside of Maryland, there were practically no Catholics; and even in that colony they were

[159] *Ibid.*, pp. 65-81.
[160] *Ibid.*, pp. 39-68.
[161] Sweet, *op. cit.*, pp. 433-440; Goodell, *Slavery and Anti- slavery*,
pp. 144-150; Robinson, *op. cit.*, pp. 253-256; Matlack, *op. cit.*, pp.
308-354.

out-numbered, especially after they lost control of the colony. As a result the Church exercised little influence on the development of the colonies. Moreover, it must be remembered that there was a great lack of priests in America at the time. John Carroll, the Prefect-Apostolic of the American Colonies reported to the Sacred Congregation for the Propagation of the Faith at the end of the Revolutionary War that there were only nineteen priests to serve 19,000 Catholics, of whom 3,000 were slaves.[162]

Turning to the controversy itself, it is well to note that many Catholics were slave owners. Some of them owned large numbers, as for example, Charles Carroll of Carrolton. Catholic priests and religious orders also owned slaves. The Jesuits followed the system of the day and used Negro slaves on their estates.[163] Archbishop Carroll evidently continued to hold at least one slave, for in his will he gave instructions that Charles, his black servant, should received his freedom.[164] Likewise the Capuchins and the Ursuline nuns retained slaves.[165] Accordingly, since priests and religious accepted the prevailing system of employing slaves, laymen felt free to do the same. Hence from the very beginning, slaves were held by Catholics with no remorse of conscience.

In stating the Catholic position, in all fairness, it must be pointed out that the leaders of the Church always stressed the duties the master had toward his slave, and the duties the slave had to his master. Each had rights, which had to be respected and honored. Later it will be shown that

[162] Peter K. Guilday, *The Life and Times of John Carroll, Archbishop of Baltimore, (1735-1815)*, (2 vols., New York: The Encyclopedia Press, 1922) 1: 225-27.

[163] Rice, *American Catholic Opinion in the Slavery Controversy*, p. 27.

[164] "Will of Archbishop Carroll" *American Catholic Historical Society Researches*, 8: 52-55.

[165] Roger Baudier, *The Catholic Church in Louisiana*, (New Orleans: A. W. Hyatt Stationery Mfg. Co. Ltd., 1939), pp. 131-132, 164.

Archbishop Kenrick very explicitly outlined these duties and obligations.[166]

Moreover, the Catholic clergy explicitly condemned the slave-trade, but, relying on the conservative teachings of the leaders of the Church concerning slavery, and keenly aware of the influences of the social and economic conditions of the time, they came to regard abolitionists as enemies of religion, of public order, and of the Union, which they, as naturalized citizens, had sworn to support.[167] Brownson sums up their position as follows:

> There is no doubt that the majority of our Catholic population is strongly opposed to the abolitionists, and regard them, very unjustly, however, as the real authors of the formidable rebellion now threatening our national life; but we do them injustice, if we supposed them to be really in favor of Negro slavery, or opposed on principle to emancipation. We think their hostility to the abolitionists, since the breaking out of the Civil War, very unwise, unpolitic, un-called for, and calculated to give aid and comfort to the enemies of the nation; but we think it grows more out of their attachment to the Union, than out of any sympathy with slavery, or with the rebels.[168]

This opposition to abolitionism was prevalent in the North, and, all the more in the South, where Catholics as well as Protestants rallied to the defense of the southern way of life, which they felt was endangered by northern aggression.[169] The only difference was that the South laid greater stress on the conservatism of the Catholic theory of slavery, while the North hoped for eventual abolition.[170]

[166] John LaFarge, "The Survival of the Catholic Faith in Southern Maryland," *CHR*, 21 (1925), 18; Carter Godwin Woodson, *The Education of the Negro Prior to 1861*, (New York & London: Knickerbocker Press, 1915), pp. 107 f.

[167] Rice, *American Catholic Opinion in the Slavery Controversy*, p. 109.

[168] Brownson, "Slavery and the Church," *Works* 17: 317.

[169] Rice, *op. cit.*, p. 131.

[170] *Ibid.*, p. 139.

Then, too, the South was conscious of the social problem engendered by the presence of a large number of Africans who were not far removed from African barbarism, and therefore not qualified to assume immediate unconditional freedom.[171]

Various reasons were given by Catholics for their opposition to the abolitionists. They are here listed indiscriminately. The majority of Catholics were adherents of the Democratic party. Since, in their mother countries they had been oppressed, on coming to this country they attached themselves to the party which made the loudest profession of liberty and equality, and which appeared most liberal toward foreigners and especially to Catholics as naturalized citizens. Catholics were democrats by conviction before coming to this country so they naïvely assumed that the Democratic party here represented their previously held views. The opposing parties, whether Federalist, Republican or Whig, were always less friendly to foreigners and Catholics.[172]

The Irish Catholics were led to party fanaticism in their fight against Protestant Europe. They continued this staunch party adherence on coming to America. Hence, when the Democratic party became anti-abolitionist, the Irish Catholics followed. Moreover, they looked upon abolitionists with suspicion as being addicted to Sabbath-worship, disunionism, woman's rightism, amalgamationism, free love, and most of all "Englishism." They were led by the democrats to regard abolitionists as miserable fanatics. But it must be remembered, Brownson warns, that this hostility to abolistionism was cherished without in the least being attached to slavery or desirous of perpetuating a social condition always discouraged by the Church.[173]

These years were times of revolutionary upheavals in Europe which were characterized by anti-clericalism and

---

[171] *Ibid.*, p. 143.
[172] Brownson, *Works*, 17: 317.
[173] *Ibid.*, p. 318; Rice, *op. cit.*, pp. 102 f.

hostility to religion in general, especially to the Catholic
Church. Hence the Catholics had a fear of joining radical
movements. At that time in this country the Protestant
nativist movements had broken out in the Know-Nothing
movement. The Catholics had to battle this movement on
one side and the Black Republicans or abolitionists on the
other. The Catholics were attacked on both sides of the
slavery issue. In all this turmoil the Catholics wanted to
avoid radical movements, which they knew from experi-
ence to be harmful to them.[174] Then, too, the Irish Catholics resented the influence of the British Anti-Slavery Society in the abolition movement, and the Germans were
uneasy about the rationalist and free-thinker emigrants who
were active in the abolition movement.[175]

Likewise Catholics feared that if the Federal government
abolished slavery, there would be a gradual centralization of
power in that government. They held that the question was
one of states' rights.[176]

Again, they reasoned that many of the things advocated
by some of the abolitionists were against the teachings of
the Church. They reasoned that the right to possess property was derived from the natural law, but not all are
entitled to hold the same amount. The teaching of the abolitionists was against this. To confiscate slave property
without compensation to the legal owners, was wrong.[177]
Then, too, many of the leaders of the movement advocated
private judgment in matters of religion. The good Catholic obviously distrusted them.[178]

Again the Irish immigrants feared the encroachment of
the workingman of the lower level, if they were emanci-

[174] Rice, *op. cit.*, pp. 90, 91, 93, 96, 103.
[175] Brownson, "The Presidential Nominations," *Works*, 15: 490;
Rice, *op. cit.*, p. 154.
[176] Rice, *op. cit.*, p. 113.
[177] Brownson, *Works*, 17: 20 f; Rice, *op. cit.*, p. 98; England,
"Letters to Forsyth." *Works*, 5: *passim*.
[178] Rice, *op. cit.*, p. 98.

pated. Coupled with this, they had an antipathy for Negroes as a race.[179]

In considering the attitude of the hierarchy it must be remembered that around 1831, at the outbreak of the abolition movement in its most vigorous forms, the Bishops in the United States were still quite busy with many problems such as the control of church property, appointment of pastors, the flood of immigrants, organized bursts of violence, such as the burning of the Ursuline convent of Charleston, which took place in 1834.[180] Likewise it must be remembered that most of its members had come from Europe and looked upon reform movements as the Revolutionaries of the Old World.[181] On the other hand many of them really loved the Negro and actually showed their interest in him.[182]

Their general opinion was that no fundamental tenet of Catholicism was at stake. Slavery in itself is not contrary to the natural law, and hence it not wrong, provided the rules for just servitude, laid down by the theologians are observed.[183]

They did lay down regulations to protect the dignity and personality of the slave, and to prevent the master from misusing his power.[184] But they feared centralizing power in the federal government, realizing the many conflicts between Church and State in the Old World. They preferred

[179] Brownson, *Works*, 17: 328; Rice, *op. cit.*, pp. 124-130.

[180] Peter K. Guilday, "Trusteeism," *Historical Records and Studies of the United States Catholic Historical Society*, 18: (March 1928), 7-73; Ray Allen Billinton, *The Protestant Crusade* (New York: Macmillan Co., 1938); Sister M. Gilbert Kelly, O.P., *A History of Catholic Immigrant Colonization Projects in the United States 1815-1860* (New York: United States Catholic Historical Society, 1939).

[181] Rice, *American Catholic Opinion in the Slavery Controversy*, p. 154.

[182] Stephen L. Theobold, "Catholic Missionary Work Among the Colored People of the United States," *RACHS*, 35 (1924), 325-344.

[183] Cf. England, "Letters to Forsyth," *Works*, 5: *passim.*

[184] Cf. *infra*, Chapter III.

that the slavery issue be solved on a local basis.[185] Then,
too, they wanted to stay aloof from political matters with
which slavery had become integrated.[186] At the same time
they felt that the slavery issue would split the Union, which
they sincerely sought to avoid.[187] At times they seem to
have gone so far in their defense of slavery that they gave
weight to the pro-slavery argument.[188] By avoiding all in-
volvement in the civil strife, the Catholics Church emerged
from the struggle with a united front, while the Protestant
Churches, as has been observed, were split asunder.[189]

The hierarchy seems to have taken the lead in avoiding discussion of the slavery issue. Archbishop Spalding
claimed that no political discussions were allowed in the
synods or councils held during the controversy, therefore
only the questions connected with faith and morals were
considered.[190] At the Council held in 1840 the letter of
Gregory XVI condemning slave-trade was read.[191] The
pastoral issued at the end of the Council of 1843 contains
what could be construed as a condemnation of Abolitionism
and an admonition of the faithful to practice "fidelity in
fulfillment of all engagements," "obedience to the laws of
the nation," and "respect for civil authorities."[192]

Regarding the Council of 1852, Guilday[193] says that the
wisdom of the fathers of the Council was outstanding in

[185] Rice, *op. cit.*, p. 114.

[186] *Ibid.*, p. 63.

[187] *Ibid.*, p. 146.

[188] *Ibid.*, pp. 156 f.

[189] Theoblod, *RACHS*, 35 (1924), 332 f.

[190] Theobold, *art. cit.*, *RACHS*, 35 (1924); 333, Peter K. Guilday,
History of the Councils of Baltimore (1791-1884) (New York: Macmillan & Co., 1932), p. 170.

[191] John England, *Works*, ed. by the Most Reverend Sebastian G.
Messmer, (Cleveland, Ohio: The Arthur H. Clarke Co., 1908), 5:
190 f.

[192] Peter K. Guilday, (ed) *The National Pastorals of the American
Hierarchy (1792-1919)* (Washington, D.C.: National Catholic Welfare Council, 1923), p. 154.

[193] Guilday, *History of the Councils of Baltimore*, p. 182.

keeping silence on the slavery issue, since it was a political question, dividing parties and churches into antagonistic groups. Many expected a decree at the close of the meeting, but the bishops would not break with their policy which vigorously opposed discussions on political matters. The pastoral issued at the end of the Council contained a plea for civil allegiance.

To make this treatment of the views of the hierarchy more complete, it might be well to note briefly the writings of some of the important ecclesiastics.

Archbishop Kenrick's biographer says that in the period of uncertainty and vague dread, all eyes turned toward Kenrick. Questions directly or indirectly relating to national issues were addressed to him by prelates and clergy, all perplexed by their consciences over what was best for the good of the Church and of the nation. Kenrick gave no offense to either side, he said, acting as a minister of religion with charity to friend and foe alike.[194]

Kenrick published the first edition of his *Theologia moralis* beginning with 1840. He stated in the text that he desired to give practical moral principles to aid priests in dealing with slaves and masters. If one consults the whole text, he will find scattered throughout it a comprehensive treatment of the problems.[195] A second edition of the work came out in 1860, with a few minor changes in the facts connected with the doctrine on slavery. In the preface of the last edition he stated that it was necessary to deal with problems, which his predecessors had dealt with from different points of view. He explicitly mentioned slavery, which he said existed in some states and which gave rise to a host of problems, which were not dealt with by the European writers of recent centuries. At this period of time, some faint indication of his feelings on the matter

[194] John J. O'Shea, *The Two Kenricks* (Phila.: John J. McVey, 1904), pp. 199-202.

[195] Francis Patrick Kenrick, *Theologia moralis*, (3 vols.; Philadelphia: Eugene Cummiskey, 1840-1843).

is found in the letters that he wrote to Eliza Allen Starr. He considered the situation in the South, in December of 1860, quite gloomy,[196] and hoped for a speedy dissolution of the Southern Confederacy. Professing not to be a political partisan, he looked to the president as the only providential means to save the national institutions and win back to the Union the seceding States.[197] In two of his letters he makes reference to the Catholic Mirror.

> The Catholic Mirror is scarcely loyal enough for your taste. Courtney Jenkins, a lawyer is editor. The sympathies of Marylanders generally are with the South, especially since we are treated as conquered people. I do not interfere, although from my heart I wish that secession had never been thought of. Shall we ever again be a united people? The issues of war are uncertain. Providence may strengthen the government by the means taken to destroy it. The danger is, that in becoming strong, it will cease to be free.[198]

Again he says:

> The Catholic Mirror does not reflect my sentiments or views. It is conducted by Courtney Jenkins, a lawyer of good principles and sincerely attached to the faith, but of strong southern sympathies. I avoid interposing not to give annoyance. I have had nothing to do with the controversies that have recently filled its columns.[199]

Jenkins, in the Catholic Mirror claimed to have little interest in slavery itself, but he desired to protect the South against outsiders. He claimed that the higher law would impel us only to mitigate the evils of slavery. In fact he thought that the higher law would even forbid the emancipation of the slaves, without some assurance of betterment.[200]

[196] *The Life and Letters of Eliza Allen Starr,* edited by Rev. James J. McGovern (Chicago: Lakeside Press, 1905), p. 141 f.

[197] Letter of March 8, 1861, *Ibid.,* p. 145.

[198] Letter of August 5, 1861, *Ibid.,* p. 148.

[199] Letter of Nov. 11, 1862, *Ibid.,* p. 163.

[200] Rice, *The American Catholic Opinion in the Slavery Controversy,* pp. 149 f.

In the later edition of his text, Kenrick indicated the futility of abolition societies. He mentioned that under the Constitution neither the Federal Government nor another State may meddle in the affairs of a State. He then noted that, in some of the northern States, societies for the abolition of slavery had arisen, but that they could accomplish nothing save by moral persuasion, which the southern States vehemently reject. Congress itself, he said, can do nothing about the abolition of slavery, except in the District of Columbia.[201] Moreover he noted that although there is great freedom of the press in the United States nevertheless the southern States have passed laws, carrying severe penalties for those who print or distribute books opposing slavery. His only comment is that hence it is no wonder that the Pope forbids books that are contrary to faith and morals.[202]

Archbishop Hughes of New York admitted that there were moral evils resulting from slavery. He also taught that slavery is not contrary to the natural law. He seems to have been impressed with the physical well-being of slaves in Cuba. He mistrusted the abolitionists' exaggerations and feared the emancipation of the Negro, having been influenced by the refugees from the massacres of Santo Domingo whom he had met as a young priest.[203] Archbishop Hughes came into public notice through his alleged controversy with Orestes Brownson. Brownson had originally been opposed to abolition.[204] Later as a war measure he advocated emancipation.[205]

[201] Francis Patrick Kenrick, *Theologia moralis* (2 vols.; Mechlin: H. Dessain, 1860-1861), Tr. V, cap. 3, no. 7.

[202] *Ibid.*, tr. XIII, cap. V, n. 61.

[203] Most Rev. John Hughes, *Complete Works*, ed. by Lawrence Kehoe. (2 vols.; New York: Lawrence Kehoe, 1865) 2: 219-223.

[204] Brownson, "The Church and the Republic," *Works*, 12: 11 f; "Slavery and the Mexican War," 16: 25-29; "The Higher Law," 17: 1-16; "The Fugitive Slave Law," 17: 16-39; "Slavery and the Incoming Administration," 17: 54-77, etc.

[205] "Slavery and the War," *Works*, 17: 144-178. Brownson, while staunchly advocating emancipation as a war measure, made a clear

A few months later there appeared in the Metropolitan Record, on October 12, 1861, an unsigned article that was very pro-slavery in tone. This article was attributed by Brownson and others to Archbishop Hughes. The writer of the article claimed that slavery was not a divine institution but had at least the Divine permission of God's providence. He almost seemed to justify slave-trade because of the benefits that came to the Negro. He said that he was aware of the moral conditions surrounding slavery, but seemed to pass them over lightly, saying that they were not much different from those of the laborers in the North. Brownson answered the article in his Review in January of 1862. He took it part by part and analyzed it critically.[206]

One of the most prominent ecclesiastics to enter the slavery controversy was Bishop England of Charleston, who wrote a famous series of letters to John Forsyth, Secretary of State. These letters were occasioned by the presidential elections of 1840. The bishop was drawn into the affair by General Duff Gree, the editor of the Baltimore Pilot and Transcript, who favored Harrison. He attempted to identify England with Van Buren, who had given offense to many Americans in 1830, when, as Secretary of State, he had written a courteous letter to the Pope. The slavery issue was predominant in the campaign. Forsyth, Secretary of State to Van Buren, in an address in Georgia, in August of 1840, declared that Harrison might be considered the first anti-slavery candidate for the presidency, and that he was forced upon the people of the South by a combination of anti-masonry and abolitionism. He associated the Catholic Church with this combination, offering as his proof the Apostolic Brief of Gregory XVI on the slave-trade. Forsyth attributed the Brief to O'Connell's influence, since at that time O'Connell was agitating for abolition in the

distinction between natural rights, to which all men are entitled and civil and social rights, which men must merit. Cf. Brownson, *Works*, 17: 536-560, 319.

[206] Brownson, "Archbishop Hughes on Slavery," *Works*, 17: 178-210.

British dominions. To arraign the Pope as an abolitionist Forsyth knew would further antagonize the southerners against the Catholics.

Bishop England came forth in defense of the Holy See, saying that the Holy Father, far from condemning domestic slavery, endorsed it. He cited the ecclesiastical legislation concerning slaves and slavery, with an amazing number of comments from the Fathers and canonists. These eighteen letters appeared in the United States Catholic Miscellany in 1840 and 1841.[207] England proved that slavery was not contrary to the natural law, was always permitted by the Church, and that the Pope in his bull condemned only the slave-trade.[208] Dr. Rice says that there was no challenge of Bishop England's stand and that it seemed to be accepted as the authoritative Catholic opinion.[209] Another instance of his voiced opposition to abolitionism was his attending a meeting in Charleston to protest the flooding of the South with abolition material, to defend the "southern constitutional rights" and "property against all attacks—be the consequences what they may."[210]

An example of a member of the hierarchy belonging to the Confederacy was Bishop P. N. Lynch of Charleston who was sent as commissioner of the Confederacy to the Holy See. He wrote a letter to the Hon. J. P. Benjamin, Secretary of the State of the Confederate States dated June 20, 1864, in which he noted that he had had an audience with the emperor of France who had asked about the demeanor of the Negroes. He replied that they had never been more quiet and submissive; that the tumult of war had seemed to have oppressed them with fear. Certainly they were never more docile and obedient. He told the

[207] Peter K. Guilday, *The Life and Times of John England First Bishop of Charleston, 1786-1842*, (2 vols.; New York: The American Press, 1927) 2: 471 f. The contents of these letters will be discussed in the following chapter.

[208] England, *Works*, 5: *passim;* Theobold, *RACHS* 35 (1924), 335 f; Guilday, *England* 2: 156; Rice, *op. cit.*, pp. 68-70.

[209] Rice, *op. cit.*, p. 70.   [210] Guilday, *Life of England*, 2: 156.

secretary that the French were in high praise of the gallant fighting of the Confederates, but that they were highly prejudiced against slavery.[211]

Bishop Lynch wrote a pamphlet from Rome explaining the southern position on emancipation.[212]

The Catholic press, too, was opposed to abolitionism. As emancipation came closer with one or two exceptions Catholic papers attacked it with a vigor that led them virtually to endorse the perpetuation of slavery for an indefinite period of time.[213]

Some pro-slavery Arguments. Having seen the arguments used by the abolitionists, it is only fair to view the arguments principally used by those who favored slavery.

In this controversy both sides made much use of the Sacred Scriptures. This was quite effectual because of the post-Reformation habit of referring all cases of moral conduct to the Bible, a practice universal in the United States. Both the New and Old Testaments were used. Justification was found there for all that slavery entailed.[214] Proponents of this argument fought against an amalgamation of the two races. They maintained that the white race must retain its supremacy. This was just one step from the justification of slavery as a social necessity.[215] They

[211] *Amer. Cath. Hist. Researches*, 22 (1905), 248-259.

[212] He also sent a general letter to Archbishop Hughes, condemning the Northerners for taking up anti-slavery and breaking up the Union, which the latter answered. Cf. Hughes, *Works*, 2: 513 ff.

[213] Rice, *The American Catholic Opinion in the Slavery Controversy*, pp. 72-85; Theobold, *RACHS*, 35 (1924), 336.

[214] John Henry Hopkins, *A Scriptural, Ecclesiastical and Historical View of Slavery from the Days of the Patriarch Abraham to the Nineteenth Century* (New York: W. J. Pooley & Co., 1864), pp. 7-18; William Sumner Jenkins, *Pro-Slavery Thought in the Old South* (Chapel Hill: University of North Carolina Press, 1935), pp. 200 ff; La Roy Sunderland, *Anti-Slavery Manual* (2nd ed.; New York: Peercy & Read, 1837) pp. 49-65; Lloyd, *The Slavery Controversy;* pp. 162-193; Rev. F. A. Rose, *Slavery Ordained of God* (Philadelphia: Lippincott & Co., 1857).

[215] Lloyd, *The Slavery Controversy*, p. 243.

further held that the blacks were inferior beings,[216] not fitted for political and social rights and privileges of the white men. They appealed to the experiments of emancipation of Haiti, Jamaica, Liberia and Santo Domingo. They particularly paraded the gruesome events of Haiti.[217]

It was further maintained that, if the slaves were manumitted, they would find it difficult to struggle for existence. Only menial tasks, it was said, would be open to the emancipated Negroes.[218] To lend force to the argument an appeal was made to the condition of the Negroes in the free States. Brownson has the following to say:

> The slaves if emancipated, thrown upon their own resources, and compelled to provide for themselves, would very generally sink to the level of these free Negroes. They would have all the responsibilities of free men, and all the disadvantages of slaves, without any of the compensating advantages of either. The simple difference of color alone would suffice to keep them a distinct and degraded class, and therefore a dangerous class in society.[219]

The material, educational and religious advantages the Negro had in America over the Negro in Africa were also delineated.[220]

An attempt was made to show that often the master was like a patriarch, whose counsel and sympathy were sought by the slaves in order to settle disputes and quarrels. To see the master return was one of the great joys on some distant and neglected plantations.[221]

[216] Harper, *Pro-Slavery Argument*, pp. 13-16, 56-60; John H. Van Evrie, *Negroes and Negro Slavery* (New York: VanEvrie, Horton & Co., 1861), *passim*.

[217] Lloyd, *op. cit.*, pp. 244-249.

[218] *Ibid.*, p. 261.

[219] Brownson, *Works*, 17: 42.

[220] Lloyd, *op. cit.*, pp. 250-255; Harper, *Pro-Slavery Argument*, p. 95.

[221] Sims, *Pro-Slavery Argument*, p. 249; William Sumner Jenkins, *Pro-Slavery Thought in the Old South*, (Chapel Hill: University of North Carolina Press, 1935), pp. 209-211.

Slaves, it was maintained, had no anxiety for the future,[222] and in general were better off than the agricultural laborers and factory operators in England and the northern states.[223]

From the point of view of the whites, slavery was looked upon as a necessity for their safety. They often argued from the disturbance in Haiti or Santo Domingo, that if the Negro would be set free, he would never permit the master to live, nor could he maintain a civilized community of his own.[224] Again, slavery was considered a necessity in order to relieve the whites from the danger of labor in the hot climate, and from the degradation of manual labor of any kind. Moreover, slavery would permit the whites to to be free from military service.[225]

Hence, slavery was looked upon not as a system which by effort might be justified, but even as a great good. John C. Calhoun, from his seat in the Senate, on February 6, 1837, said, "But let me not be misunderstood as admitting by implication that the existing relations between the two races in the slaveholding States is an evil; for otherwise I hold it to be a good, as it has thus far proved to be to both....."[226] This was the theory practically settled upon by the entire South.[227] Hence, if slavery were endangered by the union of free and slaveholding States, the Union must give way. "Come what may," wrote Hammond in 1845, "we are firmly resolved that our system of domestic slavery shall stand."[228] The protagonists of slavery looked upon their adversaries as the worst of mankind, who had

[222] Harper, *Pro-Slavery Argument*, pp. 26, 49; Sims, *Ibid.*, p. 226.

[223] Hammond, *Pro-Slavery Argument*, pp. 135-138.

[224] Hopkins, *View of Slavery*, pp. 249-256; Sunderland, *Anti-Slavery Manual*, pp. 79-82, notes that there were no disturbances in Haiti until eight years later when masters tried to reduce them to slavery again.

[225] Harper, *Pro-Slavery Argument*, pp. 79 ff.

[226] John Calhoun, *Speeches*, edited by Richard K. Cralle, (New York: D. Appelton & Co., 1856) 2: 630.

[227] Harper in *Pro-Slavery* Argument, pp. 17-24.

[228] Hammond, *Pro-Slavery Argument*, p. 169.

the intention to "excite Negroes to desperate attempts and particular acts of cruelty and horror," to bring about "a complete equalization of blacks and whites" and "to scatter among our southern brethren, firebrands, arrows, and death."[229]

Southerners thought that to admit anything wrong in slavery was to give up the principle that it was a beneficent institution.[230] Hence, when attacks were made against slavery, they promptly came to defend their position. They denied that it inspired violence in the whites. When confronted with accusations about cruelty, they promptly claimed that the abolitionists greatly over-rated the thing, and that punishment was necessary because of the nature of the Negroes. They further insisted that economic necessity required the slaves be well-treated. When they were reminded of the slaves' lack of freedom in being forced to work for another, they spoke of how well fed and clothed the slaves were in comparison to the white laborers of the North. Admitting that occasionally families were broken up, they maintained the same thing happened in industrial areas, and therefore this point was greatly exaggerated.

In attempting to refute the argument that the slaves were given no education and religious instructions, they pointed to instances where the slaves were encouraged in religious works and how many planters hired clergymen for them. When they were told that slavery was accursed by God, they would remind their accusers that the Sabbath was kept better in the South than in Puritan New England.

The Declaration of Independence, they said, did not apply to Negroes, or else Jefferson and the other signers of the document would have manumitted their slaves. The rights of human beings are not fixed, they maintained, but fluctuate in quantity and quality on a graduated scale, and depend on intelligence and education. They fiercely denied that there was as much miscegenation and sexual crime

[229] Harper, *Pro-Slavery Argument*, pp. 93 f.
[230] Dew, *Pro-Slavery Argument*, pp. 426-428.

between masters and overseers with the slaves as was maintained, because the law and natural repugnance would discourage such practices.[231]

Economically, the planters saw nothing but ruin for both races coming from general and immediate emancipation. As far as the Negro was concerned, they thought that emancipation could not last for "the law would make them free men and custom and prejudices, we care not what you call it, would degrade them to the condition of slaves."[232] The slaves themselves, they opined, were unfit for freedom,[233] and under slavery they were better off than they were as savages in Africa.[234] The planters felt that the evils of the free blacks after emancipation would also help to bring economic chaos.[235]

From another standpoint it was reasoned that, if the slaves were freed, the land would be worth nothing.[236] The planters argued in this way. Following the destruction of capital invested in slaves, the replacement of labor would be a problem. They claimed that the labor of free Negroes, not under force of punishment, would be ineffective, and that the supply of white laborers would be inadequate. As a result, extensive cultivation of the staples of the South would come to an end.[237]

Furthermore, planters feared they would become bankrupt by the annihilation of slave property. They would then be unable to continue agricultural pursuits in the South. An example was made of the valueless land left in the British West Indies after emancipation. Thus by the decline of the cultivation of the southern staples between

---

[231] Lloyd, *The Slavery Controversy*, pp. 126-161.

[232] Harper and Dew, *Pro-Slavery Argument*, pp. 85-88, 357-376.

[233] Lloyd, *op. cit.*, pp. 194-207.

[234] Frederick Olmsted, *A Journey in the Seaboard Slave-States, with Remarks on their Economy* (New York: Dix and Edwards & Co., 1856), p. 622.

[235] Lloyd, *op. cit.*, p. 223.

[236] Harper and Dew, *Pro-Slavery Argument*, pp. 85-88, 357-376.

[237] Lloyd, *op. cit.*, p. 207.

two-thirds and three-fourths of the foreign commerce of the United States would be destroyed. Not only did slavery provide for the Negroes and the planters, but for millions of free men residing in other States. With the destruction of southern agriculture, northern manufacturers would be without materials, factories would be forced to close. As a result, the laborers in these sections would become destitute from want and misery.[238]

But, even apart from such reasoning, they often played up the sacredness of vested property.[239] This argument is summed up by Hammond:

> Supposing that we were all convinced and thought of slavery precisely as you do, at what era of 'moral persuasion' do you imagine you could prevail on us to give up a thousand million of dollars in value of our slaves and a thousand million of dollars more in the depreciation of our lands.[240]

[238] Lloyd, *op. cit.*, pp. 207-209.
[239] Dew, *Pro-Slavery Argument*, pp. 385-390.
[240] Hammond, *Pro-Slavery Argument*, p. 141.

CHAPTER III

SLAVERY AS UNDERSTOOD BY KENRICK AND THE THEOLOGIANS CONTRASTED WITH EXISTING LAWS AND CUSTOMS IN THE UNITED STATES

In the foregoing chapter a brief summary of the controversy concerning slavery was given. In this chapter an attempt will be made to define slavery. Each article will be divided into two parts. In the first part the ideas of Kenrick and the Catholic theologians will be explained and in the second part the laws and customs prevailing in the United States will be given. It is felt that this is of prime importance. In general—especially among the abolitionists —people speaking of slavery, meant slavery as it existed in its most cruel form in the United States. The theologians, on the other hand, were writing of slavery as defined traditionally in the manuals of theology. Many misunderstandings could have been avoided if terms had been more clearly defined. Then too, the opinions expressed by Catholic theologians would have seemed less odious. It should be noted that when the theologians speak of slavery they refer only to the right of the master to the life-long service of the slave. They do not consider the slave as chattel property of the master as did the popular opinion of the day. From the fact of life-long service, flows the other relations between the two. These will be discussed in this chapter.

I. DEFINITION OF SLAVERY

Kenrick and the Theologians. Kenrick, along with the other theologians, defines slavery as: the state of perpetual subjection by which one is held to give his labors to another in return for his manitenance.[1]

The attitude of the theologians to the effect that the slave maintains his right as a person, is fairly well summed up by Kenrick who quotes Cardinal Gerdil.

> Slavery is not to be understood as conferring on one man the same power over another that men have over cattle. Wherefore, they erred, who in former times refused to include slaves among persons; and believed that however barbarously the master treated his slave he did not violate any right of the slave. For slavery does not abolish the natural equality of men; hence by slavery one man is understood to become subject to the dominium of another to the extent that the master has a perpetual right to all those services which one man may justly perform for another; and subject to the condition that the master shall take due care of his slave and treat him humanly.[2]

[1] Francis Patrick Kenrick, *Theologia moralis*, (Mechlin: H. Dessain, 1860-1861) tr. V, cap. VI, n. 40. This edition will be cited throughout the dissertation unless otherwise indicated. Any changes between this and the first edition will be noted. Cf. D. Lyonnet, *De justitia et jure*, Appendix I, par. I; Migne, *TCC*, 15: 844; Joseph Carrière, *Praelectiones theologicae de justitia et jure*, (3 vols.; Louvain: C. J. Fonteyn, 1845), Pars I, Sec. I, cap. III, p. 32; Gerdil, Giacinto Sigismodo, "Compensium institutionum civilium" *Opere edite ed inedite* (14 vols; Rome, 1806-1809) 7: L. I. p. 317; Antonius Diana, *Resolutiones morales* (10 vols.; Venice, 1728) 7: tr. 8, p. 289—defines it as "a constitution of the *Jus Gentium*, by which one is subjected to the dominium of another contrary to nature."

[2] Kenrick, *op. cit.*, tr. V, cap. VI, n. 39; Gerdil, *op. cit.*, p. 317 "Servitus non ita intelligenda est, quasi homo in hominem eam dominii rationem habere queat, quam habet in pecudem. Qua in re turpiter olim errarunt qui, servos in personarum numero censeri nolebant; et quamtumvis inique et crudeliter dominus servum habuisset, nullam tamen a domino injuriam ei servo fieri autumabant. Etenim servitus aequalitatem naturae inter homines non delet; proinde per servitutem sic homo in dominio alterius esse intelligitur, quatenus dominus jus perpetuum et universum habet in omnes servi operas, quas quidem ab homine homini praestari fas est; et ea quidem lege, ut curam servi gerere dominus debeat, eique officia humanitatis omnia studiose praestet, ut alibi declaravimus."

In the definition given above it must be noted that by slavery one is obliged to give his "services" to another in return for only his maintenance. Konings stresses the fact that the word "services" is used in the definition of slavery to indicate that slavery in the sense often accepted here in the United States in no case can be licit because slaves are not considered *persons,* but are numbered among *things,* which the master can use or destroy as he wills.[3]

Thus slavery does not give to the master direct ownership or the right of property over his slaves for this belongs to God alone, but only the right to use[4] the services of his slaves.[5]

A right is defined as a moral power which a person has and which other persons are bound to respect, to do something, or retain something, or exact something from another.[6] Perfect rights are those so closely connected with man's nature and personality that they are quite indispensable for the attaining of his end. These cannot be suspended without the consent of the persons, and in some cases they cannot even be surrendered by free will.[7]

Catholic theology stresses the fact that the slave does not lose his right to spiritual goods, and in these matters he is not subject to the master. Hence, he suffers a real injustice if by fraud or force he is induced to sin. To consent to any treatment, which is calculated to defeat the end and purpose of man's being is beyond his right; he cannot give his soul to servitude; for it is not man's own rights which are here in question, but the rights of God, the most sacred and inviolable of rights.[8]

[3] A. Konings, C.SS.R., *Theologia moralis* (2nd ed., New York: Benziger Bros., 1876), 1: p. 259, n. 595.

[4] *Dominium utile.*

[5] Konings, *op. cit.,* 1: p. 258, n. 595; Thomas A. Iorio, *Compendium theologiae moralis* (5th ed. Naples: M. D. D'Auria, 1934), n. 528.

[6] E. Cahil, S.J., *The Framework of a Christian State* (Dublin: M. H. Gill & Son, 1932), p. 284.

[7] *Ibid.,* p. 286.

[8] Leo XIII, "Rerum novarum," *Acta Leonis XIII,* 11: 127: "...Ani-

The slave, moreover, retains his rights to his life and members. Hence the master is guilty of a grave injustice to the slave if he cruelly beats, mutilates or otherwise hurts him, or weighs him down with too much work, or fails to provide sufficient and proper clothing.[9]

The slave retains the right to his good name. Hence he can suffer a real injustice in this regard from his master. For in this case as with regard to harm to his life and members he is considered as a free man, not as a slave.[10]

Since he does retain his rights to life and members and his good name he is owed restitution even from his master if he suffers injustice in these goods.[11]

In the controversy regarding abolition many members and groups of the Protestant Churches took part in emanci-

maque servitutem servire velle, ne sua quidem sponte homo potest; neque enim de juribus agitur, de quibus sit integrum homini, verum de officiis adversum Deum, quae necesse est sancte servari." cf. Joannis De Lugo, *Disputationes de justitia et jure* (Lugduni: Sump. Laurentii Atnaud et Petri Borde, 1670), disp. III, Sec. 3.

[9] De Lugo, *op cit.*, disp. III, Sec. 2, no. 19; Ludovicus Molina, *De Justitia et jure* (6 tom. coloniae Allobrogum: Fratres de Tournes, 1759), 1: tr. II disp. 38, no. 3; Diana, *op. cit.*, 7: tr. 8, resol. 4; Cahil, *op. cit.*, p. 286; Gerdil, *Opera edite*, etc., (Florence, 1850) 7: prop. III, p. 541.

[10] De Lugo, *op. cit.*, Disp. III, Sec. 3; no. 19; Gerdil, *Opera edite ed inedite*, (Florence: Giuseppe Celli, 1850), *De jure*, 7: prop. III, p. 541. Diana points out that a master sins gravely objectively if he treats his slaves with contumely, v.g., calling them dogs. Cf. Diana, *Resolutiones Morales* 7: tr. 8, resol. 42, p. 303.

[11] All the thologians admit that the slave suffers a real injustice if he is injured in goods of the body or soul by the master or another. They differ about restitution. De Lugo, holding that restitution can only be made in the same kind, finds restitution difficult. If money is to be paid he holds that it goes to the master. Cf. De Lugo, *op. cit.*, Disp. III, sec. 2; no. 20; on the other hand Molina thinks that restitution is to be made, and in the case of the master being guilty, different means are suggested, including liberty if the crime is very serious. If money is paid by a third party it is to go to the slave. Cf. Molina, *op. cit.*, 1: tr. 2, disp. 38, n. 3; Diana, *op. cit.*, 7: tr. 8, resol. 31, p. 301. Lessius, *op. cit.*, Sec. I, cap. IV, dub IV; Migne, *TCC*, 15: 480-482.

pation movements, teaching that slavery was instrinsically evil, while Catholics were generally on the opposite side. While there seems to be an enormous divergence between their views, in reality the actual difference was at times almost imperceptible. Thus in the excellent report made by the Congregational ministers concerning slavery one finds that their view was quite close to that of the Catholics.

This report stated that no man could acquire the right of ownership over another, excepting the case of punishment for crime, and the case where one sells his own time, liberty, skill and strength. But there are some things that man cannot relinquish justly and hence these cannot be bought, such as the rights of conscience, freedom to do the right and refuse the wrong, capacity of improvement, and the right to practice his religion. It concludes that if slavery were a contract it would be relieved of its odium, but even then it would be void because it would take away from man what he cannot give, for the laws of the States and their customs would make this contract too broad.[12]

There is no doubt but that slavery as it was found in the United States exceeded the limits allowed by the natural law; for it denied the slaves those rights which they could not even voluntarily relinquish.[13] Kenrick, in justifying at least temporary continuance of slavery demanded that certain rights of the slaves be secured.[14] This conclusion of the Congregational ministers that slavery by contract would be void rests on the fact that they were considering slavery as they found it supported by law and custom in the United States.

Whatever might have been the status of slaves had Catholic principles been accepted, the actual conditions found in

[12] *Report of the Committee on Slavery to the Convention of Congregational Ministers of Massachusetts, presented May 30, 1849* (Boston: T. R. Marvin, 1849), p. 80. Cf. J. Morce, D.D., *Discourse delivered at the American Meeting-House in Boston, July 14, 1808* (Boston: Lincoln & Edwards, 1808), pp. 10 f.

[13] Cf. *infra,* this chapter.

[14] Cf. infra, chap. III, and chap. IV.

the laws and customs of the country unmistakably exaggerated the right of the master, in fact—as will presently be noted—they took from the slave some perfect rights.

Slavery according to Law and prevaling customs in the United States. The civil law of South Carolina,[15] Georgia,[16] and Virginia,[17] to cite but a few instances, regarded the slave as chattel, which could be bought, sold, and otherwise freely disposed of by the master. In Louisiana they were considered as real chattel.[18] This status of the slaves was further brought out by decisions of the courts, where they were acounted as chattels,[19] personal estate[20] and for many purposes, real estate.[21]

[15] Act of Assembly, 1740, Joseph Brevard, *An Alphabetical Digest of the Public Statute Laws of South Carolina* (2 vols.; Charleston: John Hoff, 1814, 2: 229.

[16] Oliver Prince, *A Digest of the Laws of the State of Georgia, Compiled by the Appointment and under the Authority of the General Assembly,* (Athens: the author, 1837), p. 777.

[17] Act of June 18, 1822, *Code of Virginia Published Pursuant to an Act of the General Assembly of Virginia Passed on 15 August 1849* (Richmond: William F. Ritchie, 1849), p. 519.

[18] Act of 1808, *Statutes of the State of Louisiana revised by authority of the Assembly, 1857,* p. 523. It might be here pointed out that while they were considered as chattels, there were limitations regarding sale, work, and were to be baptized, married legally, fed properly, etc. In general, the laws of this state are considered by Philips to be the most humane. Cf. Philips, *American Negro Slavery,* pp. 493 f., Edward Channing, *History of the United States,* (New York: Macmillan & Co., 1919-1936), 6: 18.

[19] *Waldon's Executor* v. *Payne.* (Fall Term, 1794, 2 Wash. Rep. I, 8 cited from Jacob D. Wheeler, *A Practical Treatise on the Laws of Slavery,* (New York: Allan Pollock, Jr., 1837), p. 2.

[20] *Beatly* v. *Judy, et al* (Spring Term, 1833), I Dana Rep. 101, Wheeler, *op. cit.,* p. 2.

[21] *McDowell's Adm.* v. *Loveless* (Oct. Term, 1827), 6 Monroe Rep. 101, Wheeler, *op. cit.,* p. 2. For statutes in several colonies and territories summarized chronologically cf. J. C. Hurd, *The Law of Freedom and Bondage in the United States* (2 vols.; Boston: Little, Brown & Co., 1858); Legal regime analyzed from contrasting points of view: William Goodell, *The American Slave Code in Theory and Practice* (New York: 1853), and *Cyclopedia of Law and Procedure,*

The doctrine of the common law that the child followed
the condition of the father prevailed in the provinces until
the close of the seventeenth century. At that time, the
rule *partus sequitur patrem* was replaced by the maxim
partus sequitur ventrem, which prevailed until the end of
slavery.[22]

By decision of the court slaves were considered as chattels for the payment of debts.[23] Moreover, in North Carolina it was not an offense either at common law or by statute
to put slaves as a stake in gambling.[24]

At times little more consideration was given to the feelings and rights of slaves than to the animals. A master
could not claim trespass for an assault and battery on his
slave unless it was attended with the loss of service.[25] The
owner of a female slave was permitted to give her to one
of his children and her future increase to another.[26]

After the land in the border States had been worn out by
tobacco, the only profit that could acrue to those States
was to raise slaves for sale in the lower South. Thus the

William March, ed. (36 vols.; New York, 1910), pp. 465-495; De-
velopment of the slave code in Virginia traced in: J. C. Ballough,
A History of Slavery in Virginia (Baltimore, 1902); Legal regime
of slavery in South Carolina in the middle of the nineteenth century:
The Industrial Resources of the Southern and Western States, ed. by
J. B. C. DeBow (New Orleans, 1853), art. by J. B. O'Neall, 2: 269-
292; decisions of courts involving slavery: Jacob D. Wheeler, *op. cit.,*
George Stroud, *A Sketch of Laws Relating to Slavery* (2nd ed.;
Philadelphia: Kimbler and Sharpless, 1856).

[22] George M. Stroud, *op. cit.,* p. 1 ff. Kenrick pointed out without
comment that in Roman law, children born of a slave-mother were
held as slave for *partus sequitur ventrem.* Cf. Kenrick, *Theologia
moralis,* tr. V, cap. VI, n. 35.

[23] *Carrol, et al* v. *Connet* (Fall Term, 1829), J. J. Marshall's Rep.
201, Wheeler, *op. cit.,* p. 37.

[24] *The State* v. *Pemberton and Smith* (Dec. Term, 1829), Devereaux'
N. C. Rep. 281, Wheeler, *op. cit.,* p. 441.

[25] *Cornfute* v. *Dale* (April Term, 1800), I Har. & John's Rep. 4,
Wheeler, *op. cit.,* p. 239.

[26] *Bank's Adm.* v. *Marksburry* (Spring Term, 1823), 3 Little's
Rep. 275, Wheeler, *op. cit.,* p. 28.

domestic slave trade was begun.[27] The ability of slaves to provide offspring entered into the computation of their valuation, the morality of such generation provided no more scruples than the multiplication of brute animals to those engaged in the trade.[28] Numerous slave holders kept selected male slaves solely for breeding on their own plantation, as well as to be rented to others for the same purpose.[29]

Slaves were accorded very little if any rights in the courts. Generally speaking, Negroes, slave or free, could not be witnesses against white persons.[30] If it is alleged that such testimony would be dangerous to the lives and fortunes of the whites, it would seem to be implied that there is total lack of veracity in the slaves. Yet, they were admitted as witnesses against other Negroes, free or slave.[31]

[27] John Elliott Cairnes, *The Slave Power* (London: Macmillan & Co., 1863), pp. 127-135; Canning, *History of the United States*, VI: 22; Hart, *Slavery and Abolition*, p. 129. For slave breeding and its immoralities cf. Marshall Hall, *The Two-fold Slavery of the United States* (London: Adam Scott, 1854), pp. 24-31. Cairnes *op. cit.*, p. 136, estimated that between 1840 and 1850 about 235,000 slaves were shipped annually from the border States to the lower South. On the other hand, Winifield Hazlett Collins, *The Domestic Slave Trade of the Southern States*, (New York: Broadway Pub. Co., 1904) pp. 36-67, attempts to show that the domestic slave trade was not so extensive.

[28] Frederick Olmsted, *A Journey in the Seaboard Slave State with Remarks on their Economy*, (New York: Dix & Edwards & Co., 1856), p. 55; Phillips, *Life and Labor in the Old South*, p. 203; Phillips *American Negro Slavery*, p. 261; Collins, *op. cit.*, pp. 68-83.

[29] *The Negro in Virginia*, p. 171.

[30] Mississippi Act of June 8, 1822, *Code of Mississippi*, Compiled by A. Hutchinson, (Jackson, Miss.: Price and Fall, state printers, 1848), p. 515; Kentucky, Act of Feb. 8, 1798, William Littell and Jacob Swigert, *Digest of the Statute Law of Kentucky*. Printed under patronage of the Legislature (Frankfort, Ky.: Kendall and Russell, printers for the State, 1822), p. 1150; Alabama: "Act of June 6, 1806," *A Digest of the Laws of the State of Alabama* Compiled by appointment and under the authority of the General Assembly by Harry Toulmin. (Cahawba: Ginn & Curtis, 1823), p. 627.

[31] *Prince's Digest*, pp. 779, 780, 792; John A. Haywood, *Manual of the Laws of North Carolina arranged under distinct heads and in*

The American Law, invalidating the testimony of the Negro in any case where white people were concerned placed the Negro at the complete mercy of the whites, who could torture, maim or murder him with impunity if no white person were present. And few white people resided close to the Negroes on the plantations. Some very feeble efforts were made to remedy this, by stating that since many cruelties might be perpetrated on the slaves because there would be no white person present on some of the distant plantations, such persons would be considered guilty without evidence, *unless he cleared himself by his own oath.*[32]

Moreover, a slave could not be a party to a civil suit. Hence, it was necessary to get someone to act as guardian to institute a suit of freedom claimed. If the judgment was given in favor of the plaintiff, the ward was to be set free "but in case the judgment shall be given for the defendant, the said court is hereby empowered to inflict such corporal punishment, not extending to life and limb, on the ward of the plaintiff, as they in their discretion shall think fit."[33]

Furthermore, the slave could not be a party before a judicial tribunal in any species of action against his master, no matter how atrocious may have been the injury he received from him.[34]

While there was some diversity of law in various States concerning the criminal trials of slaves, it may be noted that trial by jury was utterly denied to the slave even in criminal accusations, which might affect his life, in the states of South Carolina, Virginia, and Louisiana.[35] Thus,

alphabetical order (Raleigh, N.C.: J. Gales, printer to the State, 1801), p. 523. However, in South Carolina they were not considered fit witnesses where parties of their own race were concerned. Cf. *Geoning* v. *Devana* (Feb. Term, 1831), 2 Bailey's Rep. p. 192, Wheeler, *op. cit.*, p. 193.

[32] Cf. 2, *Brevard's Digest*, p. 242.

[33] Act of South Carolina of 1740—2 *Brevard's Digest*, pp. 29 f—*Prince's Digest*, p. 777.

[34] Stroud, *op. cit.*, p. 38.

[35] Stroud, *op. cit.*, p. 91. In Georgia, slaves were tried before jus-

for example, in South Carolina the crimes of slaves are tried by any two justices of the peace, and any number of freeholders, not less than three nor more than five in the district where the crime is committed.

> In case the accused shall be convicted of any crime for which by law the punishment would be death, the said justices shall give judgment and award such manner of death as said justices, with the consent of the said free-holders shall direct, and which they shall judge will be most effectual to deter others from offending in like manner.[36]

Stroud pointed out that as a result of the ability to determine the manner of death as punishment, many horrid spectacles were seen. For example, the press of 1820 contained an account of the burning of a Negro woman.[37]

Slavery was intimately connected with color. Thus submission was required of the slaves not only to the will of his master, but to the will of all other white persons. For example in Georgia:

> If any slave shall presume to strike any white person, such slave upon trial and conviction by the justice or justices, according to the direction of this act, shall for the first offense, suffer such punishment as the said justice or justices shall, in his or their discretion think fit, not extending to life or limb; and for the second offense suffer death.[38]

The law of South Carolina was quite similar except that death was decreed only for the third offense.[39] No matter how dangerous the attack was upon the slave, he was compelled to submit. The only exception was if the attack were done in defense of, or at command of the master, in which case the master was responsible.[40]

tices for crimes that were not capital, but in capital crimes before a jury of white men. Cf. *Prince's Digest*, pp. 789 f.

[36] Act of 1740, 1 *Brevard's Digest*, p. 463.

[37] Stroud, *A Sketch of Laws Relating to Slavery*, p. 91.

[38] *Prince's Digest*, p. 781.

[39] Act of Assembly, 1740, 2 *Brevard's Digest*, p. 235.

[40] Cf. 2 *Brevard's Digest*, p. 235; *Prince's Digest*, p. 781.

Every Negro was presumed to be a slave.[41] Color and long possession were such prescriptive evidences of slavery as to throw the burden of proof on the party claiming his freedom.[42] However, the presumption of slavery arising from color was confined to blacks.[43]

II. MAINTENANCES OF SLAVES

Teaching of Kenrick and the theologians. In his tract on special obligations, Kenrick[44] noted that since slavery existed in many of the southern States, he desired to explain the duties of masters toward their slaves and those of slaves toward their masters, lest the priest should err in giving advice on either side. He said that masters were held to provide their slaves with good food and clothing and other necessities for since slaves depended entirely on the will of the master, if these things were denied to them they would be placed in certain danger to life; but it was not fitting, he thought, to give them more delicate things for the Holy Spirit teaches: "He that nourisheth his servant delicately from his childhood, afterwards shall find him stubborn."[45]

He pointed out that in some States the masters were accustomed to give a certain measure of Indian corn to the slaves each month, which they had to grind on a small mortar; pork meat was given in some places but in others no meat was furnished by the masters. As a result the occasion of theft easily arose.[46]

[41] *Maria, et al* v. *Surbough* (Feb. Term, 1825), 2 Rand. Rep. 228, Wheeler, *op. cit.*, p. 5; 2*Brevard's Digest*, pp. 229 f; *Prince's Digest*, p. 777.

[42] *Davis* (a man of color) v. *Curry* (Fall Term, 1810), Wheeler, *op. cit.*, p. 6.

[43] *Pilie* v. *Lalande et al.* (Apr. Term, 1829), 19 Martin's La. Rep. 648, Wheeler, *op. cit.*, p. 195.

[44] Kenrick, *Theologia moralis*, tract VIII, cap. IV, no. 93.

[45] Prov. 29: 93.

[46] Kenrick, *Loc. cit.* In view of this knowledge one wonders why Kenrick sounded a warning that the masters should not treat the slaves too delicately.

He concluded that those who permitted their slaves to go around without sufficient clothing and fail to protect them against the cold, or do not give them wholesome food, are guilty of grave sin, if thereby life is endangered.[47]

It would seem that he placed the sin in the danger to life—an obligation of charity—rather than in justice owed to the slave by contract, whereby he gives to the master his services with the agreement that his necessities are provided for. This does not seem consistent with his definition of slavery.[48]

Other theologians speak of the maintenance of slaves as being founded on justice. Thus Lyonett[49] maintained that the master has dominium only over the works of the slave with the condition that the master give to the slave that which is necessary and reasonably useful to the body and soul; for these are essential rights of human nature, which the slave cannot give up. He further added that if the contract is broken by the master by not supplying the necessities of life to the slave, it is *ipso facto* broken for the slave. Lessius[50] taught that if a slave is mistreated, for example, suffers hunger, cold, thirst, etc., he can lawfully flee from his master.

Special mention was made of the obligation of the masters toward the sick and old. Kenrick[51] taught that those who do not care for the sick, the old and those no longer suitable for labor, nor attempt to help them by remedies, or

---

[47]*Ibid.*   [48] Cf. *supra*, p. 55.

It should be pointed out that God created the earth and all it contains in order that by labor upon it men may each and all have means of developing their natural powers and of living a becoming life. Hence, a man has a natural claim to his due place on the earth's surface and cannot be legitimately excluded from access to his fair proportion of the goods of nature. Cf. E. Cahill, *The Framework of the Christian State*, (Dublin: M. H. Gill & Son, 1932), pp. 282 f.

[49] Lyonett, "De justitia et jure," Appendix I, pars. I, art. III, Migne, *TCC*, XV, par. 844.

[50] Lessius, "De justitia et jure compendium," Sec. I, cap. V, dub. V, Migne, *TCC*, XV, n. 508.

[51] Kenrick, *Theologia moralis*, Tr. VIII, cap. IV, no. 93.

preserve life to them by suitable food, sin gravely since they seem to wish to hasten their deaths. He noted that this happened to the little Egyptian boy long ago.[52]

Carrière[53] pointed out that the master has a perpetual obligation to maintain the slave. This obligation does not cease because of sickness. For if the obligation of the slave is perpetual so is that of the master. Cardinal Gerdil[54] stressed the fact that by justice the master is obliged to care for the slave in time of age and sickness.

Customs and laws. Before discussing the food given to the slaves in our country, it is well to note the accustomed diet in Africa.

On the West coast of Africa, especially in Guinea, the diet consisted of abundant vegetables, but the people were not all willingly complete vegetarians. In the jungles, animals were scarce and the men were ill-equipped for hunting. They often satisfied their craving for meat by eating locusts and larvae as tribes in the interior still do. Cannibalism was fairly common.[55]

The laws of the various States gave only vague regulations to the effect that slaves must be sufficiently fed, and that if the master failed to do this the master could be taken before a justice, who was to examine the case. If the master were guilty, arrangements were to be made for the relief of the slaves. If such neglect were the occasion of theft on the part of the slave, the master was to be held responsible for the damage.[56]

[52] The boy referred to was found in the fields by the soldiers of David who gave him something to eat and drink, for he had had nothing for thee days. After he was refreshed they brought him to David who asked him who he was and where he was going. He replied (Kenrick quotes the following words) : "I am a young man of Egypt, the servant of an Amalecite; and my master left me because I began to be sick three days ago."

[53] Joseph Carrière, *Praelectiones theologicae de justitia et jure,* (3 vols. Louvain: C. J. Fonteyn, 1845) I: p. 32, n. 42.

[54] Gerdil, *Opere edite,* etc., (Florence, 1850), VII, prop. III, p. 541.

[55] Phillips, *American Negro Slavery,* p. 5.

[56] Cf. 2 *Brevard's Digest,* p. 241, *Haywood's Manual,* pp. 524 f.

The Virginia slaves had two meals a day, breakfast from ten to eleven, and supper from six to nine or ten. The general allowance was a pint of corn meal and a salt herring or in lieu of herring a "dab" of fat meat. Sour milk was at times added as a luxury if there were an excessive supply. In harvest time meat rations were increased, but at other times the slaves received little bacon.[57] Olmsted noted that they had all the meal they wished, but would have liked more bacon. However, he added that they were often permitted to raise pigs and poultry and as many vegetables as they wanted.[58]

It seemed that meal formed the bulk of the food. This was used to make "hoe-cake," which was a thick cake made of meal mixed with water and patted into a cake, and fried on the flat edge of an ordinary hoe that rested in the ashes.[59]

In contrast to this, Robert Collins of Macon, Georgia, advised that for an adequate diet a field worker be given each week five pounds of clean pork bacon, one quart of molasses, and as much bread as was required. In the Fall they should get one pint of strong coffee sweetened with sugar each morning before going to work. Each family, moreover, should have a garden for raising its own vegetables, and children should be fed according to their needs.[60]

The cost of maintaining slaves is much discussed. The estimates run from fifteen to fifty dollars a year, which would not include medical attention.[61]

Before closing this discussion it is well to note that in many instances slaves were well fed so that they could be

[57] *The Negro in Virginia*, p. 69.

[58] Olmsted, *Seaboard States*, p. 109.

[59] *The Negro in Virginia*, p. 70.

[60] Olmsted, *Seaboard States*, pp. 692-97; R. H. Taylor, "Feeding Slaves," *JNH*, 9 (1924), 139-143. Phillips, *American Negro Slavery*, pp. 265 f describes the diet of the Hammond Plantation.

[61] Hart, *Slavery and Abolition*, p. 101; Olmsted, *Seaboard States*, p. 687; Hart, *EA*, 27: 395.

kept in good physical working condition.[62] But, on the other hand, masters were not wanting who thought it cheaper to feed the slaves badly and work them hard for a few years, perhaps eight, when they would be exhausted, than to preserve their health by proper feeding.[63] The homes of slaves consisted of log cabins of various degrees of comfort and commodiousness.[64] In general, slave row consisted of log or daub cabins that faced the big house on small farms and turned away from it on larger ones. It all depended on whether or not the master had an overseer. The favorite site was a hillside where there was good drainage close to a stream. The cabin usually had a window and a lone door that faced the street. A chimney rose at one end, built sometimes of brick but generally of intertwined sticks imbedded in packed mud.[65]

The clothing of the slaves was quite simple, and was usually issued twice a year. Olmsted[66] observed that in Virginia each year at the coming of winter the slave was issued a coat and trousers of wool or wool and cotton and in summer cotton trousers, sometimes with a jacket of the same. Likewise each year they received two pairs of strong shoes, or one pair of strong boots and one lighter pair, three shirts, one blanket and one felt hat. The women received two dresses of striped cotton, three shifts, two pairs of shoes, etc.

On the larger plantations the clothing was made from home-grown cotton. The short-staple cotton of Virginia was fashioned into the above mentioned jackets and dresses by the slaves themselves. Later the New England cotton mills developed a special "Negro-Cloth," a very coarse mixture of cotton and hemp, which went far toward outmoding homespun. The English variety of slave-cloth, osna-

[62] Olmsted, *Seaboard States*, p. 111.

[63] Phillips, *American Negro Slavery*, p. 383.

[64] Olmsted, *Seaboard States*, p. 111.

[65] *The Negro in Virginia*, p. 67; Hart, *Slavery and Abolition*, p. 102.

[66] Olmsted, *Seaboard States*, p. 112.

burgh or "fear-naught," a heavy coarse cloth, made a durable but uncomfortable garment. According to ex-slaves there were only two sizes, large and small.[67]

The usual dress, then, for men was canvas trousers and a cotton shirt with half-elbow sleeves. The women wore a cotton "shift" and a heavier dress over. The children wore a single "tow" shirt, the discarded apparel of grown-ups, or a guano bag with armholes cut in the corners. The shoes and hats were reserved for field work. The broiling sun was unbearable without protection and the baked, jagged clods of the tobacco fields were hard on bare feet.[68]

Regarding medical attention, it must be noted that some states authorized the courts to care for infirm slaves needing medical attention. The court could demand that the master compensate for money spent.[69]

Generally the planters found it necessary to guard the health and life of their slaves as the most vital interest for while the crops were merely income, the slaves were capital.[70] Hence, if the owners were not interested in caring for the slaves as a matter of principle, they did so in order that they could do more work and sell for better prices.[71] However, some writers give many instances of sick or old slaves, who had but a pittance for their support.[72] But it would seem that absolute abandonment of sick slaves was next to impossible for the slave codes, as has been indicated, provided penalties for those with means, who abandoned their slaves, allowing them to become public charges.[73]

Many masters did give kind and careful orders for the

[67] *The Negro in Virginia,* p. 71.

[68] *The Negro in Virginia,* p. 72; Phillips, *American Negro Slavery,* p. 266; Olmsted, *Seaboard States,* pp. 692-697 lists the clothes furnished on the Hammond plantation.

[69] Cf. *Prince's Digest,* p. 791.

[70] Phillips, *American Negro Slavery,* p. 301.

[71] *The Negro in Virginia,* p. 731.

[72] Elliot, *Sinfulness of Slavery,* 1: 122.

[73] Hart, *Slavery and Abolition,* p. 104.

care of the sick.[74] It is evident that hospitals which handled
Negroes did exist. Washington maintained a small hospital
at Mount Vernon for his slaves and paid a physician fifteen
pounds a years to look after them.[75] The "Surgical In-
firmary for Negroes" at Augusta had accommodations for
fifty or sixty patients. Board, lodging and nursing cost
ten dollars a month, and surgical and medical attention was
charged according to the "usual rates of city practice.[76]
For lesser ailments as well as deliverance of babies the mid-
wife was usually adequate. Each had her own secret remedies in addition to the genearlly known sensational cures.[77]

There were many cases of measles reported, as well as
whooping cough, and diphtheria. With regard to epidemics,
the Negroes were usually immune from yellow fever but
cholera at times threatened whole estates with bankruptcy.[78]
Other diseases often fatal were congestion of the lungs,
yaws, "Negro consumption," and colic. Some medical authorities diagnosed also "hebitude of mind," a general
breaking down of the will and nervous force, which overseers commonly supposed to be simple insolence and punished accordingly.[79] Hart[80] complains that too little attention was paid to the peculiar needs of women near child-
birth and that lifelong injuries among them from over-
strain were not uncommon.

III. THE SALE OF SLAVES

View of Kenrick and the theologians. Kenrick[81] admitted
that it is permissible to sell slaves, for this is a result of
their unfortunate condition, but as far as possible this
should be avoided as the mind cringes at the thought of the

[74] Phillips, *American Negro Slavery*, pp. 261-265.
[75] *The Negro in Virginia*, p. 74.
[76] Phillips, *American Negro Slavery*, p. 404.
[77] *The Negro in Virginia*, p. 75.
[78] Phillips, *American Negro Slavery*, p. 300.
[79] Hart, *Slavery and Abolition*, p. 107.
[80] Hart, *Slavery and Abolition*, p. 99.
[81] *Theologia moralis*, tr. VIII, cap. IV, n. 97.

sale of human beings. If a Catholic must sell his slave or slaves because of debts, the division of inheritance or some other grave reason, it behooves him, he said, to seek for them a Catholic master, and one who is humane and just. It is not lawful for the master to sell the slave indiscriminately to anyone who may wish to buy. He does, however, give two cases in which the master would be excused for selling his servant indiscriminately. They are: the case of a slave sold at auction by the authority of the law, and the case of the slave so vicious that the owner fears death to the family and to himself, unless the slave be sent away. In the first case the owner would be allowed to hand the slave over to the auctioneer, and in the second he would be allowed to sell him to anyone that he would meet willing to buy him. However, in the latter case care must be taken lest misfortune happen to the buyer, who would be unaware of the character of the slave.

Kenrick further bemoaned the circumstances that often surrounded the sale of slaves, in fact, condemned those who placed slaves in prisons awaiting sale, where they led a life that could not be imagined. But again he noted that at times the sale of slaves took place in the distribution of inheritance, or by the authority of the state for punishing crime or for satisfying creditors. In such cases it was at times necessary that the masters submit slaves to sale. If it were done without fraud or injury they could hardly be considered guilty of sin, even though the slaves underwent an unhappy condition. Nor in such cases was it in their power to secure their marriage rights and to provide for their salvation.[82]

---

[82] Kenrick, *op. cit.*, tr. VIII, cap. IV, n. 99. "Equidem quum eorum venditio aliquando contingat in haereditatis distributione, aliquando legis auctoritate ad crimina punienda, vel ad satisfaciendum creditoribus, opus est ut aliqui et ei vacent; quam si efficiant nulla fraude, vel injuria, vix rei haberi poterunt, etsi conditionem infelicem subeant mancipia: nec enim penes eos est vel conjugii jura sarta tecta servare, vel eorum saluti providere." Kenrick's excusing the master from sin, who separates the husband and wife, etc., referred to cases where

The theologians are in agreement with Kenrick in this matter of sale. Carrière[83] said that on first glance it seems terrible to put up for sale a man made to the image and likeness of God, but once slavery is admitted it follows that slaves can be sold, for the master can transfer his rights to the labor of slaves, for this can be the object of a contract, and if they are justly despoiled of their liberty they belong to the seller and if they are treated kindly by the buyers nothing is *per se illicit*. Gerdil[84] warned that in selling a slave caution must be had that such a person has been subjected to slavery by a just title. If prudent doubt arises concerning this and it cannot be solved after diligent investigation the slave, who has been bought must be manumitted.

The sale of slaves in the United States. Already in colonial days there existed on a small scale the sale of slaves from the North to the South. But by the end of the eighteenth century the internal trade began to be noticeable. One of the causes of this was the dis-establishment of slavery during and after the Revolutionary War in the North. As soon as the African trade closed, the internal trade began to assume the aspect of regular business, al-

the law required the sale. It should be noted that while this seems very harsh to us today, yet in the case where a husband is punished by imprisonment, the wife, although innocent, is deprived of her marriage rights.

[83] *De justitia et jure*, I, p. 37, n. 47.

[84] *Opere edite*, etc., (Florence 1850) 7: prop. III, p. 541. Konings writing after emancipation gave a list of ways that one making a general confession should be examined regarding slavery, then a thing past. He noted that a master sinned and was at that time held to restitution, who had taken part in the slave trade, or if he bought as a slave one that he knew to have been unjustly despoiled of his liberty. But if the person was held by a just title he could sin by separating a married person from his mate or a child from his parent without grave reason. Or he sinned if in selling a slave, especially a Catholic slave, he gave no attention to procuring a Catholic master and one who would be humane and just. Cf. A. Koings, *Theologia moralis* (2 vols. 2nd ed.; St. Louis and New York: Benzinger Bros., 1876) I: p. 259, n. 596.

though for years it continued to be of a small scale. The domestic slave trade reached its heights in the times of peace and prosperity, from 1815 to 1860, with the peak coming prior to the panic of 1837.[85]

The economic problem in Virginia and neighboring states was the principal cause of the sale of slaves from the point of view of those selling. The decrease of productivity of the worn-out tobacco land and the curtailment of foreign markets during and after the war of independence plunged Virginia into a depression. The Negro became a burden rather than a necessity.[86]

This started a trade in slaves. The slaves took the place of tobacco. The Virginia slave traders in this period enjoyed an affluence rivaled only by tobacco merchants of the previous century. Every city had scores of commission merchants dealing in slaves. At the opening of the Civil War Richmond had eighteen Negro traders, eighteen general collecting agents, and thirty-three auctioneers, all dealing in human goods.[87] Quite probably thousands were sold to the South from the northern slave states, North Carolina, Virginia, Maryland to the east of the mountains, and Tennessee, Kentucky and Missouri to the west of them.[88] The income from agricultural products in those states was not equal to one percent on the valuation of real and personal property, the balance of the income was made by sale of slaves to "the South." The premium on the production of children was so great that each child born was worth in a very short time about two hundred dollars.[89]

[85] Phillips, *American Negro Slavery*, pp. 187-190.

[86] *The Negro in Virginia*, p. 159. Collins, *The Domestic Slave Trade of the Southern States*, pp. 21-36.

[87] *The Negro in Virginia*, pp. 164 f.

[88] Channing, *History of the United States*, 6: 22; *The Negro in Virginia*, p. 163.

[89] Channing, *Ibid.* The following average price was estimated from the valuation of prime field hands convicted of capital punishment in Virginia. 1780—$465; 1790—$275; 1800—$375; 1810—$400; 1820—$600; 1830—$450; 1840—$900; 1850—$700; 1860—$1200. Cf.

The cause of these sales from the side of the buyers was
the great demand for slave labor in the deep south. An
obstacle to this cheap labor was the ban of the slave trade
in 1808. As the deadline approached ships rushed to South
Carolina and Georgia, but the demand was far from satisfied. Virginia, which had abundant supplies, put aside all
scruples and became the breeder and seller of slaves.[90]

The internal slave trade contained many of the cruelties
found in the African slave trade.[91] Olmsted[92] described in
detail the sale of some slaves by the dealers. They seem to
have been sold like animals, and the exposure of the ordinary goods in a store was no more public than the sale of
slaves in Richmond. The men at times were obliged to strip
in order to have their bodies closely examined. Firms would
have a buying house in a border State. The agent would ride
through the country to buy likely Negroes.[93]

They were transported in various ways. At times they
were loaded into freight cars, which Olmsted[94] said he saw
daily pass on their way to the south. Others were transported by overland coffles, which were encountered by
travellers.[95] This coffle chain was sometimes one hundred
feet long, having links of iron as thick as a finger. There
were handcuffs holding the left wrist of one slave and the
right of another. There was a ring connecting each wrist
band. The end of the coffle chain was then passed through
the ring and the slaves were made to walk forward until
its entire length was filled. They all had to keep in step

U. Phillips, "Slave Crime in Virginia," *AHR* 20 (1914-1915), 340;
Hart, *Slavery and Abolition*, pp. 128 f.

[90] *The Negro in Virginia*, p. 160.

[91] Olmsted, *Seaboard States*, p. 177 ff.; Hart, *Slavery and Abolition*,
p. 128.

[92] *Seaboard States*, pp. 30-40.

[93] Hart, *Slavery and Abolition*, p. 125; Olmsted, *Seaboard States*,
p. 647.

[94] *Seaboard States*, p. 55.

[95] Phillips, *American Negro Slavery*, p. 197; Buckingham, *Slave
States*, 2: 553; Olmsted, *Texas Journey*, p. 88.

by walking and swinging the heavy chain in unison. At intervals, every few days, the slaves would be changed around so as to ease the chafed wrists. "Nigger traders" roamed the state adding to their coffles at each stop.[96]

Once the slaves had arrived at the town where they were to be sold they were deposited in public jails, taverns, or some traders had stockades of their own. Some of these were decent, others not.[97] They were then advertised for sale in the newspapers.[98]

The few indications of law concerning the sale of slaves seem to have been made to protect the property interests of the owners rather than of the slaves. Louisiana seems to be the only state in which there was a law preventing the violent separation of parents from their children, or even of married persons from each other. Moreover, if at public sale in this State there were a slave who was disabled through old age or otherwise, and who had children, such slaves were to be sold only with such of his children whom he or she may think proper to go with.[99]

By the force of the revised code of Mississippi slaves descending from an intestate could be sold by order of the Orphans' Court, where equal division could be made.[100] However, when division of slaves could not be made without the separation of infant children from their mothers, compensation could be made in money,[101] or the court could

---

[96] *The Negro in Virginia*, p. 168.

[97] Phillips, *American Negro Slavery*, p. 194.

[98] Phillips, *Life and Labor in the Old South*, p. 157; Goodell, *Slave Code*, p. 54 f.; Sunderland, *Anti-Slavery Manual*, pp. 101-117. *The Negro in Virginia*, pp. 159-174, discusses the breeding of slaves for sale and its concomitant cruelties.

[99] Act of 1806—*Louisiana Statutes* (1852) p. 523; the Act of 1829 placed penalties for violations of the above act—*Louisiana Statues* (1852), p. 550.

[100]Cf. Wheeler, *A Practical Treatise on the Laws of Slavery*, pp. 50, 183.

[101] *Fitzhugh et ux.* v. *Foot, et al.* (Apr. Term, 1811), 3 Call's Rep. 13, Wheeler, *op. cit.*, p. 184.

order the sheriff to hire them out.[102]

It will be remembered that Kenrick[103] sounded a warning to those who would sell vicious slaves, namely, that they should caution the buyer lest harm unexpectedly befall him. There are indications that such sales did take place. At times they were sold to the deep south instead of being punished by death or imprisonment.[104]

However, cases of sales were invalid at times if the buyer was in ignorance of the character of the slave bought. Parole evidence was admissible to prove the declaration of a vendor concerning a rehibitory vice of slaves at or before the sale but not the testimony of strangers.[105] Drunkenness was considered a mental not a physical defect and was not a ground for rehibition,[106] but fraudulent concealment of it was grounds for rescinding the contract.[107] Moreover, if in the sale of a slave, his or her state of health was concealed or misrepresented the purchaser was absolved from the contract.[108]

After having mentioned the many cruelties connected with the internal slave-trade it would be unfair if a word were not said about indications of benevolence that can be easily found.

The universal contempt in which the slave-traders were held was so great and so general in the southern com-

---

[102] *Jackson* v. *Macy* (Spring Term, 1808), Hardin Rep. 582, Wheeler, *op. cit.*, p. 184.

[103] Kenrick, *Theologia moralis* tr. VIII, cap. IV, no. 97.

[104] Phillips, *American Negro Slavery*, pp. 192 f; Hart, *Slavery and Abolition*, p. 123.

[105] *Icar* v. *Suars* (Jan. Term, 1835), 7 La. Rep. 517, Wheeler, *op. cit.*, p. 139.

[106] *Xenes* v. *Taquinto, et al* (Apr. Term, 1829), 19 Martin's La. Rep. 678, Wheeler, *op. cit.*, p. 133.

[107] *Gaillard* v. *Labat, et al* (Dec. Term, 1835), 9 La. Rep. 17, Wheeler, *op. cit.*, p. 134.

[108] *Smith* v. *Rowzee* (Spring Term, 1821), 3 Marshall's Rep. 527, Wheeler, *op. cit.*, p. 119.

munities as to produce social ostracism.[109] But on the other hand the kindest masters might get into debt or die, causing property to be divided according to the unfortunate laws and customs. Auction sales were at times pathetic.

In order to protect faithful servants from long distance sales there were frequently two prices, one for sale in the neighborhood and a higher one for sale to the lower south.[110] Likewise many Virginia owners would insist that families be kept together, especially that mothers be not separated from their babies. There was little guarantee, however, that this promise would be kept.[111]

At times, too, the personal equation was quite a factor in the sale or hire of slaves to another. Some were sold for punishment, others for the effect that such a sale would have on the morale of their fellows, some owners were impelled by financial stress to commission their slaves to find buyers of their own choice; some purchases were prompted by belief that new management would prove more congenial and fruitful than the old; other transfers were made for the benefit of couples, who desired marriage[112]

Tender scenes like the following were known. When a certain group of slaves was auctioned in settlement of an estate the ties of affection between them and their mistress were so strong that she bought them regardless of cost. The agent admitted that the excessive cost was the result of by-bidding. The court, while calling the price a valid one, reduced it to the market level.[113]

IV. ABDUCTION OF FREE NEGROES

The teaching of Kenrick and the theologians. On two

[109] Phillips, *American Negro Slavery*, p. 200; Hart, *Slavery and Abolition*, pp. 123, 125.

[110] Phillips, *American Negro Slavery*, p. 192.

[111] *The Negro in Virginia*, p. 169.

[112] Phillips, *Life and Labor in the Old South*, p. 216.

[113] Helen T. Catterall, *Judicial Cases Concerning American Slavery and the Negro* (Washington, D.C.: Carnegie Institute, 1926) I: 96.

occasions Kenrick warned that it is seriously sinful to abduct a free Negro and reduce him to slavery. First in his chapter on slavery he warns that those sin who take away by force those who are unwilling to go into slavery.[114] Again, in treating of those things over which one can gain dominium, he said that those who induce Negroes by force or trickery to go from a free state to a slave state are held to vindicate their liberty at their own expense. Those who paid money for them likewise are obliged to restore their liberty in as far as they can without most grave difficulty even if they will not be able to recover the money paid.[115] For liberty is natural to man and hence it is an atrocious crime to bring free men into slavery.[116]

Kidnapping in Practice. The principle that persons of color are to be considered slaves unless proved free, prepared the way for man-stealing. Free men going about their lawful business could be arrested if no documentary evidence could be immediately adduced, thrown into jail, advertised as runaways. If no master called for them in a given time—as would have been the case if they had been slaves—they were sold at auction as unclaimed fugitives in order to derive proceeds from the sale to defray expenses of their detention. "The unrighteous doctrine of presumption from color, steps in and consummates the iniquity and the freeman and his posterity are doomed to hopeless bondage."[117]

Likewise the laws in other respects set the stage for loss of freedom.

> In case any slave shall be emancipated or set free, otherwise than according to the act regulating emancipation, it shall be lawful for any person whatsoever to seize and convert to his own or her own use, and to keep as his or her own property

[114] Kenrick, *Theologia moralis*, tr. V, cap. VI, no. 40.
[115] "quatenus id absque gravissimo discrimine sit possible."
[116] Kenrick, *op. cit.*, tr. X, cap. III, no. 12.
[117] Stroud, *A Sketch of Law Relating to Slavery*, p. 56.

the said slave so illegally emancipated or set free.[118]

Furthermore, in South Carolina if a free Negro harbored, concealed or entertained a runaway slave or a slave charged "with any criminal matter" he would forfeit the sum of ten pounds currency for the first day and twenty shillings for every succeeding day. And in the case where such forfeitures could not be levied, or where such free Negro should not pay the same, together with the charges attending the prosecution such free Negro would be ordered by the justice to be sold at public out-cry and the money arising by such sale would in the first place be paid to the owner and the remainder, if any, would be paid by such justice into the hands of the public treasurer.[119] In Georgia by the Act of December 19, 1818 free Negroes were not permitted to come into the State. Those who did could be arrested and on conviction had to pay one hundred dollars or they were liable to be sold as slaves.[120] In Mississippi every Negro found in the State who negligently failed to procure or renew his certificate of freedom could be sold by court order.[121]

Likewise, slaves, who had been freed and had no reason to suppose they were anything else than free men could be seized years later for a defect in the legal process of manumission.[122]

The abduction and sale of free Negroes was an element of some importance in the domestic trade. Free Negro children were frequently kidnapped and sold into slavery. Gangs of kidnappers flourished. There is little basis for establishing any number but "it was probably equal to

[118] S. C. Act of 1800, 2 *Brevard's Digest*, p. 256; cf. N. C. Act of 1777, *Haywood's Manual*, p. 525.

[119] Act of 1740, 2 *Brevard's Digest*, p. 237.

[120] *Prince's Digest*, p. 795.

[121] Act of June 18, 1822, *Miss. Revised Statutes* 1848), p. 525.

[122] Buckingham, *Slave States*, 2: 32.

and possibly exceeding the number of Negroes escaped from bondage."[123]

These cases of kidnapping took place especially between the years 1793 and 1850. In the North, there was practically no slavery, but many of the free blacks under ruse of the fugitive law of 1793 were kidnapped and taken to the South.[124]

Various methods were used for kidnapping. The most common in places where the courts were friendly to slavery was to arrest a man on a false pretense, and when he appeared in court without opportunity to secure papers or witnesses, to claim him as a fugitive. Sometimes the gangs would carry out their purpose through some small deception after having observed a slave for a time. This was done especially when they feared taking him to court. Other times the kidnappers were so bold that they resorted to simple force without the slightest attempt at concealment. But at times there would be interference and rescue by indignant civilians.[125]

V. WORK OF SLAVES

Teaching of Kenrick and the theologians. Under "Special Obligations" Kenrick[126] treated the work of slaves. He taught that masters should give to the slaves work that does not exceed their strength or ability, lest they be given the occasion of idleness, since the slaves lack the enjoyment of letters; by idleness they easily fall into crimes. Those who are of an evil disposition are to be subdued by labor; but those of a milder disposition are to be more mildly and kindly treated. He then quoted the following passage:

[123] Edward B. Reuter, *The American Race Problem* (New York: Thomas Y. Crowell Co., 1938), p. 5; McDougall, *Underground Railroad*, chap. 38.

[124] McDougall, *Fugitive Slaves*, p. 27; Marchall Hall, *Two-fold Slavery in the United States, with a Project of Emancipation* (London: Adam Scott, 1854) pp. 83-88.

[125] McDougall, *op. cit.*, pp. 36-40.

[126] Kenrick, *Theologia moralis*, tr. VIII, cap. IV, no. 94.

"Torture and fetters are for a malicious slave; send him
to work, that he be not idle. For idleness hath taught much
evil. Set him to work: for so it is fit for him. And if he
be not obedient, bring him down with fetters, but be not
excessive towards any one, and do no grievous thing without judgment. If thou have a faithful servant, let him be
to thee as thy own soul: treat him as a brother."[127] He
added that such was the manner advised by St. Paul when
he sent Onesimus back to Philemon when he said: "Not
now as a servant, but instead of a servant, a most dear
brother." Such action, however, does not demand familiar-
ity between servant and master.[128]

Cardinal Gerdil pointed out that only slaves who had
been reduced to that condition for a capital crime could be
subjected to work where there is grave danger to life; the
others can be given only ordinary work, and if they are
asked to do extraordinary work, such demand would only
be lawful if compensation accompanies it, such as freedom
to be granted after a time.[129]

Kenrick sounded a special warning concerning overseers.
He said that since the overseers without the knowledge
of the master often imposed burdens upon the slaves that
are too hard and often treat the slaves cruelly, the masters
had an obligation to select men with humane qualities for
that position.[130]

Kenrick[131] in his treatment "de servis" under the general
heading of ownership also noted that at times the master
gave the slaves the right to hire themselves out—which is
prohibited by law because of abuses, he said—for a monthly salary. He held that if slaves by their own industry

[127] He omitted the last phrase of the passage: "... Because in the
blood of the soul thou has gotten him." Cf. Ecclesiasticus, 32: 28-31.
[128] Kenrick, *op. cit.,* tr. VIII, cap. IV, no. 94. In the first edition he
added that it is enough that the master treat him benignly. 1841 ed.
I: p. 370, no. 94.
[129] Gerdil, *Opere edite,* etc., (Florence 1850) 7: Prop. III, pp. 541 f.
[130] Kenrick, *Theologia moralis,* tr. VIII, cap. IV, no. 94
[131] Kenrick, *Theologia moralis,* tr. X, cap. IV, no. 48.

earned a greater salary, they could lawfully retain the excess.

Laws and customs. The master generally could determine the kind, degree and time of labors to which the slave should be subjected.[132] And by the mere fact that some states made laws such as the following, it can be argued that there must have been some abuses in that regard.

> Whereas many owners of slaves and others who have the care, management and overseeing of slaves, do confine them so closely to hard labors, that they have not sufficient time for natural rest: Be it therefore enacted: That if any owner of slaves or other persons, who shall have the care, management, or overseering of any slaves, shall work or put any such slave or slaves to labor more than fifteen hours in twenty-four hours from the twenty-fifth day of September to the twenty-fifth day of March, every such person shall forfeit any sum not exceeding twenty pounds, nor under five pounds, current money, for every time he or she or they shall offend thereon at the discretion of the justice before whom the complaint is made.[133]

Commenting on this law Goodell and Stroud pointed out that in comparison with the law concerning prisoners it was very severe. For in the states of Maryland, Virginia, and Georgia the laws forbade that the criminals in their penitentiaries should be compelled to labor more than ten hours a day, and not exceeding nine hours in some portions of the year and eight the months of November, December and January.[134]

Occasionally a squad of Negroes would revolt because of the length or of the severity of their labors. The revolt would take the form of a strike, in which the squad would "lie out" in the swamps, all the while attempting to make an adjustment with the overseer or even a compromise,

[132] Stroud, *Sketch of Laws Relating to Slavery*, p. 13.

[133] South Carolina Act of Assembly of 1740, 2 *Brevard's Digeat*, p. 243. Cf. Mississippi Act of June 13, 1822, *Revived Code* (1848), p. 317.

[134] Goodell, *Slave Code*, p. 129; Stroud, *op. cit.*, p. 15.

through the slaves of the neighboring estates. At times
they would just wait until the return of the master. At
times the conclusion of the affair was tragic to both
sides.[135]

Work was especially difficult for women. The single
women could bear the burden of the field work but pregnant women found it hard. Former slaves insist that many
slaves preferred to marry women from other plantations
so that they would not have to see them trying to keep up
with the row.[136]

On the other hand, some tobacco planters complained,
according to Olmsted,[137] that the Negroes never worked
until they tired themselves out, rather they would rarely
put in one-half day's fair work, as they were always ready
to go out to frolic at night. He also noted that owners drain-
ing tobacco plantations usually used Irishmen. On asking
one planter why, he was told: "It's dangerous work and
a Negro's life is too valuable to be risked at it. If a Negro
dies it's a considerable loss, you know."

In Virginia from Christmas to New Year's the slaves
were free excepting the household servants. Christmas was
a very special time of celebrating for the slaves.[138]

It is well to remember that all power of the master over
the slaves could be exercised, not only by himself, but by
any one whom he might depute as his agent.[139] Only Louisiana had an express law on this matter of delegation, but
usage and the precedent of the courts usually existed.[140]

Whenever there were as many as twenty slaves it was
common to employ an overseer.[141] Quite often it was to
the advantage of the overseer to force the slaves to greater
production. Phillips in speaking of the Robert Carter

---

[135] Phillips, *American Negro Slavery*, p. 304.
[136] *The Negro in Virginia*, p. 62.
[137] Olmsted, *Seaboard States*, p. 91.
[138] *Ibid.*, pp. 101-103.
[139] Stroud, *op. cit.*, p. 28.
[140] Goodell, *Slave Code*, p. 199.
[141] Hart, *Slavery and Abolition*, p. 118.

plantation says that each unit of plantation size was in charge of an overseer, who received as his pay one-ninth of the crop made by his group.[142] In the nineteenth century the rise of slave prices intensified the occasion for conserving the lives, health and contentment of the slaves. As a result the old system of overseers on shares was abandoned as crudely exploitive and they were engaged on a fixed wage. Occasionally a contract called for an additional bonus under certain conditions.[143]

Concerning overseers in general, the great variety of their functions, their scale of operation and their personal qualities make broad statements hazardous.[144] Yet, from the literature one would be inclined to presume that they were quite often a great source of injustice to the slaves.[145]

Slaves were hired by the day, month, or more commonly by the year. The employer was required to provide shelter, food, clothing and medical services in addition to a stipulated wage, which of course went to the master.[146]

The price of hiring varied with the fluctuations of prosperity. In the lower south, full hands were hired for considerably less than one hundred dollars a year in 1800 but for two hundred dollars in 1860[147] In Virginia it was quite often the practice to give a weekly allowance of seventy-five cents to the slaves hired, with which they would board themselves. Little of this could be saved, but hired servants usually did not have to account to the master for the money earned on the side.[148] However, some States had laws which forbade masters to permit their slaves to hire themselves out. If such was done, it became lawful for any

---

[142] Phillips, *Life and Labor in the Old South*, p. 226.

[143] Phillips, *Life and Labor in the Old South*, p. 307.

[144] Phillips, *American Negro Slavery*, p. 279.

[145] Hart, *Slavery and Abolition*, p. 118; Stroud, *op. cit.*, p. 29; Phillips, *Life and Labor in the Old South*, p. 310.

[146] Phillips, *Life and Labor in the Old South*, p. 181; *The Negro in Virginia*, p. 51.

[147] Phillips, *Old South*, p. 181; Olmsted, *Seaboard States*, p. 46.

[148] *The Negro in Virginia*, p. 48.

person and the duty of the sheriff to apprehend such slaves. The master was forced to pay a fine of not less than ten dollars and not more than twenty dollars.[149]

This hiring of slaves prevailed extensively in all the southern towns because of the eagerness of short term employers to avoid the risks of speculation involved in buying slaves.[150] Since this hiring was profitable, many owners saw to it that the slaves become artisans. The slaves themselves were aware of the fact that skill often determined their status and tried hard to improve their artisanship.[151]

The main supply of slaves for hire came from the children, especially sons but sometimes also the daughters of the cooks, housemaids, and the like of the merchants, lawyers, and others who had very limited need of servants.[152] At times, too, because of the general custom of hiring slaves, Negroes serving time in jails, either slave or free, were hired out to privtae contractors.[153] The co-ordination of the demand and supply of hired slaves was facilitated by brokers.[154]

To the average owner, the morals of the slave were of little concern. Yet it must be remembered that the renting out of female slaves exposed them to great moral dangers.[155]

The system of hiring out was responsible for much of the ill-treatment of the Negroes. At times they were beaten quite severely by the hirer or overseer.[156]

VI. PUNISHMENT OF SLAVES

Teaching of Kenrick and the theologians. In his tract

---

[149] Cr. Mississippi Act of June 18, 1822, *Code of Miss.* (1848), p. 516; Kentucky Act of December 1802, 2 *Littel and Swigert's Digest*, p. 1159.

[150] Phillips, *American Negro Slavery*, p. 204.

[151] *The Negro in Virginia*, p. 56.

[152] Phillips, *American Negro Slavery*, p. 407.

[153] *The Negro in Virginia*, p. 56.

[154] Phillips, *American Negro Slavery*, p. 409.

[155] *Ibid.*, p. 408.

[156] *The Negro in Virginia*, p. 152.

on special obligations of masters and servants, Kenrick[157] pointed out that slaves were to be punished lest impunity cause boldness; but at the same time cruelty was to be entirely avoided. He noted that the apostle admonished masters to show themselves kind to their servants.[158] Hence those, who in a fit of anger, beat or cause to be beaten, a slave for a light cause are guilty of sin and the sin is the greater, the lighter the cause and the more violent the beating, especially when there is danger to life or members, he taught. The excuse that the slave is considered the master's property does not avail in the eyes of God, even though the civil law would not punish a master for excessively beating his slave.

To substantiate this view Kenrick quoted St. Thomas[159] who maintained that it was permissible for parents to whip their children and masters their slaves for the sake of correction, according to the proverbs: "He that spareth the rod hateth his son but he that loveth him correcteth him betimes," and "Withhold not correction from a child, for if thou strike him with the rod, he shall not die. Thou shalt beat him with the rod; and deliver his soul from hell."[160] And "Torture and fetters are for a malicious slave; send him to work that he be not idle."[161] Since, then, the child is under the power of the father and the slave under the master, Kenrick said that he can lawfully be whipped for the sake of correction and discipline. The master must use moderation, however, for St. Paul says: "And you, fathers, provoke not your children to anger," and "and you, masters, do the same things to them, forebearing threatenings."[162]

---

[157] Kenrick, *Theologia moralis*, tr. VIII, cap. IV, no. 95.

[158] "And you, master, do the same towards them, and give up threatening knowing that their Lord who is also your Lord in heaven, and that with him there is no respect of persons." Ephesians, 6: 9.

[159] 2a, 2ae, q. 65, art. 2.

[160] Prov. 23: 13 f.

[161] Eccles. 33. 28.

[162] Ephesians, 6: 6, 9; Kenrick, *op. cit.*, tr. VIII, cap. IV, no. 95. Kenrick omitted the rest of verse 9: "... knowing that the Lord of

It should be pointed out that the early theologians clearly taught that a master sins grievously by cruelly punishing his slave, especially if he endangers his health or life.[163] Likewise, he sins grievously if he beats his slave for a slight fault.[164]

Kenrick[165] also pointed out that in punishing a slave the master must take care lest he inflict irreparable injury, which may only be done by the supreme power. He quoted St. Thomas[166] to the effect that the state is a perfect society and as such has the complete power to coerce. Hence, the state can inflict mutilation, whereas the father and the master is head of the family, which is only an imperfect community. They enjoy imperfect power of coercion such as whipping, which does not inflict irreparable harm.

He noted that in order to keep the masters within the limits of their power the Old Law gave liberty to slaves, who were deprived of an eye or a tooth. "If any man strike the eyes of his man-servant, or maid-servant and leave them but one eye, he shall let them go free for the eye which he put out. Also, if he strike out the tooth of his man-servant or maid-servant, he shall in like manner make them free."[167]

both of them and you is in heaven. And there is no respect of persons with Him."

[163] Molina, *De justitia et jure*, tom. IV, tr. 3, disp. 2, no. 14.

[164] Diana, *Resolutiones morales*, 7: tr. 8 resol. 42, p.303. Some theologians thought that the master should be forced to sell a slave if the master is found guilty of cruelty.

[165] Kenrick, *op. cit.*, tr. VIII, cap. IV, no. 95.

[166] 2a, 2ae, q. 65, art. 2, ad 2um.

[167] Exodus, 21: 26 f. He also paraphrases the following text of the Old Law: "He that striketh his bond-man or bond-woman with a rod and they die under his hands, shall be guilty of crime. But, if the party remains alive a day or two, he shall not be subjected to the punishment because it is his money." Exodus, 21: 20 f. In the later edition Kenrick noted that by the law of Maryland a servant became free if the master was guilty of excess in punishing three times or if he was guilty of not supplying things necessary for life. Kenrick, *op. cit.*, tr. VIII, cap. IV, no. 95.

The theologians unanimously teach that man does not have direct dominium over his life and members, but has only the use of them. The power of life and death is attributed to God as something special,[168] which would not be special if each man had full dominium.[169] Since, then, man has only the use of his life and members, the master cannot claim dominium over them.[170]

Under the title of restitution, Kenrick,[171] pointed out that if a slave is given capital punishment by the civil power, the price of the slave should be given by the government to the owner.

Under reparation of special injuries, Kenrick[172] noted that if someone killed a slave, he owed restitution to the master of the slave. The amount was to be estimated according to prudent judgment concerning the value of such slave.

Some theologians go further in the matter of restitution for slaves who have been killed. De Lugo[173] admitted that some taught that two-fold restitution must be made if a slave is injured or killed, namely to the master and to the slave or his family. But, he feels that restitution to the latter is due only after the sentence of a judge on account of the principle that they are goods of a different kind. He admitted, however, that there is a precedent set by the juridical law of Exodus.

Twice Kenrick emphatically condemned lynching. First, in treating of the fifth commandment, he noted that in some places private citizens assume the right of judging criminals and punishing them immediately even by death. He taught that such process is void of all justice and public order, and is an enormous crime. The power that several

---

[168] Wis. 16: 13.

[169] Lyonnet, *De justitia et jure*, Migne, *TCC*, 15: no. 842.

[170] Lessius, *De justitia et jure*, Lib. 2, cap. 4, dub. 10; Carrière, *De justitia et jure*, I: pp. 32, no. 43.

[171] Kenrick, *op. cit.*, tr. X, cap. III, no. 183.

[172] *Ibid.*, tr. X, cap. V, no. 218.

[173] De Lugo, *De justitia et jure*, disp. III, sec. II.

citizens usurp for themselves belongs only to a perfect community and not to individuals. The pretext of acting for the safety of the community does not avail. He noted that the Constitution forbids that men be despoiled of life, liberty or property without the due process of law.[174]

Again in his treatment of things over which dominium can be had Kenrick after showing that God alone has the right of life and death, explained that the state for the good of the whole can use capital punishment and noted that often this power is appropriated by individuals who, impelled by anger and revenge, punish criminals without any process of law. Such a practice, he says, is to be reprobated as contrary to the divine law, which threatens pestilence and slaughter to the country.[175]

Laws and customs concerning punishment. The stories of brutality of the slave days must be read in their relation to an era in which human suffering elicited scant sympathy, when a public hanging drew curious crowds, when mentally deranged persons and imbeciles furnished amusement for jeering onlookers and when society sought not to reform the criminal but to place upon him a mark that would serve as a safeguard and warning.[176]

Public sentiment generally condemned the cruel treatment of slaves; but still it did occur during fits of passion and often without deliberation. It was especially perpetrated by overseers, who were sometimes men of intelligence and piety, but more often brutal, licentious and drunken men, unfit for responsibility.[177]

The community condoned a certain amount of cruel punishment; otherwise planters would not have printed descriptions of scars and brands to identify slaves in advertising for those who had escaped.[178] Then, too, in the

---

[174] Kenrick, *op. cit.,* tr. III, cap. IX, no. 142. *Constitution* art. 5.

[175] Kenrick, *op. cit.,* tr. X, no. 8.

[176] *The Negro in Virginia,* p. 150.

[177] Olmsted, *Seaboard States,* pp. 45, 97; Elliott, *Sinfulness of American Slavery,* 1: 183 ff.

[178] Phillips, *American Negro Slavery,* p. 320.

early history of the country some rather cruel punishments were publicly performed, such as the following: if a Negro or Indian, not a Christian, gave false testimony he was sentenced to have one ear nailed to the pillory for one hour and then cut off, after which the second ear was to be treated similarly. Thirty-nine lashes accompanied the dismemberment.[179] As late as 1808 slaves were burned alive and for supposed complicity in setting fire in Augusta in 1830 a slave woman was executed and quartered.[180]

One sees quite a contrast between this condonation of cruelty on the part of American society and the customs practiced in countries under the influence of the Church. For example, if a slave fled to a church because of the cruelty of his master, he enjoyed the immunity of the sanctuary. He was to be restored to the master only after the latter had taken an oath not to act cruelly toward him in the future. If the cruelty was excessive, the master was obliged to sell him. If the cruelty was light or the crime committed small, and only small punishment would be expected, he was returned to the master after the master had taken the the oath. But, if it was feared that another would inflict punishment on him, then he enjoyed immunity.[181]

The spirit and extent of slave punishments in the United States depended upon a combination of two contradictory conceptions: The Negro was looked upon as a child, who must be thumped into obedience; at the same time he was looked upon as an adult, capable of understanding responsibility and willfully defying his master.[182]

By 1821 all states declared that the malicious and deliberate murder of slaves by whomever perpetrated, was punishable by death. Earlier in some instances they were punished only by fine.[183]

---

[179] *The Negro in Virginia,* p. 151.
[180] Hart, *Slavery and Abolition,* p. 116.
[181] Sanchez, *Opera moralia,* Lib. IV, cap. I, dub. 8, no. 30.
[182] Hart, *Slavery and Abolition,* p. 113.
[183] Cf. *James' Digest,* p. 392—Act of Assembly of S. C., Dec. 20,

In most of the states where the murder or mutilation of slaves was proscribed by law, there was often a legal escape. Note the wording of the Act of the state of North Carolina of 1798, section 3:

> "Be it enacted that if any person hereafter be guilty of maliciously killing a slave, such offender shall, on the first conviction thereto, be adjudged guilty of murder and shall suffer the same punishment as if he had killed a free man; Provided always, this act shall not extend to any person killing a slave outlawed by virtue of any Act of Assembly of this State, or to any slave in the act of resistance to his lawful owner or master, or to any slave dying under moderate correction."[184]

The slaves who committed crimes—if tried at all—were tried by those who would be inclined to be severe to them, especially in matters that related to their treatment of white people. Thus a slave in North Carolina on trial for a capital felony was entitled to a jury, but that jury was to be made up of slave-owners.[185] In South Carolina[186] and in Virginia[187] they were tried by justices and free-holders courts.

Although the testimony of slaves could never be admitted against white persons, a slave being tried for a grave crime could be convicted on the testimony of another slave although this evidence was uncorroborated by pregnant circumstances.[188]

The following chart shows an alarming and unjust difference in the punishment of whites and slaves.

1821; *Va. Revised Code (1849)*, p. 723; Act of N. C. of 1798; Constitution of Ga., art. 4, sec. I; *Miss. Revised Code (1848)*, p. 781.

[184]*Haywood's Manual*, p. 530.

[185] *The State* v. *Jim, a Neg. Slave* (Dec. Term, 1826), Devereaux's N. C. Rep. 142, Wheeler, *op. cit.*, p. 212.

[186] Act of 1854, *James' Digest*, p. 392.

[187] *Rev. Code*, p. 789. Phillips, *American Negro Slavery*, pp. 493 f; analyzes crimes committed by Negroes in Baldwin Co., Ga.

[188] *The State* v. *Ben, a slave* (Dec. Term, 1821), I Hawk's N. C. Rep. 434, Wheeler, *op. cit.*, p. 204.

CRIME	PUNISHMENT		
	WHITES	FREE NEGROES	SLAVES
1. Murder of 1st degree	death p. 723	death p. 723	death p. 723
2. Murder of 2nd degree	5-18 yrs. p. 723	5-18 yrs. p. 723	death p. 753
3. Voluntary manslaughter	1-5 yrs. p. 723	1-5 yrs. p. 723	death 2nd off. p. 753
4. Attempting to administer poison to a person or a persons or poisoning a well, spring or reservoir	3-5 yrs. p. 723	3-5 yrs. p. 723	death p. 753
5. Administering a drug to a woman to destroy an unborn child; if child is destroyed — unless done in good faith to save life of woman or child	1-5 yrs. p. 724	15 yrs. p. 724	death 2nd off. p. 753
6. Maliciously shooting stabbing, etc., with intent to disfigure, maim or kill	1-10 yrs. p. 724.	1-10 yrs. p. 724.	death 2nd off. p. 753
7. Unlawfully shooting, stabbing, etc., in commission of or attempting to commit a felony	1-5 yrs. p. 724	1-5 yrs. p. 724	death 2nd off. p. 753
8. Committing a robbery if armed with dangerous weapon	5-10 yrs. p. 724	5-10 yrs. p. 724	death p. 753
9. —if not armed	3-10 yrs. p. 724	3-10 yrs. p. 724	death p. 753
10. Threatening a person to extort money	1-5 yrs. p. 724	1-5 yrs. p. 724	death 2nd off. p. 753
11. Rape or carnal knowledge of a female under 12 yrs. or of one			

PUNISHMENT

CRIME	WHITES	FREE NEGROES	SLAVES
past 12 against her will	10-20 yrs. p. 524	death or 10-20 yrs. at discretion of jury p. 753	death p. 753
12. Attempting by force or fraud to have carnal knowledge of white females	not provided for	same as #11	death p. 753
13. Taking away a white female against her will with intent to marry her or defile her or to have her married to another or defiled by another	3-10 yrs. p. 724	same as #11	death p. 753
14. Selling a free person as a slave	3-10 yrs. p. 725	3-10 yrs. p. 725	death p. 753
15. Maliciously burning in the day time a dwelling house, jail, pile of wood, cowhouse, etc. the property if worth at least $100	3-5 yrs. p. 727	3-5 yrs. p. 727	death p. 753
16. Same, if less than $100	1-3 yrs. p. 727	1-3 yrs. p. 728	death 2nd off. p. 753
17. Burglary	5-10 yrs. p. 728	3-10 yrs. p. 728	death p. 753
18. Simple larceny of goods of $20 of more	1-5 yrs. p. 729	1-5 yrs. p. 729	death 2nd off. p. 753
19. Administering poison to a horse, cattle, etc.	1-5 yrs. p. 732	1-5 yrs. p. 732	death 2nd off. p. 753
20. Maliciously obstructing, removing or injuring any part of a canal, railroad, or any bridge or fixture thereof, etc. to			

CRIME	WHITES	PUNISHMENT FREE NEGROES	SLAVES
endanger the life of a traveler.	3-5 yrs. p. 732	3-5 yrs. p. 732	death p. 753
21. Counterfeiting a coin	2-10 yrs. p. 734	2-10 yrs. p. 734	death 2nd off. p. 753
22. Crime against nature	1-5 yrs. p. 740	1-5 yrs. p. 740	death 2nd off. p. 753[189]

[189] The numbers refer to the pages of the *Revised Code of Virginia* (*1849*). The punishment of the slaves was based on the following two regulations: "If a slave ... commits an offense for the commission of which a free negro, at the time of committing the same, is punishable with death, or by confinement in the penitentiary for not less than three years, he shall be punished with death. But unless it be an offense for which a free white person, if he had committed it, might have been punished with death, such slave instead of being punished with death, may at the discretion of the court, be punished by sale and transportation beyond the limits of the N. D." *Revised Code of Virginia*, p. 753.

"If a slave commits an offense for which a free Negro, if he had committed it, might be punished by confinement in the penitentiary for a period of less than three years, such slave shall be punished by stripes; and if, having been once sentenced for such an offense, he afterwards commits an offense for which a free Negro, if he had committed it, might be punished by such confinement, he shall be punished by death, or at the discretion of the Court, by sale and transportation as aforesaid." *Revised Code of Virginia*, pp. 753-754.

Occasionally one finds that authorities placed the value of a Negro's life equal to that of a white. A petition was sent to Governor Pierce M. Butler asking pardon for Nazareth Allen, who had been condemned for killing a Negro boy. The last paragraph of the Governor's answer issued on Oct. 30, 1830, is as follows: "That the crime of which the prisoner stands convicted was committed against one of inferior grade in society is a reason for being cautious of intercepting the just severity of the law. This class of our population is subjugated to us as well for their protection as our advantage. Our rights in regard to them are not more imperative than their duties and the institutions which for wise and necessary ends, have rendered them perculiarly dependent, at least pledge the law to be to them peculiarly a friend and a protctor. The prayer of the petition is not granted." *United States Catholic Miscellany*, 18 (Nov. 17, 1838), 158.

At times slaves were spared the death penalty by being sold and shipped to other territories.[190]

It is well known that lynching was practiced in slave days. The lynch law may be said in large part to be the special product of the sparseness of the population and of the resulting weakness of legal machinery, if one follows the view of Phillips.[191] The victims of lynchings were not only rapists but Negro malefactors of sundry sorts, occasionally white offenders as well.[192]

But, generally speaking, the lynch law was used to punish the murder of whites or attacks upon women committed by Negroes. Such crimes were considered the rebellion of the inferior race against the superior.

As the years rolled on, lynchings increased. Of the forty-six recorded murders of owners and overseers by Negroes between 1850 and 1860, twenty culprits were legally executed, and twenty-six lynched of whom nine were burned at the stake.[193]

Mutilation was never clearly defined, although the lobes of the ears were usually cut off. It served a two-fold purpose in that it identified criminals, Negro and white, and served as a warning to others. Castration of Negroes was unlawful except on conviction of an attempt to rape a white woman.[194]

Toward the end of the eighteenth century the earlier severity was considerably mitigated. For example, in 1806 Louisiana passed an act that placed a penalty on persons who would beat the slave unjustly or mutilate him. If found guilty they were fined between $200 and $500, *unless they cleared themselves by their own oath.*[195]

[190] Phillips, *Life and Labor in the Old South*, p. 165; Phillips, *AHR*, 20 (1914-1915), p. 339, says that from 1859 to 1863 most sentences were commuted to labor or public work.

[191] Phillips, *American Negro Slavery*, p. 512.

[192] *Ibid.*, p. 511.

[193] Hart, *Slavery and Abolition*, p. 117.

[194] *The Negro in Virginia*, p. 152.

[195] La. Statutes (1856), p. 550. Older laws were more severe.

In case any person shall wilfully cut out the tongue, put out

Whipping was by far the most frequent form of punishment. *The Negro in Virginia*[196] gives several testimonies of living slaves to the effect that many masters felt that slaves needed a whipping at regular intervals, just so that they would know what punishment would be theirs if they were disobedient.

Whipping was used quite extensively since imprisonment was no penalty for the slave, who could not be kept employed yet who must be fed.[197] Sometimes trivial offenses brought lashings. It was not so much the wrong that demanded punishment but rather the effect the chastisement would have on the others.[198]

These whippings were usually inflicted with an English cat-o'-nine-tails, which was a yard long rope of twisted rawhide. An expert flip of the weapon would draw blood from rib to rib.[199] From the law of South Carolina quoted above it can be judged that whipping must have also been done with horsewhips, sticks and the like.

Some laws were passed which provided only flimsy protection.[200] Stroud[201] pointed out that a conviction could be made only "upon sufficient information"; yet a Negro free or slave could never give testimony against a white person.

the eye, castrate, or cruelly scald, burn or deprive a slave of any limb, or member of shall inflict any other cruel punishment other than by whipping or beating with a horsewhip, cowskin, switch or small stick, or by putting irons on, or confining or imprisoning such slave, every such person, for every such offense shall forfeit the sum of one hundred pounds current money."—Act of S. C. of 1740, 2 *Brevard's Digest*, p. 241.

Any person, who shall maliciously dismember, or deprive a slave of life, shall suffer such punishment as would be inflicted in case like offense had been committed on a free white person, and on like proof, except in the case of insurrection of such slave, and unless such death should happen by accident in giving such slave moderate correction.—Constitution of Ga. art. 4, sec. 1, *Prince's Digest*, p. 786.

[196] p. 155.
[197] Hart, *Slavery and Abolition*, p. 112.
[198] *The Negro in Virginia*, p. 155.
[199] *Ibid.*, p. 151.
[200] Cf. *Prince's Digest*, p. 376.
[201] Stroud, *Sketch of Laws Concerning Slavery*, p. 20.

In North Carolina the master was not liable to an indictment for a battery committed by him upon his slave.[202]

Even in the rare cases where the master could be convicted, such conviction carried with it only a fine. In no state except Louisiana could the slave redeem himself or obtain a change of masters, even though cruel treatment may have rendered such change necessary for his personal safety.

On the other hand, in order to protect society some states attempted to remove the temptation of masters to conceal the felonies of slaves, by passing laws providing public compensation for those sentenced to death or deportation.[203]

Phillips[204] quoted a South Carolinian as saying a master robbed by his own slave would not institute judicial process for that "would add the loss of the value of the Negro to that of the article stolen." If, on the other hand, the slave stole from a neighbor, a conference was usually held and some punishment was prescribed informally for the neighbor never knew when one of his slaves would steal.

If a slave was killed by a third party the proper rule to determine the amount of damage was the value of the slave at the time of his death, this same to be paid by the master.[205]

The South Carolina law reads as follows:

"If a Negro or other slave, who shall be employed in the lawful business of service of his master or owner, overseer, etc., shall be beaten, etc., by any

[202] *The State* v. *Mam* (Dec. Term, 1829), 2 Devereaux's, N. C. Rep. 263, Wheeler, *op. cit.*, p. 244.

[203] U. Phillips, *AHR*, 20 (1914-1915), 336-340. In North Carolina on an indictment against a slave for a capital offense, the master could not be compelled to testify—*The State* v. *Charity*, (Dec. Term, 1830, 2 Devereaux's N. C. Rep., Wheeler, *Treatise on the Laws of Slavery*, p. 214.

[204] Phillips, *Life and Labor in the Old South*, p. 165.

[205] *Richardson* v. *Dukes* (Jan. Term, 1827), M'Cord's Rep. 156, Wheeler, *op. cit.*, p. 202.

person or persons, not having sufficient cause or
lawful authority for so doing, and so shall be
maimed or disabled by such beating from perform-
ing his or her work, such person or persons so of-
fending, shall forfeit and pay, to the owner or
owners of such slave, the sum of fifteen shillings
current money per diem, for every day of his lost
time, and also the charge of the cure of such
slave."[206]

In the foregoing discussion many of the abuses and injustices of the American institution of slavery were mentioned. Certainly in some instances there were grave violations of both justice and charity.

How far slavery, as a system was inhuman and
barbarous is difficult to decide. Charges of cruelty
were fiercely pressed by the abolitionists, who
threw out a drag-net for every case that came to
their knowledge; and they proved beyond question that there were many awful instances of bar-
barity which public opinion did not check.[207]

Bishop England said that "The general treatment of the
Negroes in the diocese of Charleston is kind and affection-
ate, far, very far more so than that of the bulk of Irish,
agricultural or other labourers."[208] Moreover, in an editorial
in his newpaper, possibly written by him, there is a complaint registered that the treatment of the slaves is misrepresented. The author said that he would never create
the system, nor would he feel it necessary to will its abolition. Being aware of its difficulties he considers it the task
of the legislatures to change its conditions. There remains
one duty, namely, that the master treat the slave kindly
and the legislature protect.[209]

On the other hand, England, in a letter to the Cardinal
Prefect of the Sacred Congregation for the Propagation of
the Faith said that he would stay on in his work in the

---

[206] *Brevard's Digest*, pp. 231 f.

[207] Hart, *Slavery and Abolition*, pp. 120-122.

[208] "Early History of the Diocese of Charleston," *Works* (Messmer), 4: 318.

[209] *U. S. Cath. Miscellany*, 18 (Nov. 17, 1838), 158.

United States no matter how great the difficulties became and "no matter how great may be my disgust with the condition of the slaves, brought into my diocese under a system which perhaps is the greatest moral evil that can desolate part of the civilized world."[210]

Other priests also complained of the treatment of the Negroes received from their masters. For example, Father Mosley, writing to his sister in 1774 said:

> ... The Negroes that do belong to the Gentlemen of our Persuasion and our own, are all Christians, and instructed in every Christian duty with care: some are good, some very bad, some docile, some very dull. They are naturally inclined to thievery, lying and much lechery. I believe that makes them worse thieves and liars. And the innate heat of the climate of Africa and their natural temper of constitution gives them a great bent of lechery. The Negroes of all other persuasions are much neglected, as you imagine, and few ever christened.[211]

Nuesse,[212] in his study, concluded that there is no doubt that the slave-trade was cruel and debased those who engaged in it, but on the plantations owners were generally cognizant of some responsibility for the humane treatment of the laborers they owned. This was sometimes merely an appreciation of the economic advantage of decency, but as a rule it was a species of benevolence toward inferiors of a sharply demarcated class.

But taken at the best the institution as it was practiced in the United States failed to secure for the slaves those natural and inalienable rights which Kenrick and the theologians staunchly claimed for them.

[210] Original in the Irish College, Rome, quoted from Guilday, *Life of England*, 1: 531.

[211] Edward J. Devitt, S.J. (ed)., "Letters of Father Joseph Mosley, S.J., and some extracts from his Diary, 1757-1785," *RACHS*, 17 (1906), 299.

[212] Nuesse, *The Social Thought of American Catholics 1634-1829*, p. 40.

CHAPTER IV

KENRICK'S OPINION ON THE LAWFULNESS OF SLAVERY

It was necessary to first explain the definition that Kenrick and the theologians gave to slavery and to consider the obligations and limitations imposed on masters of slaves by those theologians. With these explanations as a basis this chapter will consider the teaching of Kenrick and the theologians concerning the lawfulness of slavery in general. Then, Kenrick's opinion concerning the lawfulness of American slavery will be given and discussed.

I. SLAVERY NOT CONTRARY TO THE NATURAL LAW

Kenrick's teaching concerning the origin of slavery. Before discussing the lawfulness of domestic slavery, an inquiry should be made into the basic principles upon which slavery rests. To carry this out, an analysis of Kenrick's treatment of the subject will be compared with that of some of the principal theologians.

Kenrick[1] began by saying that although by right of nature, all men are equal, still by the *jus gentium* both dominium of jurisdiction and of property are conceded to man over man. He defined *jus gentium* by dividing it into *primaevum* and *secundarium*. *Jus gentium primaevum* comprises those principles which are common to all nations by the very dictates of nature; *jus gentium secundarium* comprises those which by common consent are determined by equity. *Jus gentium* is further divided into *necessarium* and *voluntarium*. The former means the right which is derived from the law of nature accommodated to nations so

[1] Kenrick, *Theologia moralis*, tr. V, cap. VI, no. 35; tr. III, cap. I, No. 6.

100

that the relationship of nations ought to be ruled by it. To this right belongs the obligation of one nation not to injure another and the obligation of keeping a promise once it is made. *Jus gentium voluntarium* refers to those principles of action which cultured nations have agreed should be observed from a sense of equity. Many of these principles are gathered from custom, others from written pacts.[2]

Kenrick defined dominium of jurisdiction as the legitimate power of governing one's subjects, v.g., a bishop with regard to the salvation of souls in his diocese, or civil rulers in matters pertaining to public order. Dominium of property, according to Kenrick, is the right of disposing of a thing as one's own, unless the law, or a pact, stands in the way, just as a child is master of his goods, but the law forbids him to dispose of them. He makes reference to the Epistle to the Galatians, "Now I say, as long as the heir is a child, he differeth nothing from a servant, though he be lord of all."[3] *Dominium plenum* is the free right to dispose of the article and its fruits as one's own. *Dominium non plenum* is the right to dispose of the thing alone, or of its fruits.[4]

Kenrick did not say whether he had in mind complete or partial dominium, but obviously it is not merely partial, for not only does the master have the right to use the labor of his slaves but he also has the right to sell them. The difficulty lies in the fact that in the definition of complete dominium he said that it entails the free right of disposing of a thing, or its fruits, as was seen above.[5] Thus the

---

[2] Kenrick, *op. cit.* tr. V, cap. I, no. 2.

[3] Gal. 4: 1. Kenrick, *op. cit.*, tr. X, no. 4.

[4] Kenrick, *op. cit.*, tr. X, cap. II, no. 4.

[5] Merkelbach in explaining the phrase *perfecte disponendi*, says it is the right to use the fruits or to dispose of the substance of the thing, in a word, the right of destining it to all uses, or of alienating, selling, giving, changing, using, enjoying, or destroying the thing, or as the ancients said, of abusing it, i.e., of using it to destruction. Benedictus Henricus Merkelbach, O.P., *Summa theologiae moralis*, (3 vols. Paris: Desclee; 3rd ed., 1939), 2: 167, no. 159.

term "complete dominium of property," without limitations,
would be too broad to be applied to slavery. Kenrick, although he does not seem to have placed any limitation in
his definition, at another point does say that masters' rights
are limited.[6]

However apparently there arises a contradiction in saying that all men are free and equal and yet allowing an
approval of slavery, since it had been introduced by the
jus gentium. Kenrick held that man has not the power
to dispense from the law of nature nor can this law be
abrogated by custom or agreement of men; but those things
that are permitted by the law of nature can be forbidden,[7]
and thus is induced an order of things in which the natural
faculty of many is restricted. By right of nature, all things
are common to all men, and each can use them in accord
with his needs, but by the agreement of men, a most just
division was made, and on account of this, one is not allowed to usurp the property of others. In like manner,
man is born free, but by agreement of men, during a war,
the liberty of man is taken away, and from this arises a
condition, namely slavery, which is not repugnant to the
law of nature, although it is not very fitting.[8]

The influence of Christianity on slavery. The nations of
antiquity maintained that because of unbridled passions of

[6] Cf. *supra,* chap. III. Noldin points out that dominium may be
limited in two ways: the exercise of right is limited if a certain use
is against another virtue, e.g. to use one's goods for getting intoxi-
cated, or for a sin of impurity, or juridically if by justice one must
abstain from a certain use, or the right itself is limited, if certain
rights are excepted, so that one did not have complete dominium,
v.g. a house is acquired by heredity, but with a third party having
the right of dwelling there, or if in the social order, on account of
the common good, certain limits are place, v.g. the right of building
is restricted. H. Noldin, S.J., *Summa theologiae moralis,* (3 vols.
Innsbruck: F. Rauch, 1936), 2:345, no. 357. Hence one would conclude that dominium of the master over the slave, is partial but
permanent... hence the master could sell only the work of the slave.

[7] "quae in lege naturae licent possunt vetari."

[8] Kenrick, *op. cit.,* tr. III, cap. I, no. 16.

men, wars were started which gave rise to a human necessity from which slavery was thought to be justified. For
slavery existed as a consequence of captivity, in war; and
being a consequence of public wars, sanctioned by the rules
of actions between nations, it was at that time a principle
of international law, insofar as any international law could
be said to exist.[9]

Under the old Roman law, the slave was considered as
a brute animal. He could not legally marry, he had no right
to his mate, or his child, he could not even bear a name,
regarded properly as such, but, like a horse or dog, was
called after his master's fancy. He was considered incapable of virtue or honor. His testimony was not acceptable.
His children belonged to the master as commercial assets.
Although at times he was highly trained in arts and crafts,
still he could be scourged, maimed or crucified, like any
other slaves under the old Roman law, for any motive
whatsoever of the master.[10] Hence, in its legal acceptation
of the day, slavery was that condition of a person, in which
the law permitted the application of his physical and mental
powers to depend, as far as possible, upon the will of another who was himself subject to the supreme power of the
state, and in which he (the slave) was incapable, in view
of the law, of acquiring or holding property, and of sus-
taining those relations out of which relative rights proceed, execpt as the agent or instrument of another. In
slavery, strictly so-called, the supreme power of the state
in ignoring the personality of the slave, ignored his capacity for moral actions, and committed the control of his
conduct as a moral agent to the master, together with the

[9] Hurd, *The Law of Freedom and Bondage,* I: 150 f; Paul Allard,
"Esclavage," *DAFC, I:* 1457-1459.

[10] Joseph Husselein, S.J., *Social Wellsprings* (Milwaukee: Bruce
Publishing Co., 1943), pp. 91 f; *DAFC,* 1: 1459-1475; *DTC* 5: 457-
461; Victor Cathrein, S.J., *Philosophia moralis* (Friburg: Herder
& Co., 1907), p. 354; Hurd, *op. cit.,* 1: 153 f.; Augustin Cochin, *The
Results of Slavery* (Boston, 1863), p. 285.

power of transferring his authority to another.[11]

While exhorting slaves and serfs to obey existing laws, the Church always insisted that their inalienable rights be safeguarded, and that they be not subjected to any inhuman and over-oppressive conditions. Hence, she never approved or even tolerated absolute slavery of that type that prevailed in Europe in pre-Christian times. Such slavery disregarded inalienable rights and was essentially unjust and immoral. All the while the Church worked for the gradual emancipation of the slaves. This gradual emancipation brought about by Christianity is beautifully expressed by Pope Gregory XVI (1831-1846) whom Kenrick quoted:

> When indeed the light of the gospel first began to be diffused, those wretched persons, who at that time in such numbers went down into the rigorous slavery principally by the occasions of war felt their condition very much alleviated among the Christians. For the Apostles, inspired by the Divine Spirit taught, in fact, the slaves themselves to obey their carnal masters as Christ and to do the will of God from the heart; but they commanded the masters to act well toward their slaves and to do to them what is just and equal and to forebear threatenings; knowing that there is a Master both of these and of themselves in the heavens, and that with Him there is no respect of persons.[12]

"The Catholic Church has ever deplored the cruel slavery, in which multitudes of men are detained, to the great detriment of their souls, and has never ceased to labor to remedy so great a calamity."[13] The Church did this first by her

---

[11] Hurd, *op. cit.*, 1: 42 f. Cf. M. A. Barrow, *Slavery in the Roman Empire* (New York: Lincoln MacVeagh, 1928); W. W. Buckland, *The Roman Law of Slavery* (Cambridge University Press, 1908).

[12] "In supremo" (3 Dec. 1839), *Collectanea S. Cong. de Prop. Fide*, 1: pp. 503 f, no. 891. Translation taken from pamphlet edited by W. George Read (Baltimore: John Murphy, 1844), p. 9. Cf. Kenrick, *op. cit.*, tr. V, cap. V.

[13] Statement issued by the Bishops of the province of Bordeaux assembled in Council at La Rochelle in 1853, *RACHS* 25 (1914), 28.

doctrine; then by the recognition of slaves as equal to a free man before the altar.[14] In the very early ages, slaves found entrance not only to the priesthood, but even to the papacy itself.[15] At the same time the Church labored to obtain manumissions for the slaves. Many of the early Fathers and Popes sold sacred vessels in order to buy freedom for the slaves.[16] Especially in the fourth and fifth centuries, when the Church emerged from the catacombs, many slaves were manumitted.[17] Religious orders were founded for the purpose of freeing slaves, even those in foreign and pagan countries.[18] The Church used her influence with the Christian emperors to have the rights of slaves as human beings restored and their general conditions bettered.[19]

In this work of freeing the slaves the Church did not proceed abruptly and radically.

> She looks to the preservation of society, to its well-being as well as to the liberation and well-being of the slave. This is wise and just, for social changes should as far as possible be effected without social shocks or convulsions. [20]

Pope Leo XIII[21] expressing his great happiness that the slaves in Brazil were to be freed, warned in his letter of 1888, that manumissions should be done in orderly fashion without public disturbance, and in a way that would be useful to the freed slaves.

In this way, then, the Church helped the slaves of the

---

[14] Husslein, *op. cit.*, p. 92.

[15] *Ibid.*, p. 92. Quite possibly Pius I was a slave. Cf. Donald Attwater, *A Dictionary of the Popes* (London: Burns, Oates and Washbourne. Ltd., 1939), p. 9.

[16] Leo XIII, "In plurimis" *Acta Leonis*, 8: 182-185.

[17] Husslein, *op. cit.*, p. 92; J. Balmes, *European Civilization* (Baltimore and New York: John Murphy Co., 1850), pp. 94-111.

[18] Leo XIII, "In Plurimis," *Acta Leonis*, 8: 184 f; *DAFC*, 1: 1508-1512.

[19] Allard, *DAFC*, 1: 1475-1485; *DTC* 5: 481-485.

[20] Brownson, *Works*, 17: 343.

[21] Leo XIII, "In plurimis," *Acta Leonis*, 8: 190 f.

old Roman days to obtain their rights, later, slavery was discarded and the slaves became serfs,[22] and finally, they became free.

The theologians and slavery. All the theologians admit that every kind of slavery is full of dangers. It is not fitting to human dignity that a man spend his whole life and all his activity for another, receiving only his upkeep. Slaves usually degenerate to an abject condition; on the other hand, slavery fosters pride, avarice, and cruelty in the masters.[23]

If slavery be defined as perpetual service rendered to another for no compensation beyond food and clothing it is not *per se* contrary to the natural law. For man, provided he retains his essential and inalienable rights, is not prohibited from obligating himself to another for perpetual service in return for his upkeep. Since a man can hire himself to another for twenty years, he can do so for life, with the understanding that the master will care for him in old age. Then, too, if man can be lawfully deprived of his life by execution, and of his liberty by incarceration, why can he not be punished for crime by slavery?[24]

But a slavery that takes away all the human rights of slaves is contrary to the natural law. In this type of slavery the master makes himself the immediate end of the slave, hardly recognizing him as a person, who has God as his immediate end, and who has rights necessary to attaining that end.[25]

It must be clearly borne in mind that no theologian, while theoretically justifying slavery as lawful, attempted to

[22] *DTC*, 5: 176-181, Allard, *DAFC* 1: 1495-1505.

[23] Cathrein, *Philosophia moralis*, (ed. of 1907), p. 355, no. 463; *DTC*, 5: 503.

[24] Cf. Instruction of the Holy Office, 20 July, 1866, *Collectanea S. Cong. de Prop. Fide*, I: no. 1293, p. 719; Cathrein *op. cit.*, (ed. of 1907) p. 355, no. 464.

[25] Cathrein, *loc. cit.*; E. J. Cahill, *The Framework of a Christian State*, (Dublin: M. H. Gill & Sons, 1932) p. 317.

justify slavery as it actually did exist.[26] Historical slavery, whether under the old Roman law, or as often practiced in America, was contrary to the natural law, because it violated rights that the slaves have from the natural law. No slave may be the property of another as a chattel, but may owe service to another for life. The natural rights to life, limb, subsistence, fair treatment, marriage, cohabitation, and the like, must be secured.[27] Likewise the rights of the slave to be instructed and to practice his religious duties cannot be taken from him lawfully.[28]

With these basic principles in mind, the doctrine of slavery, as developed by St. Thomas and other recognized theologians will be investigated.

By the time of St. Thomas—thanks to Christianity—the old Roman slavery had completely disappeared. There remained only serfdom as a vestige of the ancient bondage and this a step in the gradual transition from slavery to free labor. The rights of masters over slaves were strictly confined to disposal of their services. The ancient rights over the slaves' body had completely disappeared.[29]

In the twelfth and thirteenth centuries, the princes abolished the complicated gradation of tenures and reduced serfdom everywhere to a uniform servile condition. This raised the lower ranks to a higher standard.[30] Since the abuses of the old system had practically disappeared, the scholastic writers wrote very little about slavery and made few comments concerning the tyranny of masters.[31]

Speaking of the natural law, St. Thomas taught that a principle can belong to the natural law in two ways: first

[26] Henry Davis, S.J., *Moral and Pastoral Theology* (New York: Sheed and Ward, 4 vols., 5th ed., 1946), 2: 269.

[27] Davis, *op. cit.*, 2: 269.

[28] Cf. *infra*, chap. 5.

[29] George O'Brien, *An Essay on Medieva Economic Teaching* (New York: Longmans, Green and Co., 1920), p. 9.

[30] Bede Jarrett, O.P., *Social Theories of the Middle Ages* (Westminster, Md.: Newman Bookshop, 1942), p. 105.

[31] O'Brien, *Op. cit.*, p. 100.

because nature itself indicates a certain idea, v.g., injury
is not to be done to another; or secondly, because nature
does not indicate the contrary, v.g., we could say that for
man to be naked is of the natural law for nature did not
give him clothes, but art invented them. In this sense,
the possession of all things in common and universal freedom, are said to be of the natural law, because the distinction of possessions and slavery is brought in, not by nature,
but by human reason or the benefit of human life. Accordingly the law of nature was not changed, but something was
added.[32]

In discussing whether the law of nations and the natural
law are the same, St. Thomas says[33] that, absolutely speaking, the fact that this man is more a servant than another
is not according to natural law, but only is so because of
some consequent utility, inasmuch as it is useful to this
man that he be ruled by a more wise man, and to the other
that he be helped by the first. Thus slavery pertains to the
jus gentium and is natural only in the second manner, not
in the first manner.

Man is ordered to another when he is employed for the
utility of another, who is dominating him, and since one's
own good it considered very precious, slavery has the note
of sadness, because the prized good is exercised for the
sake of another, which can be done only with the "poena"
of the subjects. Therefore, slavery could not exist in the
state of innocence.[34]

Sin is possible only when there is free choice, preceded
by ratiocination. Sin fetters freedom. Since by sin man
falls from the order of reason, consequently he falls from
his dignity as a human being into the slavish state of beasts
and then can be disposed of in accordance with his useful-
ness to others.[35] Thus, men of St. Thomas' time thought

[32] 1a, 2ae, qu. XCV, art. V, 3um.
[33] 2a, 2ae, qu. LVII, art. 3; *De Reg. Princip.*, II, 10.
[34] Pars I, qu. XCVII, art. 4.
[35] 2a, 2ae, qu. 64, art. 2 ad 3.

that slavery was begot by sin. Since in all ages some men were found less affected by sin than others and hence were more prudent in their judgments, others turned to them for government. The better men are, the more freedom they can have; but it would be absurd to suppose that all men are capable of complete freedom. The rapacity of kings should be prevented; yet should it prove too difficult to restrain, it should be borne with patience as the price of peace. The citizens of that age did not disdain liberty as a political ideal, but were uncertain as to whether it could be realized. Peaceful living rather than civic independence was insisted on as the basis of communal life. Freedom was not an end in itself in the Middle Ages. No one was urged to strive for freedom for the mere purpose of being free, but for the purpose of fulfilling the law. Thus the *Magna Charta* itself illustrates the fact that little reference was made in those days to the hardness of unfree life. Not freedom, but justice, not liberty but law, was the social ideal of the day.[36]

During the fifteenth century the slave traffic began anew. In the Counter Reformation to this and other evils, which developed out of the Renaissance, Lessius and De Lugo wrote rather thorough treatises on moral theology. Because of the thoroughness of their treatment and because of the fact that since their work influenced the succeeding centuries, it is well to consider their treatment on the subject of slavery.

Lessius[37] taught that all men are equal, because they have the same nature, are from the same parent, and are called to the same end. Nevertheless by nature one is more apt to be a servant, and another to be a master. Slavery was created by both civil law and the law of nations. He used Sacred Scripture to show that various laws regulated slavery. Is slavery contrary to nature? Not in so far as it is against reason and natural precept; but it is against

[36]Jarrett, *op. cit.*, pp. 96-98.
[37] Lessius, *De justitia et jure*, Lib. 2, cap. 4, dubitatio 9.

the primitive condition of nature. But, since men have sinned, slavery is not against nature, just as medicine is contrary to nature for a well man, but not for the sick man.

De Lugo[38] held that it is licit for one man to have dominium over another as his true slave. This is evident, thought he, from Sacred Scripture, the Fathers, the councils, and from reason. In giving his argument from reason, De Lugo, stating that slavery is licit, said that the freedom of man does not invalidate the argument. By right of persons, slavery is contrary to nature which makes all men free. The sense of this is that nature does not prohibit slavery but it is beyond the intention of nature, which of itself intended all men to be free. Slavery was induced because of unjust wars, sins, and other miseries in order to avert greater evils.

Thus, slavery to the early theologians was a punishment for crime and sin, inflicted to avoid greater evils. In our day, however, one is prone to think of it as an institution whereby one man by brute force seizes another, even though he is innocent, and by means of a whip forces him to perform dreadful labors.

Kenrick's Justification of Slavery in General. Kenrick relied on Sacred Scripture, both the Old and New Testaments, the Fathers, and the Councils of the Church, to prove that slavery in itself is lawful.

In referring to the Old Testament Kenrick merely noted that slavery was ratified in the old law. He referred to chapter 21 of the book of Exodus, and chapter 25 of the book of Leviticus.[39]

It is interesting to note that slaves in Jewish history were of two classes, foreigners—claimed by capture or purchase —or fellow Hebrews, who had been sold by their parents,

---

[38] De Lugo, *Disputationes de justitia et jure,* Tom. I, *Disput, VI,* sec. II.

[39] Kenrick, *Theologia moralis,* tr. V, cap. VI, no. 35.

or had sold themselves to meet debts. The treatment of the two types was quite different.[40]

The duty of treating Hebrew servants otherwise than slaves, and above all their retention for a limited time only, was deemed so important that the subject was placed next to the decalogue, at the head of the civil legislation.[41] There were careful regulations regarding the amount of labor to be done, possible self-redemption, treatment of the bond-maids, and the parting gift, and the like[42]

Besides these slaves, the Jews were permitted to buy men and women from the strangers of the surrounding nations. These foreign slaves were held in absolute bondage and were inherited by their children like other property but their condition was far from intolerable. The law definitely limited the power of the master.[43] Then, too, the law alleviated the condition in many ways, e.g., it forbade the return of a fugitive slave to his master by those among whom he sought shelter.[44] Their religious status could be used to defend the thesis that they were made an integral part of the community. The males were to be circumcised and as such to be admitted to the eating of the Passover.[45] The slaves of priests could eat of the holy meats.[46] They were not to be required to work on the Sabbath. Their need of this rest was mentioned as one of the grave motives for the institution of the Sabbath.[47]

Thus the Jewish treatment of slaves was never allowed to become cruel or debasing. The Mosaic legislation insisting on the rights of the bondsman, placed limitations on the power of the master, and inculcated clemency. The Jews

[40] G. Woosung Wade, *Old Testament History* (New York, 1904), p. 156.
[41] Exodus, 21: 2-11.
[42] Leviticus, 25: 39-54; Deuteronomy, 15: 12-18.
[43] Leviticus, 25: 44 ff.
[44] Deut. 28: 15.
[45] Gen. 17: 27; Exodus, 12: 44.
[46] Leviticus, 22: 11.
[47] Exodus, 23: 12.

were frequently reminded to be kind to the slaves, recollecting how much their own ancestors had suffered during their serfdom in Egypt.[48]

Kenrick also appealed to the New Testament. He noted that St. Paul did not reprobate slavery existing among the nations, but rather counselled slaves to obey their masters in patience, urging masters to treat their slaves with justice and meekness.[49]

There is no explicit condemnation of slavery in Christ's doctrine. Christ as well as the Apostles accepted the political and social conditions of His time, leaving His teaching to work out its consequences in the Christian Church during the course of history. St. Paul especially developed the doctrine of the unity of mankind. St. Paul sent back to Philemon his runaway slave named Onesimus, but he asked that the slave be received as himself.[50]

An acceptable explanation of the passages of the New Testament that indicate the duties of masters and slaves can be attributed to Bishop England, who labored for the Church in America during the same troubled times in which Archbishop Kenrick wrote his text of moral theology. In the celebrated letters to John Forsyth, he pointed out that slavery is not incompatible with the natural law for it had

[48] J. Abelson, "Slavery (Jewish)," *Encyclopedia of Religion and Ethics*, 11: 610. The theologians appeal to these passages of the Old Testament to show that slavery is not inconsonant with the natural law. Cf. Lessius, *De justitia et jure*, Lib. 2, cap. 4, dub. 9; De Lugo, *De justitia et jure*, Tom. I, disp. VI, sec. II; Carrière, *Praelectiones de justitia et jure*, I: no. 44.

[49] Kenrick, op. cit., tr. V, cap. VI, no. 35. In this passage he quoted from Eph. 6: 5 and 9.

[50] Epis. to Philemon. Cf. Leonard D. Agate, "Slavery (Christian)" *Encyclopedia of Religion and Ethics*, 11: 602. Scriptural texts were used frequently in the slave controversy. The following are samples of American works of the 19th century: A. B. Barnes, *An Inquiry into Scriptural Views of Slavery* (Phila., 1857); M. J. Raphael, *Bible view of Slavery* (New York, 1861); J. B. Lightfoot, *St. Paul's Epistle to the Colossians and Philemon* (London, 1879); M. R. Vincent, *The Epistle to the Philippians and Philemon* (Edinburgh, 1897).

been outlawed neither in the Old nor in the New Testament. To substantiate this view he quoted copiously from both sections of the Bible.[51] In another letter he said that he had shown that the Saviour did not repeal permission to hold slaves, but that He promulgated principles calculated to improve the condition of the slaves, and perhaps in the course of time, to extinguish slavery completely.[52]

Kenrick likewise appealed to canonical legislation to show that slavery can be lawful.[53] He noted, that having before her eyes the words of St. Paul, the Church in the Council of Gangra anathematized those who, under the appearance of religion, induced slaves to leave their masters.[54]

The Synod of Gangra was held about the middle of the fourth century. The passage referred to is Canon 3, which reads as follows: "If any one teaches a slave, under the pretext of piety, to despise his master, to forsake his service, or not to serve with good will and entire respect, let him be anathema."[55] It appears from this canon and the fifth article of the Synod letter, which is in accordance with it, that many slaves had assumed the monastic habit and had left the service of their masters to lead an ascetic life.[56]

Kenrick added, however, that the Church had as always favored liberty and had exhorted masters to manumit their slaves, so that little by little slavery disappeared.[57] As an

---

[51] Letters of Oct. 13 and 21, 1840, *Works* (Messmer), 5: 196-211.

[52] Letter of Oct. 28, 1840, *Works* (Messmer), 5: 211.

[53] This discussion will be limited to legislation referred to by Kenrick. For other legislations of councils, etc., the reader can be referred to Bishop England's Letters, *Works*, (Messmer), 5: 211 ff.

[54] Kenrick, *op. cit.*, tr. V, cap. VI, no. 35.

[55] Mansi, 2: 1102: "Si quis docet servum pietatis pretextu dominum contemnere, & ministeriis recedere, & non cum benevolentia & omnia honore domino suo inservire, sit anathema."

[56] Rev. Charles Joseph Hefele, D.C., *A History of the Councils of the Church*, (Edinburgh: T. & T. Clark, 1876), 2: 326-329.

[57] Kenrick, *op. cit.*, tr. V, cap. VI, no. 35. Kenrick, in his early edition, added the following sentence which was left out in the later edition: Referring to the Church counseling liberty—"haec humanis-

example he cited the third council of the Lateran. This
council opened in March of the year 1179 under Pope Alexander III.[58] The council has twenty-seven canons. The
twenty-sixth decreed that neither Jews nor Saracens should
have Christian slaves in their homes, under any pretext.
Those presuming to live with them, were to be excommuni-
cated.[59]

In the later edition Kenrick added a paragraph containing a quotation from St. Augustine which speaks of the
various grades and powers in the Church and in society
permitted by God, and makes an application to slavery
showing that slaves meritoriously serve Christ through
their masters. Christ did not make freed men out of slaves
but good slaves out of bad ones.[60]

Apparently he added this to complete his arguments just
as the other theologians do, namely, by showing that neither
the Inspired Word, nor the Fathers nor the councils taught
that slavery was against the natural law. This above mentioned passage was also quoted by Bishop England in his
letter to Forsyth.[61]

It may be noted that there are several texts from the
Fathers that seem to be contrary to slavery, but there are
several that also seem to be contrary even to private property. Slavery was not founded by the Divine Law but the
Fathers respected it as conformable to the human law.[62]

---

sima sanctio sequioribus saeculis infirmata, commercio indicto in-
fando." Cf. Kenrick, *op. cit.*, 1840, ed., tr. V, cap. VI, no. 35, I: 256.

[58] Henry Joseph Schroeder, O.P., *Disciplinary Decrees of the General Councils* (St. Louis, Mo. and London: B. Herder Book Co.,
1937), p. 214.

[59] Mansi, 22: 209.

[60] Kenrick, *op. cit.*, tr. V, cap. V, no. 36.

[61] John England, *Works*, (Messmer), 5: 219-220.

[62] O'Brien, *An Essay on Medieval Economic Teaching*, pp. 90-91;
P. Janet, *Histoire de la science politique dans ses rapports avec la
morale* (2 vols. Paris: Felix Alcan, no date), 1; 318-321, *DTC*, 5:
504-506.

II. Titles of Slavery Recognized by Kenrick
and the Theologians

Several responses of the Holy Office in effect say that slavery is lawful if the slave is held by a valid title.[63] The titles generally accepted by the theologians are: capture in war, punishment for crime, sale, and nativity. Kenrick recognized all four of these. Each of these lawful titles will now be discussed.

Capture in war. In passing, Kenrick[64] mentioned that those who w ere captured in war were formerly reduced to slavery when it seemed wise to the victors to spare their lives.

The theologians maintained that this custom was introduced by mercy. Thus instead of killing the victims of war they reduced them to slavery.[65] The title rests on the assumption that for the peace of the nations it was lawful to kill the unjust aggressors and if it was justifiable to kill them it was certainly permissible to place them instead under the yoke of slavery where they would no longer harm the nations by aggression. The theologians insisted that the one captured must have been a participant in an unjust war before this title is valid. Thus Lessius[66] taught that one taking part in a just war being captured is not and cannot be a slave. If justice is ambiguous both can be captured but when it is seen that justice favors one side then the members of that side held in slavery must be granted liberty without price.

The theologians maintained, however, that even children can be made slaves. Cochin raised the question about the right to enslave the wife and children of a man conquered

---

[63] Sept. 12, 1776; June 20, 1866; Mar. 20, 1686—*Collectanea S. Cong. de Prop. Fide*, I, no. 230, 515, 1293.

[64] Kenrick, *Theologia moralis*, tr. V, cap. V, no. 35.

[65] De Lugo, *De justitia et jure*, Disp. VI, sec. II, no. 11, p. 126. Cf. Carrière, *De justitia et jure*, 1: p. 36, no. 45; *DTC* 5: 508.

[66] Lessius, *De justitia et jure*, Lib. 2, cap. IV, dub. IV.

in war since one is not allowed to kill them.[67]   An answer
is found in De Lugo[68] who said that this right to reduce
an unjust aggressor extends to children, for while they cannot be killed, they can be made slaves for they are part of
the hostile government, and it is the government that is
being punished in its children. Lessius[69] observed that even
the children of a hostile government can be enslaved; for
just as they partake in the benefits of their country so also
can they partake of the burdens.

It should be pointed out that this title of capture in war
is valid only when the captives of war are worthy of such
a penalty because of personal crimes or those of the community.[70] Later through the influence of the Church the
custom which had the force of law forbade Christians to
be taken as slaves by Christians. But if Christians were
taken by pagans, in a just war, they could be enslaved,
for the law of nations was the same for all.[71]

Punishment for Crime. The second title is punishment
for crime. Kenrick[72] noted that those who committed
atrocius crimes were often afflicted with slavery. He gave
an example from canon law. The citation noted, says that
those who sell arms, aid in any manner whatsoever, the
Saracens, are to be despoiled of their property by the
Catholic princes and are to be made slaves of those who
capture them, if they are captured, and they are to be ex-
communicated.[73]

The liceity of using slavery as a punishment for crime
is admitted by all the theologians. For if a man can be deprived of his life for crime, he certainly can be deprived

[67] Cochin, *The Results of Slavery*, p. 336.
[68] De Lugo, *op. cit.*, Disp. VI, sec. II.
[69] *Op. cit.*, Lib. 2, cap. IV, dub. IV.
[70] Cathrein, *Philosophia moralis* (ed. 1907) p. 356, no. 466.
[71] Molina, *De justitia et jure*, Tom. I, tr. II, disp. 33, no. 2.
[72] Kenrick, *Theologia moralis*, tr. V, cap. V, no. 35.
[73] Taken from Lat. III, chap. 24. Cf. C. 6, X, "de Judaeis Saracenis
et eorum Servis," V, 6.

of his liberty, they said.[74] St. Thomas[75] observed that
slavery is an impediment to the use of power and thus men
naturally flee it. Thus slavery is a punishment and because
it is dreaded it can serve as a deterrent to crime.

The next title is that of *sale*. Kenrick[76] noted that the
paternal power was considered so great that the civil law
granted parents the right to sell their own children if that
were necessary to relieve their needs, but with the intention of redeeming them if their fortune improved. He referred in his note to Roman law. This citation points out
that justice most certainly forbids parents to sell, give
away, or pledge their own children under any pretext to
another. But it then goes on to state that it is lawful in
cases where one, because of very great poverty or need,
sells his children for the sake of necessities of life. But even
then the condition is placed that later either the person
who sells the child, or the child himself or any third person may redeem him by offering a just price or by presenting a slave to replace him.[77]

Kenrick[78] observed further that at times persons have
sold themselves in order to secure for themselves the necessities of life.

The theologians of the day apparently approved of this
law. Thus Lessius[79] observed that parents by the law of
nature might lawfully sell their children, since they are
part of the parents depending on them for their very existence. A parent then may make any contract for a child,
that the child might make for itself if it were *sui juris*.
A person may sell himself, a parent therefore may sell
the child. But, he added, that according to the civil law of
the day four conditions were required for the validity of
such a sale: it may be done only in the case of extreme pov-

[74] De Lugo, *op. cit.*, Dist. VI, sec. II; Lessius, *op. cit.*, Lib. 2, **cap.**
IV, dub. IV. Carrière, *op. cit.*, 1: p. 36, no. 45; *DTC* 5: 508.

[75] 1a, 2ae, qu. II, art. IV, ad 3.

[76] Kenrick, *op. cit.*, tr. V, cap. V, no. 35.

[77] *Corpus juris civilis* Bk. IV, Tit. 43, "De patribus qui filios suos
detraxerunt."

erty; only the father not the mother may sell the children (the mother could by the law of nature); they may sell only a child who has not reached his majority; the child may be recovered later by paying a just price or offering another slave.

They further taught that it is lawful for a free man to sell himself, for if he may oblige himself to labor for an anticipated salary for a given time, he may do the same for the duration of his life.

Man is master of his liberty just as he is of his good name and money. But they thought that in order that this be done without sin there must necessarily be a reason, for otherwise it would be the careless throwing away of liberty which is a greater gift than good name or fortune. Lessius and De Lugo[80] both note the six things required by civil law for the validity of the sale of oneself: the person must be over twenty years of age; he must intend to participate in the price given; that he permit another to sell him so that he actually can participate in the money given; the buyer must believe that the person he buys is a slave, thus a person is not permitted to sell himself but must do so through another; the person must know that he is free before the sale; that the seller knows that he is free. If any one of these conditions is missing the sale would be invalid in countries which retained the principles of Roman law, for they considered these prescriptions binding in conscience. In other countries and under other laws these requirements would not be necessary.

Carrière[81] while he did not think anyone would do such a thing in his day and age—which is the same period in which Kenrick wrote—admitted that if otherwise one could not provide the necessities of life or pay his debts, such a

---

[78] Kenrick, *loc. cit.*

[79] Lessius, *op. cit.*, Lib. 2, cap. IV, dub. IV.

[80] Lessius, *op. cit.*, Lib. 2, cap. IV, dub. IV: De Lugo, *op. cit.*, disp. VI, sec. II, no. 14; *DTC*, 5: 508-509.

[81] Carrière, *op. cit.*, I: p. 36, no. 45.

role is not completely repugnant. For, he said, a man is obliged to take care of his needs and may not demand that they be given gratis if he is able to work for them.

It should be pointed out that this title of sale when used by the theologians means the voluntary sale of oneself or of a child by its parents. However, a master may sell a slave that he legitimately holds by a just title.[82]

Kenrick[83] accepted the title of *nativity* without any discussion or qualification merely stating that children born of a slave mother are slaves, for *partus sequitur ventrem*. He referred to Roman law on the matter which taught that it was "explorati juris" that the child follows the condition of the mother, not the state of the father in this matter.[84]

Many theologians find little difficulty in accepting this title. St. Thomas[85] observed that in civil law "Partus sequitur ventrem." This is reasonable, he said, because the offspring has its formal complement from the father but the substance of the body from the mother. Slavery is a corporal condition because the slave is a quasi-instrument of the master in working. Thus the offspring in liberty and slavery follows the mother but in things that pertain to dignity—because these are *ex forma rei*—it follows the father, such as in the case of honor of heredity, etc.

Lessius[86] too, noted no difficulties. But he merely stated that the child is a slave if the mother is such at the time of birth, since the child is the "fruit" of a slave.

De Lugo,[87] after making the same observation as Lessius, said that he could understand the justice of this title in

---

[82] Cf. *supra*, pp. 105-107.

[83] *Theologia moralis*, tr. V, cap. V, no. 35.

[84] Liber I, Cod. III, tit. XXXII "de Rei vindicatione."

[85] Supp. Qu. LII, art. IV.

[86] Lessius, *op. cit.*, Lib. 2, cap. IV, disp. IV, Migne, *TCC*, 15: 506.

[87] De Lugo, *De justitia et jure*, Disp. VI, sec. II, no. 15-19; Cf. Carrière, *De justitia et jure*, I: 36, no. 45, who is in agreement with De Lugo.

the case of the punishment for crime or in the case of the children of slaves who were captives of an unjust war, for then the punishment is extended to the children just as ill-fame falls upon them. But in the case where the mother sells herself he did not see how she can oblige unborn children to slavery since the mother never can sell a living child into slavery and the father can do so only in the case of extreme necessity and then is obliged to redeem it and the owner is obliged to accept the price and return the child. Thus he was convinced that this title needs the sanction of the civil law. Hence, a country for a good reason may permit a mother to thus obligate her children to slavery just as it permits a tutor to oblige his ward and compels the ward to accept the obligation. But if the mother sells herself in another province where the principles of Roman law are not in force and later is removed to a place where they do apply, the child cannot be held as a slave, since it would be presumed that a contract of sale is made according to the law of that land in which it is written. Likewise, if a person who is made a slave as punishment in a territory where the law does not bind the offspring, is later transported to a territory where the law does oblige, the offspring cannot be held as slaves. The buyer is obliged to inquire about the lawfulness of the titles of the slave bought, for the seller cannot give to the buyer a right that he himself does not possess.

Cathrein[88] noted that this title of nativity was admitted by all nations and was one which made slavery a stable institution. But, he asked, how can this be just? Some say that the slave mother belongs to the master and therefore the master may acquire the "fruits" coming from her. But man cannot be considered a "fruit," for he is a person, on whose account all fruits were made, and who is essentially the subject of rights.

Others point out, he said, that the master has the right to all the labors of the slave-mother, thus he has a right

[88] Cathrein, *Philosophia moralis*, (ed. of 1907), p. 356, no. 467.

to compensation for the labors that she spends upon the infant, and for its food and clothing. But even though this right is conceded, it is not permitted to infer that the infant, in payment for this expense, should serve as a slave for his whole life, and much less that he could never acquire anything.[89]

He then gives two reasons that could possibly justify the title of nativity: (1) from the doctrine of many of the theologians one cannot be punished in the internal goods of the body or soul except for personal crimes; but in the external goods—liberty and riches—one may be punished for crimes which the community committed, and of which he is a part. Hence, such penalties could descend upon the offspring. But according to present customs of waging war, one could be deprived of liberty for crimes that may not be personal; formerly it had been otherwise. The nation waging an unjust war was punished by slavery partly as a penalty for the most grievous crimes committed by them and partly as an efficacious defense of the victors. Also it must be remembered that formerly once they had begun a war they continued it unto complete slaughter. Slavery in such a case was considered a more moderate penalty.[90]

(2) Once slavery had become universal and had planted its roots in all the social institutions, justly or unjustly, its sudden abrogation would have been very detrimental to the whole society and to the slaves themselves. Often they were ignorant persons, without any property, and without sufficient protection, slavery having become the foundation of the whole social order. It would seem that public custom or the law in these circumstances could supply or complete to the title of nativity that which it lacked from the right of nature to be a just title.[91]

[89] *Ibid.*

[90] *Ibid.*, pp. 356-357, no. 467.

[91] *Ibid.*; Davis, *Moral and Pastoral Theology*, 2: 269, agrees with this solution as the only one justifying this title. Cf. *DTC*, 5: 509; Brownson, *Works*, 17: 340-341.

III. Kenrick's Opinion on Domestic Slavery

Kenrick[92] considered domestic slavery under the general title of *Jus Gentium*. It might be looked upon as a corollary to his general teaching on slavery, which is treated in that place, for he considered it as being instituted by the *Jus Gentium*. By domestic slavery is meant slavery as it existed in some States of the Union by law of the State and had existed for many years.

At first thought one presumes that the slaves in this country were held either under the titles of sale or nativity, but neither can be the case. As was noted, when the theologians speak of sale, they refer to a person selling himself or his child or a slave held by a just title. Sale, as used in the United States, consisted in the sale of a slave by one person to another. The lawfulness of such a sale would depend upon the validity of the title under which the seller held the person sold.

According to the theologians, the title of nativity is used to denote those who can be held as slaves because they are children of parents who are justly held as slaves. Some say, as has been seen, that this title requires the support of the civil law before it can be considered valid.[93] But, as with sale, the validity of this title depends largely upon the validity of the title under which the parents or at least the mother is held in slavery. Realizing this, Kenrick did not even allude to those two titles for this justification of domestic slavery.

Kenrick proposed the question: What is to be thought of that domestic slavery which existed generally in the southern States as far as the descendants of those who were abducted from Africa and reduced to slavery are concerned?[94] He grieved that since men prize liberty so highly, there were so many slaves who were prevented by the then existing laws from being educated, and at times even from

---

[92] Kenrick, *Theologia moralis*, tr. V, cap. VI, no. 38.
[93] Cf. *supra*, 176-178.
[94] Kenrick, *Theologia moralis*, tr. V, cap. VI, no. 38.

practicing their religion. But since such is their condition, nothing contrary to the Civil law should be attempted, he thought, in order to liberate them, nor should anything be said or done which would make them bear their yoke badly. Rather, the prudence and charity of the clergy should be exerted to teach them Christian morals, and to encourage them to obey their masters and to venerate God, the Supreme Lord of all; the masters likewise should be encouraged to show themselves just and meek so that they will lighten the conditions of the slaves by humane treatment, and the desire of salvation, as the apostle had taught. He warned that those who neglected the words of the apostle, and moved by humanity attempted to overturn the order of things, often made the condition of the slaves worse. To strengthen his admonition he quoted the words of Gregory XVI (1831-1846):

> For the apostles inspired by the Divine Spirit, taught, in fact the slaves themselves, to obey their carnal masters, as Christ and to do the will of God from the heart; but they commanded the masters to act well before their slaves and to do to them what is just and equal, and to forebear threatenings; knowing that there is a Master both of them and themselves in the heavens, and that with Him there is no respect of persons.[95]

After giving this pastoral advice Kenrick[96] again reverted to the original question and asked if the masters could retain as slaves those whose ancestors were unjustly brought from Africa. He replied that it seemed to him they could; for he held the defect of the title was to be considered as validated by the lapse of a very long time, since otherwise, the condition of society would be uncertain, with very great danger resulting to the people. They indeed sin, who capture unwilling persons by force in order to enslave them; but it is not unjust to keep descendants

[95] "In supremo," *Collectanea S. Cong. de Prop. Fide*, I: p. 504, no. 891, translation from pamphlet edited by W. George Read (Baltimore: John Murphy, 1844).

[96] Kenrick, *op. cit.*, tr. V, cap. VI, no. 40.

of such victims in slavery, for the offspring are born in that condition and are not able to reject it.

In discussing this view of Kenrick, it will be necessary to take up the following points: slave-trade, prescription with its possible application to domestic slavery, the right of the slave that was restricted, the power of the state to legislate for the common good.

IV. DISCUSSION OF KENRICK'S OPINION

The slave-trade. Slave-trade might be defined as forcibly taking human being from their native lands and selling them as slaves to men of other nations—giving no thought as to whether or not they were enslaved by a just title—completely disregarding their natural rights. Kenrick, in accord with constant Catholic teaching, held that such an act is sinful, gravely sinful.[97]

Such capture and enslavement were denounced by several popes. For example Pope Urban VIII (1623-1644)[98] on

---

[97] Kenrick, *op. cit.*, tr. V, cap. VI, no. 40. Kenrick, *op. cit.*, (1840 ed.) I: 256 noted that Joseph Carrière, whose work on justice and rights was published in Paris in 1839 attempted to justify the slave-trade. He added that if he had seen the letter of Gregory XVI, he would not have stated that opinion for he was most attentive to the Holy See. Carrière was vicar general of Paris and professor of moral theology at the seminary of San Sulpice.

In the opinion mentioned, Carrière said that their sale is useful to the Negro, for in their own region they are frequently murdered, by the sale of many the population is decreased, thereby lessening wars, and they live a better life in America. He does admit that their work in America is very heavy, that many cruelties are perpetrated in capturing the Negroes and in shipping them to America. He admitted, too, injustice in the wars from which they are captured. Carrière, *De justitia et jure*, 1: pp. 37-43, no. 48-54. Kenrick omitted his comment on Carrière in his later edition, but cites the reference concerned in a footnote without any explanation. Perhaps this is because the edition of Carrière's work printed in Louvain in 1845 contains the same opinion, even though the letter of Gregory XVI was issued six years (1839) previously.

[98] "Letter to the Collector of Portugal, Apr. 22, 1639." *Bullarium diplomatum et privilegiorum sanctorum rom. Pontificum* XIV (1868), 712.

April 22, 1639, forbade all men to despoil men of their liberty, to sell or buy them, or to separate them from their wives or children, to remove from their native land and further to despoil them of their property.

Benedict XIV (1740-1758) [99] on December 20, 1741, spoke in great detail of the harm done to the natives and of the penalties for those who perpetrate such wrongs. The letter was addressed to the bishops of Brazil. He spoke of the great sadness that had come to his paternal heart that "men calling themselves Christians are so far forgetful of the sentiments of charity diffused in our hearts by the Holy Spirit as to reduce to slavery the unhappy Indians, the people of the eastern and western coasts of Brazil and other regions. . . . Much more, they sell them as common herds of slaves, they despoil them of goods; and the inhumanity which they display towards them is the principal cause of turning them away from embracing the faith of Jesus Christ by making them look upon it with horror." Pope Benedict stated that he appealed to King John of Portugal and that he reaffirmed the apostolic letters of Paul III of May 28, 1537, and of Urban VIII of April 22, 1639, which condemned these abuses. He appealed also to the bishops to do all in their power to cooperate in eradicating the abuse and invited them to enlist the help of the religious orders and laymen. Then "All infractions of these regulations shall incur an excommunication *latae sententiae . . .* in order that in the future no one would dare to reduce the Indians to slavery, to sell, to exchange, or give them away, to separate them from their wives and children, to despoil them of their goods, to transport them from one place or country to another, in fine, in any way whatsoever to despoil them of their liberty and to retain them in servitude, or to second those who act thus."

Finally, there is the oft-mentioned letter of Pope Gregory XVI (1831-1846) of December 3, 1839. In this letter the

---

[99] Letter sent to the Bishops of Brazil and other territories of Portugal, Dec. 20, 1741. *Bullarium Benedicti* XIV, 1 (1841), 123.

Pope mentioned that slavery in the early time of the Church did exist and that the apostles taught patience and meekness to the masters. He recalled how men realizing that all men are equal, often freed their slaves. "But grieving much we say it, there were subsequently from the very number of the faithful, those who, basely blinded by the lust of sordid gain, in remote and distant lands, reduced to slavery Indians, Negroes, or other unfortunate persons; or, by traffic begun and extended in those who had been made captive by others, did not hesitate to aid the shameful crime of the latter." He noted that other Roman pontiffs had reprimanded this for "from which, also, they perceived this to follow that the nations of infidels would be more and more hardened to hate our religion."

He recalled the letter of Pope Paul III of May 29, 1537, but especially the more extensive letter of Pope Urban VIII of April 22, 1639, to the Collector of the Rights of the Apostolic Chamber in Portugal, in which letter those are most seriously censured who should dare "to reduce to slavery the western and southern Indians, to sell, to buy, exchange, or give them away, to separate them from their wives and children, or despoil them of their property and goods, to conduct or send them to other places, or in any manner to deprive them of liberty, or retain them in slavery, and also to afford to those who do the aforesaid things, counsel, aid, favor or assistance, upon any pretext or studied excuse, or to preach or teach that it is lawful, or in any other manner to co-operate in the process." He recalled that Benedict XIV had given this admonition to the Bishops of Brazil.

He was saddened that although things had been somewhat remedied and the Negro slave-trade partly abandoned, still it did exist. He added: "we vehemently admonish and adjure in the Lord all believers in Christ, of whatsoever condition, that no one hereafter may dare unjustly to molest Indians, Negroes, or other men of this sort; or to despoil them of their goods; or to reduce them to slavery; or to extend help or favors to others, who perpetrate such things against them; or to exercise that inhumane trade by which Negroes, as if they were not men, but mere animals, howsoever reduced into slavery, are without any distinction, contrary to the laws of justice and humanity, bought, sold, and doomed sometimes to the most severe and exhausting labors; and moreover, the hope of gain being by that trade proposed to the first captors of the Negroes, dissensions, and as it were, witł petual wars fomented in their countries. We indeed, with apostolic authority, do reprobate all the aforesaid actions as utterly unworthy of the Christian name; and, by the same apostolic authority, do strictly prohibit and interdict that any ecclesiastic or lay person shall presume to defend that very trade in Negroes as lawful under any pretext or studied excuse, or otherwise to preach, or in any manner, publicly or privately, to teach contrary to those things which we have charged in this, our Apostolic Letter."[100]

Bishop England in his letters to Secretary Forsyth discussed this letter at length. He made the distinction between "slave-trade," which he obviously agreed is con-

---

[100] *Collectanea S. Cong. de Prop. Fide*, I: 504, no. 891: "...praedecessorum Nostrorum insistentes vestigiis, auctoritate Apostolica, omnes cujuscumque conditionis christifideles admonemus et obtestamur in Domino vehementer ne quis audeat in posterum spoliare suis bonis, aut in servitutem redigere, vel alia talia in eos patrantibus auxilium aut favorem praestare, seu exercere inhumanum illud commercium quo nigritae, tanquam si non homines sed plura putaque animantia forent, in servitutem utcumque redacti, sine ullo discrimine contra justitiae et humanitatis iura emuntur, venduntur, ac durissimum interdum laboribus exantlandis devoventur, et insuper lucri spe primis nigritarum occupatoribus per commercium idem proposita dissidia etiam et perpetua quodamodo in illorum regionibus praelia foventur. Enimvero Nos praedicta omnia tamquam christiano nomine prorsus indigna, auctoritate Apostolica reprobamus; eademque auctoritate districte prohibemus atque interdicimus, ne quis ecclesiasticus aut laicus ipsum illud nigritatum commercium velut licitum sub quovis obtentu aut quaesito colore tueri, aut aliter contra ea quae Nostri hisce Apostolicis Litteris monuimus praedicare seu quomodolibet publice vel privatim docere praesumunt,etc...."

demned by the Pope and which would be a felony here in
the United States since 1808, and "domestic slavery" which
may exist in any state by the authority of the state, over
the existence of which or the regulation of which, he said,
the federal government of the United States had no authority.[101]

. He attempted to prove that the Pope referred in his letter
only to slave-trade. He said the first class are those, "who
reduced (in remote lands) Indians, Negroes, and other unfortunate beings into slavery." "The citizens of Georgia
didn't do this," he added. The second class, he said, are
those criminals by being accessory, namely, those who encouraged or profited by such transactions. Now, he continued, since 1808, for an American citizen to go to Africa
to reduce persons to slavery or to purchase and ship for
foreign ports or any place in the United States would be
a felony. This is what the Pope meant by slave traffic.
The third class, said the Bishop of Charleston, are those
who, "buy, sell, exchange, or give away; separate from
their wives and children";—he does not comment on this—
the next expression, he said, cannot possibly apply to domestic slavery—"despoil them of their goods and possession, "for in the common and civil law the slaves have
no possessions." He continued, "carry or send them to other
regions"—which is incompatible with domestic slavery but
belongs to slave-trade; "or in any manner deprive them of

---

[101] "I now proceed, sir, to establish another distinction which I am
astonished that you overlooked. The distinction between the slave-
trade, as prohibited by the United States and the engagement in
which would be a high crime, I believe a felony, in any one of their
citizens, and the continuance of "domestic slavery" in any of the
states by the authority of that state, and with the existence or regulation of which the government of the United States has no concern
whatsoever.... The Pope neither mentions nor alludes to this latter
in his Apostolic letter, which is directed, as were those of his predecessors, solely and exclusively against the former.... The Roman
Catholic Church...has always observed this distinction; and it is
one as obvious as that which exists between the word "foreign" and
"domestic," *Works* (Messmer), 5: 189.

their liberty,"—which domestic slaves never had and of which he could not be deprived.[102]

The papal documents have been extensively quoted, for they form the background and the basis for the discussion of Archbishop Kenrick's view on domestic slavery. Bishop England's commentary was given great prominence, for he was a prominent member of the hierarchy of the day and his view seemed to be that generally of the hierarchy of that time.[103] He mentioned that Pope Gregory's letter was read at the recent council[104] and he claimed that if the fathers thought that it contained anything contrary to faith and morals, they would have been bound to communicate their difficulties with the Holy See; but such was not the case. On the other hand if they considered the doctrine of the Pope correct and if they knew of conditions in their dioceses contrary to it, they would be bound to refuse the sacraments to such as offended. Yet he says there were slave-holders who were Catholics and continued to receive the sacraments.[105]

Thus Catholics in the country admitted that the Church had always explicitly condemned the African slave-trade even though many of them were violently united in opposition to immediate repeal of slavery in the United States.[106]

[102] England, *Works* (Messmer), 5: 187-188.

[103] While it would seem that Bishop England watered down the words of the Pontiff attempting to free the slave holders of America from the sting of condemnation, his interpretation is given without comment, even though the author does not agree with it. In the first place because of the illegal continuance of the slave-trade, some slaves then living, contrary to what he said, had been forcibly taken from Africa. Moreover, the rest of the slaves of Bishop England's time were descendants of those who had been taken from Africa in the manner described by the Pope. Hence the title to them was just as faulty as that by which their parents were held.

[104] Fourth Provincial Council of Baltimore, 1840; Cf. Guilday, *History of Councils*, p. 123.

[105] "Letter to Forsyth, Oct. 7, 1840"; *Works* (Messmer), 5: pp. 190 f. It might be noted that not more than 5% of the slave-holders were Catholics.

[106] Brownson, *Works*, 17: 67 f.

The question, then, that is raised is this: Could slavery as it existed in the United States in the middle of the nineteenth century be classified as slave-trade? Daniel O'Connell, who prominently figured in the discussions on slavery in those days declared that it was. After noting that Gregory XVI had condemned all slave traffic, he claimed that it existed in a more abominable form than His Holiness could describe in the traffic, which existed in the sale of slaves from one state to another.[107] Bishop England answered this opinion in his open letter. Speaking of his audience with Gregory over his being made envoy to Haiti he quoted the Pope as saying: "Though the southern States have had domestic slavery as an heirloom, whether they would or not, they are not engaged in the Negro traffic."[108]

Prescription and its application to domestic slavery. Kenrick in proposing his question concerning the lawfulness of retaining in slavery the ancestors of those who were unjustly brought from Africa, said that he thought that the defect of the title had been remedied by the lapse of a very long time. Hence, Kenrick considered the original slaves as seized unjustly but by the time of the writing of his text he considered the title to them valid on the grounds of prescription.

Kenrick used prescription and usucaption synonymously and defined it as a mode of acquiring dominium by pos-

---

[107] Letter to the Irish Repeal Society of Cincinnati dated Oct. 11, 1843. Cf. pamphlet entitled: *The Pope's Bull and the Works of Daniel O'Connell* (New York: Joseph H. Ladd, no date).

[108] Letter of Forsyth, Oct. 7, 1840. *Works*, (Messmer), 5,: 192. While it seems to the author that the Letter of Gregory XVI had much more direct bearing on slavery as it existed in the United States than the commentator seemed to give it, this opinion is given without comment for this work is an attempt to discuss the subjective view of Kenrick, which likely was similar to that of his colleagues. The author cannot help but add that he wonders if Bishop England actually gave to the Pope a true picture of slavery existing in the United States in his day with its domestic slave-trade.

session in good faith, continued for a long time as defined by law. [109]

For a better understanding of the argument it would help to consider briefly the motives of prescription, its origin, and its force in conscience before considering the conditions necessary for prescription and their application to domestic slavery as it existed in the time of Archbishop Kenrick.

Carrière,[110] who treated prescription rather extensively, gave four motives as being those commonly accepted. First, prescription is needed for the sake of the common good, lest dominium remain uncertain over a long period of time or perhaps always. If one person holds the title and another actually possesses the thing, neither has a clear right to the thing and doubt and ambiguity would hold sway. Secondly, there would be practically eternal litigations if, after any length of time, the owners could claim a thing from the possessors, and the longer the lapse of time the more difficult it would be to arrive at a true decision. Thirdly, possessors would be besieged with an almost eternal fear that their property might be taken from them by someone who may have had a previous title. The result of this would be that fields and properties would be neglected to the disadvantage of the country. Fourthly, he who, after a certain length of time, does not seek his property from the possessor might be presumed to be willing that he shall keep it. But, he admitted, this presumption is at times deceiving, but at least the knowledge that one's goods can be taken away by prescription tends to make the owners more cautious in taking care of their property.

Now, while prescription, has some foundation in the natural law and the law of nations, it receives his force

[109] Kenrick, *Theologia moralis*, tr. X, cap. V, no. 75. In another place he referred to prescription as the exclusion of all pretension to a right founded on the length of time during which it was neglected. *Ibid.* tr. V, cap. II, no. 5. Cf. Davis, *Moral and Pastoral Theology* 2: 261; Merkelbach, *op. cit.*, 2: p. 229, no. 225; Noldin, *op. cit.*, 2: p. 380, no. 399.

[110] Carrière, *De justitia et jure*, 2: 4, no. 399.

principally from the civil law. Long possession gives a presumption of dereliction and alienation on the part of the original owner, but by proofs to the contrary one could destroy this presumption, hence, it is the civil law that really supports prescription in such a case by laying down regulations by which such contrary proofs to the contrary would be outlawed, this making the possession of property stable. But still it can be said that the natural law indicates at least the opportuneness if not the moral necessity of prescription. Hence, given the distribution of property, one might say that the nautral law makes prescription a necessity for otherwise the order of society would be very unstable, no one being sure that his property could not be taken from him by another.[111]

Kenrick[112] said that usucaption belongs to the law of nations. Carrière[113] thought that such an opinion is not to be absolutely admitted nor simply denied. If we consider the *jus gentium* as referring to those mutual offices by which the nations operate together there arises the difficulty that there is no common legislator admitted by all, who would determine the time and conditions; if, then, it is admitted by these nations, either it is so because of the natural law or because of treaties entered into by them. In the latter case such treaties would bind once they are made by force of the natural law.[114]

Moreover, as far as the fact of prescription is concerned, Carrièrre[115] stated that in most of the nations, excepting the Jews who were ruled specially, prescription is found from the earliest times, in fact it is difficult to find the beginning of it for the codices presume that it does already exist.

Here only acquisitive prescription is considered, and it

---

[111] Carrière, *op. cit.*, 2: p. 8, no. 406.
[112] Kenrick, *op. cit.*, tr. V, cap. I, no. 5.
[113] Carrière, *loc. cit.*
[114] Carrière, *op, et loc. cit.*
[115] *Ibid.*, 2: 6, no. 402.

is maintained that given the required conditions it binds both civilly and in conscience. That it binds civilly need not be proved, but that it is binding in conscience can be proved from the fact that the legislator can transfer and wills to transfer dominium in such cases.

The legislator can bind in conscience by reason of the common good. But, the common good demands prescription, for otherwise dominium would remain almost forever uncertain; otherwise there would be endless litigation; otherwise there would be constant fear of losing one's property; without it there would be great negligence on the part of owners in caring for their possessions. That the legislator wishes to transfer dominium not only to deny civil action, is evident from the purpose of the law itself, namely, the common good; moreover, the very obvious words of the civil law contain no restriction.[116] Additional force is added to the argument by the Fourth Lateran Council which recognized the validity of prescription.[117]

The theologians, Kenrick included, list five things necessary for valid prescription: an apt thing, possession, title, good faith and required time. As each of these is explained, an attempt will be made to discuss their application to domestic slavery in accord with Kenrick's theory.

A thing prescribable means anything, corporal or incorporal, which of its nature is capable of private dominium and is in no way excepted by law.[116] In this regard it is interesting to note that Kendick[119] himself taught that things taken by robbery, or by one using force, cannot be prescribed; nor can the property of one who cannot seek them back in court, such as the insane, be prescribed.

Regarding domestic slavery, it must be admitted that the labor of one in the form of slavery could possibly be

---

[116] Merkelbach, *Summa theologiae moralis*, 2: 230, no. 226.

[117] Cap. 41, Henricus Denzinger, *Enchiridion symbolorum* (ed. 18-20, Freiburg: Herder & Co., 1932), no. 439.

[118] Kenrick, *op. cit.*, tr. X, cap. V, no. 75; Merkelbach *op. cit.*, 2: p. 230, no. 227; Noldin, *op. cit.*, 2: p. 381, no. 402.

[119] Kenrick, *op. cit.*, tr. X, cap. V, no. 75.

prescribed for as has been seen, the theologians have always taught that slavery is in itself not contrary to the natural law. However, if the observation of Kenrick above is considered, one would wonder in the case of the American slaves, for they were taken by force, at least those living at that time, who had been actually taken from Africa.[120] Secondly, slaves by law in most of the states were forbidden to bring a court suit against their masters.[121] Kenrick indicated that the "property" of such people who cannot seek them back in court cannot be prescribed.[122]

The second requisite for prescription—good faith—is the practical judgment by which the possessor of a thing belonging to another is persuaded that the thing is his. Hence, it is a judgment that is objectively erroneous but made with invincible ignorance by which one sincerely thinks that he possesses the thing legitimately.[123]

To show that good faith is necessary in the beginning of the possession and in the whole course of the time required it will be sufficient to cite two ecclesiastical documents.

The Fourth Lateran Council:

We define that no prescription whether canonical

---

[120] Cf. *supra*, pp. 8-12, where it was noted that the majority of the Negroes of the trade were unjustly captured; Cf. *supra*, p. 20, where it was noted that even after the law of 1808 was passed forbidding the trade, slaves were smuggled into the country. In the years preceding 1808 many slaves were imported. Phillips estimated them as follows: 1804, 5,386; 1805, 6,790; 1806, 11,458; 1807, 15,676. Cf. Phillips, *American Negro Slavery*, p. 138. Between 1808 and 1860 conjecture places the gross of illicit importation as 270,000. Cf. *Ibid.*, p. 147.

[121] *Supra*, p. 92.

[122] Noldin, *Summa theologiae moralis*, 2: p. 382, no. 403, who refers this to lack of good faith. This is merely said from the standpoint of the natural law. It will be pointed out later that Canon Law of the day explicitly decreed that prescription could not be used with regard to liberty of persons. Cf. *infra*, p. 219.

[123] Kenrick, *op. cit.*, tr. X, cap. V, no. 76; Merkelbach, *op. cit*, 2: 234, no. 230.

or civil is valid without good faith.... Thus it is
necessary that he, who prescribes, in no part of
the time be conscious that the thing belong to another.[124]

The second is the code of canon law:

No prescription is valid unless it rests on good
faith, not only in the beginning of the possession
but in the whole time required for prescription.[125]

Applying this to domestic slavery, it should be pointed
out, Kenrick[126] admitted that it seemed that the slaves
were taken unjustly from Africa. This seems to agree with
the thought of others. For example, Molina[127] asking the
question about the justice of the Ethiopian wars of his day
in which captured Negroes were sold to the Portuguese
as slaves, said that such affairs should be considered robberies rather than wars, according to the statements of
the traders, who had freely testified without pressure. It
might be noted that a court decision was rendered in 1822
stating that the African slave-trade, abstractedly considered, is inconsistent with the law of nations, and a claim
founded upon it may be repealed in any court where it is
asserted, unless the trade be legalized by the nation to which
the claimant belongs.[128]

Thus it seems that objectively those persons were wrong
who bought Negroes as part of the African slave-trade for
they had been unjustly enslaved. But, in dealing with good
faith in prescription, we are dealing with a subjective

[124] Cap. 41, "... diffinimus, ut nulla valeat absque fide prescriptio tam canonica quam civilis.... Unde oportet, ut, qui prescribit, in
nulla temporis parte rei habeat conscientiam alienae." Denzinger,
p. 439.

[125] Canon 1512. "Nulla valet prescriptio, nisi bona fide nitatur, non
solum initio possessionis, sed toto possessionis tempore ad prescrip-
tionem requisito."

[126] Kenrick, *op. cit.*, tr. V, cap. VI, no. 40.

[127] Molina, *De justitia et jure*, tr. 2, disp. 35, no. 18-20.

[128] Cf. *United States* v. *Battiste*, Fed. Cases, no. 14,545 (2 Sunan,
240), *American Digest*, 40: 856.

judgment that is sincere and good but by invincible ignorance is objectively false.[129]

The good faith of those who bought Negroes captured in Africa on a wholesale basis might be questioned. Could they have had no doubts about the validity of the title under which such persons were held in slavery? If they doubted then, they were bound to solve the doubt by consulting moral theology on the point. The moral books of the day would have shown them that while slavery is not contrary to the natural law it is legitimate only when the persons are enslaved by a just title. The theologians admit only four just titles: sale, punishment, imprisonment from a just war, and nativity. Moreover, moral theologians and teachers should have been conversant with the array of papal documents which very definitely and explicitly condemned the slave-trade from which they derived their slaves.[130]

Now, the people of the day did not completely and universally justify the trade, for instances are found of those whose consciences troubled them at the thought of slavery under the circumstances being unjust.

In 1646 a cargo of Africans was brought from the slave-coast of Africa. The magistrates of Boston sent them back, saying that they were "bound by the first opportunity to bear witness against the heinous and crying sin of man-

---

[129] Merkelbach, *op. cit.*, 2: 234, no. 230. Bishop Dupanloupe in the pastoral cited, acknowledged that many act in good faith in holding slaves in America. *RACHS*, 25 (1914), 27.

Peter Early of Georgia had this to say in the House of Representatives in 1807: "A large majority of the people of the Southern States do not ... believe it immoral to hold human flesh in bondage. Many deprecate slavery as an evil; but not as a crime. Reflecting men apprehend, at some future day evils, incalculable evils, from it; but it is a fact that few, very few, consider it a crime. It is best to be candid on this subject. ... I will tell the truth. A large majority of the people in the Southern States do not consider slavery as an evil. Let the gentlemen go and travel in that quarter of the Union; let them go from neighborhood to neighborhood, they will find that this is a fact." Cf. *Annals of Congress*, 1806-1807, Col. 237.

[130] Cf. *supra*, pp. 186-190.

stealing."[131] An example of an individual is William Garnett, a planter, who was driven from the plantation career because of the aversion of using slaves. He felt that he was incompetent in the test of managing the slaves, for every time he found it necessary to punish one he was conscious of violating the natural rights of a being who was as much entitled to them as himself.[132]

However, in considering the possibility of lack of good faith on the part of those who held slaves, who were directly bought from slave-traders or were the descendants of such, two facts must be considered, especially as far as Catholics are concerned. These are: the fact of the ownership of such slaves by the clergy[133] and the humane treatment of slaves by Catholics.

Guilday quoted a letter written by Father John Ryan, a Dominican, to the Propaganda in 1819 in which he explained the opposition of many of the Protestant sects to slavery and then added:

> A trite topic of remark and of no trifling occasion for scandal, among these people, is furnished by the fact that the Catholic clergy are principal slave-owners in their corporate capacity; and a great portion of the Catholics lament the existence of such a system, which they consider injurious to the character of their religion, and consequently to its progress.[134]

From a letter of John Caroll to Father John Thayer, a New England convert who wanted to resign his parish because he could not reconcile slavery with his conscience, we learn the pastoral advice of that prelate. He told Thayer that he did not think that that was sufficient reason to grant an *exeat*. He told him that while he confined himself within the bonds of solid piety he might act freely and unrestrained by any ecclesiastical interference in remedy-

[131] John C. Polfry, *Papers on the Slave Power* (2nd ed. Boston: Merrill, Cobb and Co., no date), p. 3.

[132] Phillips, *Life and Labor in the Old South*, p. 210.

[133] Cf. *supra*, p. 54.

[134] Guilday, *Carroll*, 1: 684.

ing the abuse of slavery: "and when you have done your duty, if all the good effect possible and desirable does not ensue from your endeavors, you must bear that as every pastor must bear the many disorders which will subsist in spite of his zealous exhortations.... I am as far as you from being easy in my mind at many things I see and know, relating to the treatment and manner of Negroes. I do the best I can to correct the evils I see and then recur to those principles which I suppose influenced the many eminent and holy missionaries in South America and Asia where slavery equally exists."[135]

On the surface it might seem that Father Thayer could not reconcile the existence of slavery as being unjust, with his conscience. Yet, Bishop Carroll in his reply referred solely to the treatment of slaves. He made no reference to the fact of their being enslaved as bothering him but merely their cruel treatment. This is consistent with the fact that he owned slaves.

As stated above, the second point to consider is that as a general rule Catholics treated their slaves kindly and in a Christian manner. Bishop England said:

> The general teratment of the Negroes in the diocese of Charleston is kind and affectionate; far, far more so than that of the bulk of Irish agricultural and other laborers.[136]

Father Mosley in a letter to his sister on October 1, 1774 said:

> ... the Negroes that do belong to the Gentlemen of our Persuasion and our own are all Christian and instructed in every Christian duty with care.... The Negroes of all other Persuasions are much neglected, as you imagine, and few ever christened.[137]

[135] *RACHS*, 20 (1908), 58 f.

[136] "Early History of the Diocese of Charleston," *Works*, (Messmer), 4: 318.

[137] "Letters of Father Joseph Mosley, S.J., and some extracts from his diary 1757-1786," edited by Edward I. Devill, *RACHS*, 27 (1906), 299.

Can, then, the owners of slaves in the middle of the nineteenth century be said to have had good faith in their possession of slaves, who were the descendants of those who were unjustly taken from Africa, or were actually taken themselves? It seems difficult to answer. From the examples given it seems that some worried about the justice of keeping slaves procured through slave-trade. Yet, as far as the average Catholic is concerned, the normal thing would be to consult his priests. It would normally be presumed that the priests would be conversant with the papal letters quoted above and would have warned them that any participation in the slave-trade would be sinful. Yet one wonders if that were the case since many of the clergy actually possessed slaves. It would seem from sources studied that all that was publicly taught was that slavery in itself is not contrary to the natural law provided the slaves are treated kindly. It does not seem that any of them directly said that the Negroes were held by a just title in the United States. Yet at times they are falsely quoted as such. For example, Father Stephen Theobold claimed that Bishop England maintained that the Holy Father far from condemning domestic slavery actually endorsed it.[138]

One wonders how such a conclusion could be made by studying the letters of Bishop England. The Bishop pointed out that slavery itself is not contrary to the natural law. His conclusion was, "Slavery, then, Sir, is regarded by the Church of which the Pope is the presiding officer not to be incompatible with the natural law.[139] He agreed that slave-trade is definitely wrong and was condemned by the Pope, but he made a distinction between it and domestic slavery.[140] Moreover, he said that in his audience with the Pope the latter said: "Though the Southern States have had domestic slavery as an heirloom, whether they would or not, they are not engaged in the Negro traffic."[141]

[138] Theobold, *RACHS*, 35 (1924), 335 f.
[139] *Works* (Messmer), 5: 195.
[140] *Ibid.*, 5: 187.
[141] *Ibid.*, 5: 192.

How can one honestly construe these thoughts to mean
that he approved of domestic slavery in the United States
and taught that the Holy Father endorsed it? To agree
that slave-trade is wrong and then agree that slavery as
it existed in the United States is not slave-trade is quite
different from saying that said domestic slavery was just
and lawful. No statement was given on the latter. Unfortunately Bishop England died before he finished his
series of the letters and consequently never really gave
his opinion of the lawfulness of retaining slaves, whose ancestors were transported from Africa in the slave-trade.
There are some indications of his attitude which closely re-
sembles that of Archbishop Kenrick. In a note addressed
to the editor of the United States Catholic Miscellany, he
said:

> I have been asked by many a question which I
> may as well answer at once, viz.: Whether I am
> friendly to the existence or continuation of slav-
> ery? I am not, but I see the impossibility of now
> abolishing it here. When it can and ought to be
> abolished, is a question for the legislature and not
> for me.[142]

Madeleine H. Rice[143] after studying the literature of the
day concluded that at times in order to disassociate the
Church membership from abolition movements, some went
to great lengths in their defense of slavery; Bishop England in his letters on domestic slavery, Bishop Kenrick's
counsel to the clergy in the *Theologia moralis* and Archbishop Hughes in his diatribe against Brownson. Each, she
says, seem to give ecclesiastical sanctions to the slave system and in so doing contributed to the pro-slavery argument.

That these men contributed to the pro-slavery argument
is quite possible. But if one carefully studies the complete
teaching of Kenrick on slavery, it would seem false to say

[142] *Ibid.*, p. 311.
[143] Rice, *American Catholic Opinion in the Slavery Controversy*,
p. 156.

that he flatly gave ecclesiastical sanction to slavery as found in the United States in his day. Kenrick, for example, grieved that the situation existed in the country and he admitted that the slaves were originally captured unjustly, but he held that by prescription and for the sake of the common good, masters might in conscience continue to hold their slaves, provided they respect their God-given rights.[144]

Unfortunately the various historians speak of Kenrick's pastoral advice completely neglecting his theological opinion as to why domestic slavery could be lawfully maintained and neglecting to point out that he insisted that the rights of slaves be respected. For example, Theobold, in the article cited, quoted the Catholic Miscellany (no date given) :

> The line of conduct prescribed especially to the Catholic clergy is laid down by the venerable and learned Bishop of Philadelphia in his standard work, *Theologia moralis*, vol. I, tr. 5, cap. 5, tr. 3, cap. 4. From the first cited chapter the following is a translation. . . .[145]

The article then quoting the United States Catholic Miscellany gives only the part in which Kenrick regrets that so many beings are submerged in slavery, but such being the case nothing should be attempted against the law that would make them bear their yoke more unwillingly. While he does not give the date of the issue of the Catholic paper quoted, we might suppose that it is the same issue Rice quoted in her work. For she, too, in speaking of Kenrick's doctrine referred only to the part mentioned, saying nothing about the more important part, the actual theological view.[146]

While it seems that the discussion has drifted, the preceding matter is of great importance in attempting to ascertain whether or not the people owning slaves in the

---

[144] *Theologia moralis*, tr. V, cap. VI, no. 38.

[145] Theobold, *RACHS*, 35 (1924), 338.

[146] Rice, *op. cit.*, p. 71, lists the Metropolitan Magazine, June, 1855, p. 267 and the U. S. Cath. Misc., Dec. 9, 1843.

nineteenth century had good faith. The average Catholic, who might have had worries of conscience regarding the slaves he was holding, would logically go to the teachers of the Church for a solution of his problem. One would suppose that such a person would have been told that slave-trading was specifically condemned by the various popes and consequently, those slaves, that they held, who were bought from the trade and their children, were unjustly held. One would have, moreover, expected public statements to this effect by the leaders of the Church.

But quite possibly such was not the case. In the first place, as was observed, many of the clergy held slaves. Secondly, utterances of the hierarchy were concerned with the fact that slavery in itself is not contrary to the natural law, and strongly opposed to the proponents of immediate emancipation; thirdly, while these statements seem quite true and quite clear to the theologian, evidently they were interpreted by the average person as a sanction of slavery as it existed in the United States. It seems all the more likely that people living during the troubled days of the slave controversy would have accepted that interpretation, since even those who in the calm of the present write of the history, give similar interpretations. Such being the case, it is difficult to accuse the people of the middle nineteenth century of holding the descendants of those who were taken from Africa unjustly, in bad faith.

The third requisite of prescription is possession—the detention of a thing or the enjoyment of a right either personally or through another in one's name.[147] Possession is the foundation of prescription so that without it there can be no prescription. It must be dominative, peaceful and continuous, doubtless and public.

It is dominative if it is held with the intention and title of being the owner. It is peaceful when it is held without violence, but on the contrary is undisturbed and uninter-

---

[147] Kenrick, *op. cit.*, tr. X, cap. V, no. 75; Merkelbach, *op. cit.*, 2: p. 232, no. 228; Noldin, *op. cit.*, 2: p. 384, no. 425.

rupted.[148] Thus, where there is violence there is no possession but invasion of the right of another. Kenrick[149] remarked that things stolen or taken by force cannot be prescribed.

Kenrick[150] in another place said that if a nation unjustly invades another region, by the space of a very long time the title seems healed if the people submit to the invaders lest insurrection be invoked causing calamity to the people. Again, he said that by usucaption a right is prescribed against those opposing (*adversos*); but the patience of an oppressed people is not to be easily assumed in the argument of an admitted right (*juris agniti*). But presumption certainly avails after a very long space of time, if the usurped power is exercised in the utility of the people.

The case of which he spoke in the last two citations is that of one nation invading another and claiming domain over them in their own territory. Our problem concerns the case of members of a nation kidnapping men from their own country and taking them to another country where they claim servile dominion over them. Yet, there is some similarity between the two, at least enough perhaps to catch Kenrick's rather undeveloped idea of prescription over the Negro slaves.

Turning to Domestic slavery, one notes that few phases of ante-bellum life in the South were not influenced by the fear of or the actual outbreak of militant slave action.[151] Because of this fear, laws were passed restraining the personal liberty of the slave; his right to assemble in large numbers, except under the supervision of the master class, was restricted; his right to purchase firearms or weapons of deadly warfare was taken away—all in order to prevent the possibility and effectiveness of outbreaks for free-

---

[148] Merkelbach, *op. cit.*, 2: 232, no. 228.

[149] Kenrick, *op. cit.*, tr. X, cap. V, no. 75.

[150] *Op. cit.*, tr. X, cap. V, no. 5.

[151] This the conclusion of Herbert Aptheker, *American Negro Slave Revolts* (New York: Columbia University Press, 1943).

dom.[152] The idea of colonization was conceived because of
this fear of insurrection.

Despite all the precaution taken many insurrections are
recorded. While these insurrections increased in the decade
of the thirties,[153] there were about twenty-five recorded
instances of insurrection before the Revolution.[154] The best
known of these early insurrections was the "New York
Slave Plot of 1741," which resulted in the transportation
of eighty Negroes, the hanging of eighteen whites and Negroes, and the judicial burning of thirteen more.[155] At times,
considerable numbers were involved. In the insurrection
of General Gabriel in 1800, 1,000 slaves were involved.[156]

The Congregational ministers sum the situation up in the
following words:

> Slavery, at the present day is everywhere under-
> stood to imply coercion; and coercion of that kind
> and degree, to which, in general more would not
> submit, if they were not kept in subjection by
> laws framed for the express purpose of protecting
> the master, against the assertion of natural rights
> by the slave, and his claim to be regarded as a
> fellow-man and a brother.[157]

Applying the theological doctrine to this it would seem
difficult to assume that the slaves actually freely submitted
to their masters. It seems that the constant fear felt by
the people in slave-holding States as well as the recorded
instances of insurrection, plus the many instances of runaway slaves[158] indicate that the possesion of slaves by their

---

[152] Cromwell, *Negro in American History*, p. 12; Cf. Aptheker,
op. cit., passim.

[153] Sunderland, *Anti-slavery Manual*, pp. 83-91.

[154] Cromwell, *Negro in American History*, p. 12; Hart, *Slavery
and Abolition*, p. 52.

[155] Hart, *Slavery and Abolition*, p. 52.

[156] Cromwell, *Negro in American History*, p. 12; *The Negro in
Virginia*, pp. 174-188; Phillips, *Life and Labor in the Old South*,
p. 164.

[157] *Report on Slavery to the Congregationalist Ministers*, p. 14.

[158] Cf. *infra*, p. 301-314.

masters was not on the whole a peaceful possession. Noldin points out that where violence is used "vis," not possession, is had.[159]

The fourth requisite for prescription is, title, which is the *per se* sufficient reason why one thinks that the thing possessed is his own. The title is only apparent if it seems to transfer dominium but because of some defect it actually does not. It is called a colored title if it has the legal form sufficient to transfer dominium but actually does not because of some occult defect. It is a presumed title if it really does not exist but because of the fact of possession over a long period of years it is presumed by law to exist.[160]

It can be readily admitted that the masters possessed their slaves at least by a presumed title, for they were in their possession for a long time when Kenrick proposed this theory. Or, in the case of those who more recently acquired them, there was a colored title for they had bought them, even though the seller may not have had a just title to them.

The fifth requisite is specified time. This element varies considerably according to the civil codes of the various nations.[161] In our own country it even varies with the different states.[162] In countries where the civil codes are based on Roman law all things are able to be prescribed in thirty years even without a title and immovable goods held with a just title are prescribed in ten or twenty years. Movable goods in a still shorter time.[163]

In the case at hand there is a matter of the liberties of individuals of one nation being possibly prescribed by members of another nation, who have transplanted them to their territory. Hence, one could scarcely use the time

---

[159] Noldin, *op. cit.*, 2: 384, no. 405.

[160] Kenrick, *op. cit.*, tr. X, cap. V, no. 77; Merkelbach, *op. cit.*, 2: 234, no. 229; Noldin, *op. cit.*, 2: 383, no. 404.

[161] Noldin, *op. cit.*, 2: 384, no. 406.

[162] Kenrick, *op. cit.*, tr. X, cap. VI, no. 80.

[163] Merkelbach, *op. cit.*, 2: 236, 237, no. 231.

stipulated by the civil codes of the various states in the
Union to determine the issue.

Earlier in the discussion it was noted that prescription
finds its origin principally in the civil law, although the
right of private property having been admitted, the natural
law indicates at least its opportuneness. Likewise, it might
be indicated that the law of nations, too, would find it useful and fitting. But, the dfficulty arises in that there is
no authority to determine the time.

Now Kenrick[164] claimed that prescription does belong
to the *jus gentium*. He likewise gave a vague indication of
time when he said that if a people loses its liberty, having
been conquered by a more powerful nation, and thus passes
under a foreign sovereignity its rights are not to be considered lost except after the lapse of a *very long time* and
only after all hope of recapturing their liberty has vanished
and the people seem to have consented to their new condition. A nation sins against the *jus gentium* if it oppresses
a smaller nation by power and deprives it of liberty except
for the avenging of an injury from legitimate war.[165]

Thus he seems to indicate that in such a case the thing
to be considered the necessary element is the utility of
the people and their acceptance of the conqueror; further
in the chapter, he seems to consider their possibility of
recapturing their rights. This latter, in turn, agrees with
a remark that he made concerning slavery, namely, that
those sin who by force take away those who are unwilling
but it is not unjust to keep their descendants in slavery
for they are born in that condition and are not able to reject it.[166]

However, are they not possibly unjustly held in slavery
if they are by force led to believe that they cannot put off
their condition? Kenrick taught that the rights of those
who cannot reclaim them in court cannot be prescribed.[167]

---

[164] Kenrick, *op. cit.*, tr. V, cap. II, no. 5.
[165] Kenrick, *op. cit.*, tr. V, cap. III, no. 9.
[166] *Ibid.*, tr. V, cap. VI, no. 40.
[167] *Ibid.*, tr. X, cap. VI, no. 75.

But, disregarding that element for the moment, what amount of time would be required for the prescription of the liberties of the slaves? It would seem that the case at hand comes under the law of nations rather than civil law for it is a case of the liberties of members of one nation being prescribed by the members of another. Kenrick said that it requires the space of a *very long time*,[168] and he added in his statement on domestic slavery that such a space of time had elapsed.[169]

Precisely how long would that be in years? Carrière divided time for prescription into long or very long time, which he says would be the lapse of thirty years, which time extinguishes all actions real and personal; short, meaning five years; and very short meaning anything from six months to five years,[170] but it must be remembered that he was speaking of prescription in Roman civil law.

England in his letters discussing the history of slavery speaking of the "coloni" namely, those persons who were bound to the soil, divided them into; "originarii," those born there; "adscripti," those written to it; and "advenae," the stranger coming there and fulfilling the conditions without any special bargain. The latter, he says, were prescribed against after thirty years.[171]

Turning to domestic slavery, one could easily imagine that the average slave knowing the law through custom and treatment might have had no hope of redeeming his liberty. But, under such circumstances could the time, required for prescription run on? Davis says that when an owner is deprived of land by concealed fraud (by some ruse, by which he is not only deprived but defrauded by being led to believe that the claimant and not he is the

---

[168] *Ibid.*, tr. V, cap. II, no. 5, "post longissimum temporis lapsum."
[169] *Ibid.*, tr. V, cap. VI, no. 40.
[170] Carrière, *De justitia et jure*, 1: Pars. I, sec. I, cap. V, p. 4, no. 398. "longi vel longissimi, brevis, et brevissimi."
[171] "Letter to Forsyth, Jan. 14, 1841," *Works* (Messmer), 5: 250.

legal owner) time does not run until such fraud is found out or might with diligence have been known.[172]

Now, assuming that the last slaves were bought not later than 1808, when slave-trade was forbidden by law of the United States, thirty-two years had elapsed when Kenrick's first volume which contains his opinion of this problem, was published. Hence, it might be claimed that the very long time of which he spoke was spent, but the difficulty arises, as was said above, that during that time the enslaved people could have no redress, therefore was the time running or was it suspended?

Moreover, the fact that there is no authority to determine the time element in this case must be considered.

Therefore as a conclusion to this discussion of Kenrick's view attempting to justify domestic slavery on the grounds of prescription it must be said that it seems difficult to agree with such an opinion because of the accumulation of doubts raised as to the fulfillment of the conditions for prescription as taught by the theologians.

But a still more cogent reason enters this conclusion. Canon law of the day clearly decreed in several places that prescription could not be used against liberty, even if the person in question were held in slavery for a long time, even for more than forty years.[173] One wonders how it was possible for Kenrick to pass over these decrees of canon law in giving his opinion that the title by which slaves were held in his day in the United States was validated by the lapse of a very long time.

[172] Davis, *Moral and Pastoral Theology*, 2: 262.

[173] "Unde si liber homo longo tempore pro servo detineatur; etiam si quadraginta annorum curricula excesserint, sola temporis longinquitate libertatis iura minime mutilabuntur." *Decretum Gratiani*, Post Canonem XV, causa, XVI, qu. III; "Arg. contra libertatem non praescribi" Glossa Ordinaria, Can. XIV, v, servitute; "Nota hos casus in quibus non currit praescriptio. ... Et liber homo non praescribitur," Glossa ordinaria, *Decretales Gregorii* IX, C. 12, de praescript., III, 26, v, non obstante.

It is interesting to note that the court of Louisiana was in agreement with canon law in a decision given in 1824 to the effect that prescription could not be used against liberty. In the case in question the plaintiff urged that she was a descendant from one Marie Catherine, a Negro woman, now deceased, who was the slave of a certain Marie Durse, and that said Marie set free Catherine and her children, the mother of the petitioner. She complained that the defendant illegally held her in slavery, and asked to be set free and to recover damage for injury by being held in servitude. The defendant pleaded general issue and prescription. The court decided as follows:

> We shall, before entering on the merits, dispose of the exception which forms the second ground for the defense of the defendant's answer. We do so, by referring to the third partida, twenty-nine, law twenty-four, in which we find it provided, that if a man be free no matter how long he may be held by another, as a slave, his state or condition cannot be thereby changed, nor can he be reduced to slavery, in any manner whatsoever, on account of the time, he may have held in servitude. The plaintiff is entitled to her freedom.[174]

Therefore, it would seem more just to appeal to the common good for at least temporary justification of the institution, which argument Kenrick seems to indicate but does not develop. A discussion of this argument will now be attempted.

Discussion of the temporary justification of slavery for the sake of the common good. Kenrick intimated that the rights of slaves to their liberty might be limited for the sake of the common good. He spoke of the instability of society and the danger that would accrue to people if slavery were to be thrown off. He thus intimated that

---

[174] *Delphine* v. *Deveze*, 14 Martin's La. Rep. 650 (June Term, 1824), Wheeler, *A Practical Treatise on the Laws of Slavery*, p. 101.

slavery might be justified for the sake of the common good.[175]

It must be remembered that Kenrick in expressing this opinion presumed that slaves were treated in accord with the rules of morality laid down by the moral theologians. Articles written by the leaders of the Church during the slave controversy spoke of slavery theoretically as it should be found in order to be lawful, while the average person spoke of it practically as it did exist in many cases with grave injustices to those enslaved. Thus having no common ground they were really speaking of two different things.

Kenrick[176] viewed slavery as a perpetual and universal right that the master had over all the works that a slave as a man can give to man rightfully, with the master having the obligation of caring for the slave and of studiously observing all duties of humanity toward him.

It is evident that there is a necessary connection between person and society, for person is unintelligible without the community and the community is meaningless without constitutents.[177] In order to understand better an attempt will be made to establish the scholastic idea of person and its human dignity and then of society and the common good.

Person, in the classical definition is an individual substance of the rational nature.[178] Since the individual human being is a reality existing by himself, he is a substance, and since this individual is endowed with reason, he is a person.[179] It is, then, because of reason that a person is autonomous, responsible, and the possessor of per-

[177] John Rudolph Harvey, O.F.M., M.A., *The Metaphysical Relation between Person and Liberty* (Washington, D.C.: The Catholics University of America Press, 1942), p. 66.

[178] I, qu. 29, art. I, ad 1 um.

[179] "Distinctum subsistens in intellectuali natura." *Summa Theol.*, I, qu. 29, art. 3, ad 2.

[175] Kenrick, *Theologia moralis*, tr. V, cap. VI, no. 40.

[176] *Ibid.*, no. 39.

sonal rights and a dignity, which are entitled to protection and respect.[180]

Liberty of choice is the basis of human dignity for it is the condition of man's creative power. Pope Leo XIII recognized liberty as "the highest of natural endowments."[181] For St. Thomas[182] liberty is the faculty of choosing means, keeping in mind their relation to an end.

Man being a person endowed with an intellect and a free will was created for a purpose, which he ought freely to achieve. This implies that he must be able to choose the means necessary for that. The means necessary to attain that purpose necessarily requires material things for man is composed of body and soul. The more closely these material things are connected with man the more profound the right of having them. Now, if for the common good the state in the nineteenth century were to prescribe the liberty of the slaves, just what rights would be restricted?

The body of the slave is his and his alone and over it the master acquires no right by slavery. The master is obliged to feed, clothe, shelter the slave adequately and to care for him in time of need. Hence, the slave has a right to all necessary things in property, but the right of the products of one's own brain and hands go to the master.

But, even though the slaves had been emancipated would they have been completely free in claiming the fruits of their brains and hands?

The liberated slaves would obviously have had to work for others. Moreover, they would have had no unions to assist them to demand just wages and decent working con-

---

[180] *Questiones disputatae de potentia*, qu. 9, art. 1, ad 3; "Hoc . . . quod est per se agere, excellentiori modo convenit, substantiis rationalis naturae quam aliis. Nam solae substantiae rationales habent dominum sui actus, ita quod in eis est agere et non agere; aliae vero substantiae magis aguntur quam agunt. Et ideo conveniens fuit ut substantia individua rationalis naturae speciale nomen haberet."

[181] "Libertas praestantissimum," *Acta Leonis* XIII, 8: 212.

[182] *Summa theol.*, I, qu. 83, art. 4, "libertas est vis electiva mediorum servato ordine finis."

ditions. They had been trained only for work in the fields for the most part. Hence, they would have been very limited in the type of employment they could have sought. Yet they had no money to start with and would have been forced to take any type of menial work under any conditions and for any salary in order to be able to procure the most meager necessities for conserving life.

Kenrick could have logically reasoned that by a continuation of slavery at least temporarily, the slave would be deprived only of the relative necessities, possessions, superfluities and luxuries. But, this was very small when one—following the thought of the day—considers how the slaves would have been naturally restricted had they been immediately emancipated. It must be repeated that this presumes that the relationship of master and slave was morally correct according to the teaching of the theologians, as outlined. Hence, it would seem that not even the slave could be reasonably unwilling to have these his rights prescribed by the state for the common good.

Moreover, man is a rational being, whose purpose in life is to develop his personality. Thus far man has been considered as an individual and now his relationship with others must be studied.

That man is a social being by nature is evident from many reasons. First of all, historic investigations all lead to the fact that men of all times, in all lands have always lived together in some sort of a society. But, it does not seem possible that such a constant, universal and perpetual fact could have its origin in anything but nature itself.[183] Moreover, man needs society and he uses it because he in his rational nature chooses means that he realizes will be necessary to attain his purpose.

> However, it is natural for man to be a social and political animal, to live in a group, even more so than all other animals, as the very needs of his nature indicate. For all other animals nature has

[183] Matthaeus Liberatore, *Institutiones philosophicae*, (3 vols., Naples: Francisco Giannini, 1871), 3: 244.

prepared food, hair, as a covering, teeth, horns, claws as means of defense, or at least speed in flight. Man, on the other hand, was created without any natural provision for these things. But, instead of them all, he was endowed with reason, by the use of which he could procure all these things for himself by the work of his hands. But one man alone is not able to procure them all for himself; for one man could not sufficiently provide for life, unassisted. It is, therefore, natural that man should live in company with his fellows.

Moreover, all other animals are able to discern by inborn skill what is useful and what is injurious; just as the sheep naturally regards the wolf as his enemy. Some animals even recognize by natural instinct certain medicinal herbs and other things necessary for their life. Man, however, has a natural knowledge of the things which are essential for his life only in a general fashion, inasmuch as he has power of attaining knowledge of the particular things necessary for human life by reasoning from universal principles. But it is not possible for one man to arrive at a knowledge of all these things by his own individual reason. It is, therefore, necessary for man to live in a group so that each one may assist his fellowmen; and different men may be occupied in seeking by their reason to make different discoveries, one, for example, in medicine, one in this, and another in that.[184]

[184] De reg. prin. Bk. I, c. 1: "Naturale autem est homini ut sit animal sociale et politicum, in multitudine vivens, magis etiam quam omnia alia animalia, quod quidem naturalis necessitas declarat. Aliis enim animalibus natura praeparavit cibum, tegumenta pilorum, defensionem ut dentes, cornua, ungues, vel saltem velocitatem ad fugam. Homo autem institutus est nullo horum sibi a natura praeparato, sed loco omnium data est ei ratio, per quam sibi haec omnia officio manuum posset praeparare, ad quae omnia praeparanda unus homo non sufficit. Nam, unus homo per se sufficienter vitam transigere non posset. Est igitur homini naturale, quod in societate multorum vivat. Amplius; aliis animalibus insita est naturalis industria ad omnia ea, quae sunt eis utilia vel nociva, sicut ovis naturaliter aestimat lupum inimicum. Quaedam etiam animalia ex naturali industria cognoscunt aliquas herbas medicinales et alia eroum vitae. Homo autem horum, quae sunt

Other arguments could be given from the fact that man has the faculty of speech, which is given only for the sake of communication with others, from the innate benevolence that man seems to have from concept of perfectibility of human person, etc.,[185] but for the point at issue the very practical words of St. Thomas seem sufficient.

St. Thomas[186] always spoke of the relationship of man to society as that of the part to the whole. Just as every part is ordained to the whole as the imperfect to the perfect, so the individual is part of the perfect community. In his article concerning mutilation the Angelic Doctor taught that while the removal of one member of the body would be harmful to the body, still it would be permissible as a punishment for crime or as a deterrent of crime because the whole man himself is ordained to the community as to an end.[187] One of the reason that he gives to show that suicide is wrong is that the individual belongs to the community.[188] Thus the end of persons living in the community is the common good just as the whole is the end of the individual parts.[189]

Now that it is established that man is a social being and has a relationship to society, it is well to inquire into the definition of society. St. Thomas[190] defines it as a "group

vitae necessaria, naturalem cognitionem habet solum in communi, quasi eo per rationem valente ex universalibus principiis ad cognitionem singulorum quae necessaria sunt humanae vitae pervenire. Non est autem possible quod unus homo ad omnia hujusmodi per suam rationem pertingat. Est igitur necessarium homini quod in multitudine vivat, ut unus ab alio adjuvetur, et diversis inveniendis per rationem occuparetur, puta unus in medicina, alius in hoc, alius in alio."

[185] Cf. Liberatore, *op. cit.*, 3: 246 ff.
[186] 1a, 2ae, qu. 90, art. 2.
[187] 2a, 2ae, qu. 65, art. 1.
[188] 2a, 2ae, qu. 64, art. 5.
[189] 2a, 2ae, qu. 58, art. 9, ad 3.
[190] "Contra Impugnantes Dei Cultum et Religionem," *Opuscula Selecta*, vol. III, cap. 3, "Societas nihil aliud esse videtur quam adunatio hominum ad aliquid unum communiter agendum."

joined together in order to achieve something in common."
Thus civil society is a form of community in which, by
means of law and order, men seek a degree of happiness
which would not be attainable by individual effort.

The end or purpose of society is happiness, but this can
be divided into perfect and imperfect, and consequently
can become the immediate or mediate end of society. The
immediate end of society is temporal happiness. To this
purpose pertain the goods of society itself such as the administration, defense, relation of the members to it, etc.;
then also the good of those members of society which are
a) goods of the intellect, education, science, art, which
serve both the public and private good; b) goods of the
will, that is the fostering of virtue and the suppressing of
vice; c) goods of the body, public health and propagation;
d) goods of fortune, the acquisition, retention and trans-
mission of things. The mediate end is, of course, eternal
happiness in heaven. Thus it is the duty of the state to
direct temporal things so that they will not only not prejudice eternal beatitude but will rather be aids toward it.[191]
Since then man cannot attain to perfect happiness in this
life, the common good of society is only an imperfect kind
of happiness. It should, then, embrace those things by
which a human being can advance toward his final goal of
eternal happiness.[192]

Hence, it must be kept in mind that as an individual
member of society man is functionally social in accordance
with his own nature and the nature of society and hence
he must exert himself in the attainment of the common
good; whereas man as a person is something more precious than all social functions combined since he is ordained to God as to a final end.[193] Man by seeking the

[191] Merkelbach, *op. cit.*, 1: 254, no. 281.
[192] *De Reg. Prin.*, Bk. I, c. 15: "Quia igitur vitae, qua in presenti
bene vivimus, finis est beatitudo coelestis, ad regis officium pertinet ea
ratione vitam multitudinis bonam procurare, secundum quod congruit
ad coelestem beatitudinem consequendam."
[193] Harvey, *op. cit.*, p. 71.

common good of society also seeks his own particular good:

> He that seeks the good of many seeks in conse-
> quence his own good, for two reasons: first, be-
> cause the individual good is impossible without
> the common good of the family, state or kingdom.
> Hence, Valerius Maximus says of the ancient Ro-
> mans that they would rather be poor in a rich
> empire than rich in a poor empire. Secondly, be-
> cause man is a part of the house and state, he
> must needs consider what is good for him by
> being prudent about the good of the many. For
> the good disposition of the parts depends upon
> their relation to the whole.[194]

Thus the common good does not exclude the private good
for it really redounds to the private good although it does
differ specifically from it.[195] The private good is the end
to which the common good is ordered and is greater[196] and
more divine than the common good.[197]

The common good is achieved by the active cooperation
of the members of the group, working together for the
good of the whole.[198] Hence, society is made up of individuals often referred to as the multitude and of authority,
the element that unifies the group and secures order to
it.[199]

---

[194] *Summa Theol.*, 1a, 2ae, qu. 47, art. 10 ad 2: "Ad secundum
dicendum quod ille qui quaerit bonum commune multitudinis, ex conse-
quenti etiam quaerit bonum suum, propter duo: primo quidem quia
bonum proprium non potest esse sine bono communi vel familiae, vel
civitatis aut regni. Unde et Valerius Maximus (Lib. IV, cap. 4, no. 9)
dicit de antiquis Romanis quod malebant esse pauperes in divite imperio, quam divites in paupere imperio. Secundo, quia homo sit pars
domus, vel civitatis, oportet quod homo consideret quod sit sibi bonum
ex hoc quod est prudens circa bonum multitudinis. Bona dispositio
partium accipitur secundum habitudinem ad totum; quia ut, Augus-
tinus dicit (Confess. lib. III, cap. 8 ante med.) 'turpis est omnis
pars suo toti non conveniens, vel non congruens.''

[195] *Summa Theol.*, 2ae, qu. 58, art. 7, ad. 2.

[196] *Contra Gentiles*, I, 41.

[197] *Ibid.*, III, 19.

[198] Merkelbach, *op. cit.*, 2: 262, no. 263.

[199] Liberatore, *op. cit.*, 3: 264.

If this unity is to be achieved it is evident that a leader is needed to direct the multitude, for many minds make many ends.

> A little thought makes it clear that nature, or more especially the natural law, teaches the necessity of authority in the state. In order that the State may function as an organism in which each mem- does his part for the common welfare, there must be someone or some group endowed with the power to regulate and to see that things are carried out according to some adopted pattern. Otherwise confusion results, as history demonstrates. Since this necessity arises from the very nature of man and is a dictate of our own reason, we rightly look upon authority as originating, not from any man-made law but from the natural law itself.[200]

This power of the State ultimately comes from God,[201] even though the immediate origin of this power is disputed.

This leader, or group, who hold the authority exercise their power by executive, legislative and judicial acts.[202] In the exercise of this function it must be remembered that the governments are instituted to protect man's rights that are instituted for a still more comprehensive end, name-ly, the common good.[203]

The purpose of our American government is said in the Declaration of Independence to be: "to effect their safety and happiness," and according to the Preamble of the Con-stitution: "to promote the general welfare." Therefore, the authority of the government is restricted to using its power for the common good, which means that it must

[200] Walter Edward Kelley, "The Concept of the Common Good in St. Thomas" (unpublished Master's thesis, The Catholic University of America, Washington, D.C., 1939), p. 29.

[201] Leo XIII, "Immortale Dei," *Acta Leonis* XIII, 5: 121; *Summa Theol.* 2a, 2ae, qu. CIV, art. 1.

[202] Liberatore, *op. cit.*, 3: 302.

[203] Joseph V. Trunk, "The Philosophy of Civil Rights," *Proceed-ings of the American Catholic Philosophical Association*, Charles Hart ed., 15 (1939), (Reprint, Baltimore, Watkins Printing Co., 1940), pp. 21-35.

secure for society those material and spiritual goods that
are necessary and useful for attaining their purpose in
life. In the same line of thought, Pius XI said:

> ... The authority which it possesses to promote
> the common welfare, which is precisely the pur-
> pose of existence. ... Now this end and object, the
> common welfare in the temporal order, consists in
> that peace and security in which families and in-
> dividual citizens have the free exercise of their
> rights, and at the same time enjoy the greatest
> spiritual and temporal prosperity possible in this
> life, by the mutual union and co-ordination of the
> work of all. The function, therefore, of the civil
> authority residing in the State is twofold, to pro-
> tect and to foster, but by no means to absorb, the
> family and individual, or to substitute itself for
> them.[204]

The State, then, has no rights of its own independent
of the needs of those whom it governs and of the common
good for which it exists.

> The foremost duty, therefore of the rulers of the
> State should be to make sure that the laws and in-
> stitutions, the general character and administra-
> tion of the commonwealth shall be such as of them-
> selves to realize public well- being and private
> prosperity.[205]

[204] Pius XI, "Rapresentanti in terra" (Divini illius magistri),
AAS, 21 (1929), 737:

> "...ma bensì per l'autorità chè ad essa compete per il pro-
> movimento del bene commune temporale, chè appunto il fine
> suo proprio. ... Ora, questo fine, il bene commune di ordine
> temporale, consiste nella pace e sicurezza, onde le famiglie
> e i singloi cittandini godano nell' esercizio dei loro diritti, e
> insieme nel maggior benessere spirituale e materiale chè sia
> possibile nella vita presente, mediante l'unione e il coorina-
> mento della opera di tutti. Doppia è dunque la funzione dell'
> autorità civile, chè risiede nello Stato: proteggere e pro-
> muovere; non già assorbire la famigilia e l'individuo, o sosti-
> tuirsi ad essi."

[205] Leo XIII "Rerum novarum," *Acta Leonis* XIII, 11 (1892), 120:

> "Itaque per quos civitas regitur, primum conferre operam
> generatim atque universe debent tota ratione legum atque
> institutorum, scilicet efficiendo ut ex ipsa conformatione atque
> administratione reipublicae ultro prosperitas tam communi-
> tatis quam privatarum efflorescat.

Catholic philosophers repudiate the do-nothing state when they hold that the authority of the State must actually exert its authority to promote the common good so that the ultimate end of men can be reached.

> For in civil society God has always willed that there should be a ruling authority, and that they who are invested with it should reflect the divine power and providence in some measure over the human race.[206]

> In political affairs, and in all matters civil, the laws aim at securing the common good, and are not framed according to the delusive caprices and opinions of the mass of people, but by truth and by justice; the ruling powers are invested with a sacredness more than human, and are withheld form deviating from the path of duty, and from overstepping the bounds of rightful authority; and the obedience of citizens is rendered with a feeling of honor and dignity, since obedience is not the servitude of man to man, but submission to the will of God, exercising His sovereignty through the medium of men.[207]

The State, then, has an obligation to direct society toward the common good, which has a primacy over the individual good.

> The common good takes precedence of the private good, if it be of the same genus; but it may be that the private good is better generally.[208]

[206] Leo XIII "Immortale Dei," *Acta Leonis* XIII 5 (1886), 121: "Ita in societate civili voluit principatum, quem qui gerent, ii imaginem quamdam divinae in genus humanum potestatis divinaeque providentiae referent."

[207] *Ibid.*, p. 117.
"In genere rerum politico et civili leges spectant commune bonum, neque voluntate iudicioque fallaci multitudinis, sed veritate iustitiaque diriguntur: Auctoritas principum sanctitudinem quamdam induit humana majorem contineturque ne declinet a justitia, nedum in imperando transiliat: obedientia civium habet honestatem dignitatemque comitem, quia non est hominis ad hominis servitus, sed obtemperatio voluntati Dei, regnum per hominis exercentis."

[208] *Summa Theol.*, 1a, 2ae, qu. 152, art. 4, ad 3 um: "Bonum commune potius est bono privato, si sit ejusdem generis. Sed potest esse quod privatum sit melius secundum suum genus." Cf. *Summa Theol.* III, qu. 7, art. 13, ad 3um.

Now, if the common good is involved the individual can be called upon to sacrifice his private good especially if it is of the same genus, since the common good is more divine than the private good. Thus soldiers can be called upon to defend their country at the risk of their lives in time of just war, doctors can be required to assist the sick in time of plague, pastors obliged to remain in their parishes in time of contagious disease, etc. Noldin says that in such cases the natural law rather than the positive law commands such acts of heroism because it is a case of the common good being preferred to the private good.[209] But, note that such acts are for the common good. This includes the good of the individual, who makes the sacrifice, for by so doing he attains his own good by contributing to the common good.[210]

As has been seen the end of the State is the common good, the welfare of its members. The State exists to protect the rights that the individual has from nature and to promote a condition in which the individual can fully develop his personality. At times it is necessary to restrict the rights of some of the people for the good of the whole. Thus rationing in time of shortage, bankruptcy proceedings, conscription in time of war are lawful restrictions of the individual rights of some of the members of society for the common good. Rights vary in importance. When the more important rights of the people are at stake the State may restrict the less important rights of some individuals. This redounds to the good even of those whose rights are restricted.

Now, in the time of Archbishop Kenrick, slavery had become intricately entrenched in the social and economic life of the people. True, this condition had arisen in consequence of injustice to the Negroes, but nevertheless the condition existed. There were two courses open: first, the State could recognize slavery as legal and morally valid,

[209]Noldin, *Summa theologiae moralis*, 1: 146, no. 140.
[210] Cf. *Summa Theol.*, 2a, 2ae, qu. 47, art. 10, ad 2 um, *supra cit.*

at least for a time; or it could declare it illegal, emancipating the slaves at once.

To declare slavery illegal and to abolish it immediately would bring about chaos, the opponents of abolition claimed. Basically they gave two arguments—the social and the economic. In their social argument they maintained that the continuation of slavery was necessary for the good of the community, for they claimed that the Negro was an inferior being unfit for political and social rights and privileges with the white man. They claimed that emancipation would not be for the good of the Negro for he would find it hard to struggle for an existence. From the point of view of the whites, slavery was looked upon as a necessity for their safety. The slaves had received little instruction, moral or intellectual, but had been held down by force on the plantations. This force would be eliminated if slavery were abolished, and it was feared that the meager police force could not control the situation. Economically they felt that emancipation would be ruinous to the Negro, who would not be able to support himself, to the master who would become bankrupt, to the South which would not be able to cultivate its lands without slaves, and as a result to the North whose industry was connected with the South.[211]

Now, the right to control ones labor freely is not an end in itself. It is a means to an end. The end is a right and reasonable life. A reasonable amount of liberty is involved in a right and reasonable life. That element in the labor contract protects the worker from tyranny, and affords greater opportunity for advancement. Hence, it is a highly prized and very superior means to the end.

But in the slave days such a right seemed to be a very ineffective means. In fact it might have lost its moral validity altogether since it ceased to accomplish its purpose. For with the possibility of the economic and social disorders that were thought likely to follow in the wake of

[211] Cf. *Supra*, pp. 76 f.

immediate emancipation the members of society would scarcely be able to live reasonably and happily. Hence, it would seem that this was a case where the state for the common good would have been justified in restricting the right of the Negroes to control their own labor.

Moreover, such an action, while on the surface it would seem to be opposed to the words of the Declaration of Independence, in reality would not be. The "life, liberty and the pursuit of happiness" to which all men are declared entitled cannot be understood so as to interfere with either of the three. Liberty has life and the pursuit of happiness as its manifest and necessary limitations. Would complete liberty in the case we are discussing promote their primary and highest purpose?[212]

Hence, it would seem that even if Kenrick taught that slaves were held in bondage *per se* unjustly, still *per accidens* they could be held lawfully since the various states had considered it legal, and such action could be considered legitimate because of the common good.[213] Is not this perhaps Kenrick's view when he said, "It can be questioned whether the masters are permitted to keep in slavery those whose ancestors seem to have been taken by injustice from Africa? It seems to us that it must be answered in the affirmative: for the defect of the title is to be held as healed by the lapse of a very long time, since otherwise the condition of society would always remain uncertain, with very great danger to the people."[214]

[212] *The Present Crisis with a Reply and Appeal to European Advisers* (Boston: Crocker and Brewster, 1860), p. XIV. Cf. Carrière, *De justitia et jure*, pp. 37-43, and pp. 42-43, who pointed out that hastily to give slaves liberty which they would not know how to use would not be helpful to their happiness. Hence, they should be prepared for liberty by training and instruction.

[213] Kenrick did not use these terms. Cf. Cathrein, *Philosophia moralis*, (ed. 1927) p. 377, no. 548; says that because of danger to social order, custom or law could supply what is wanting to the title by the right of nature, and thus make the title just.

[214] *Op. cit.*, tr. V, cap. VI, no. 40: "Id quaeri potest utrum heri possint servos retinere, quum eorum majores injuria videantur ex Africa

While, as was noted above, it seems impossible to admit the validity of prescription for holding the slaves in bondage, it seems that the undeveloped reason at which Kenrick here hints might in itself be sufficient argument for at least a temporary continuation of slavery.

Such a solution to the problem would seem to be in agreement with the other Catholic leaders of the day. Bishop England said:

> I have been asked by many a question which I may as well answer at once, viz., Whether I am friendly to the existence or continuation of slavery? I am not, but I see the impossibility of now abolish-it here. When it can and ought to be abolished, is a question for the legislature and not for me.[215]

Again, in "The Early History of the Diocese of Charleston" he said:

> On this question it may be laid down as a maxim, that no greater moral evil can be brought upon any country than the introduction of slavery; but is a very difficult question, whether in a state, which has the misfortune of having been from a long series of years under the influence of such a calamity, an immediate or indiscriminate emancipation would be safe practicable or beneficial.[216]

Dr. Rice[217] concluded that the unofficial position of Catholics in 1860 was that it can be argued that slavery is not intrinsically wrong; they recognized the evils in the institution that eventually made emancipation desirable, but that this should come only gradually with regard for the welfare of society and the protection of the property rights of the owners; they condemned abolitionism absolutely for its methods and associations.

huc traducti? Nobis affirmandum videtur: nam tituli vitium longissimi temporis lapsu sanatum habendum est, quum societatis conditio alias incerta semper foret, cum gravissimo turbarum periculo."

215 To the editor of the *U. S. Catholic Miscellany*, Feb. 25, 1841, *Work*, (Messmer), 5: 311.

216 *Works* (Messmer), 4: 317.

217 Rice, *American Catholic Opinion in the Slavery Controversy*, p. 155.

The situation that existed in our country with regard to slavery had a parallel in Europe after the Franks and Saxons had enserfed the European masses. They might say whatever they wished about the justice of the situation in itself but after the deed was done and the established relations and conditions existed even the monarchs were powerless to abolish the institution. They could only ameliorate it.[218] No immediate absolute abolition of a great social institution has ever been effected except by Divine intervention, namely, the condition of the Jews in Egypt. In England the change from the state of slavery was attended with a certain amount of evil. It led to the increase of vagrancy which in turn led to the various laws passed from the time of Edward II to Elizabeth ending in the infamous poor laws, thought necessary because of the condition of society. All this happened even after gradual emancipation.[219]

Hence, the opinion of Kenrick that slavery could lawfully be continued for the common good seems to be a just and reasonable one from a subjective standpoint and perhaps even from an objective point of view at least if the idea was to continue it for a comparatively brief time.[220]

V. Gradual Emancipation

The obligation to strive for gradual emancipation. As

---

[218] Samuel Nott, *Slavery and the Remedy* (New York: Appleton & Co., 1857), P. XXV.

[219] *Ibid.*, p. XXVII.

[220] It might be indicated that the evils—social and economic—were not in reality as serious in reconstruction days as it was argued that they would be. Cf. A. A. Taylor, "The Negro in South Carolina," *JNH*, 9 (1924), 241-569. But this does not affect the argument given nor its justification. We were here concerned with Kenrick's *subjective* view. However, it must be borne in mind that many evils were suffered by both whites and colored in the process of emancipation. These evils quite probably would have been intensified had there been emancipation without a war. For a result of the war the Federal Government stepped in to exert its influence to protect newly emancipated Negroes.

has been noted Catholic theologians rejected the do-nothing state, holding that the authority of the state must actually exert its authority to promote the common good so that the ultimate and proximate end of men can be attained. Further it was observed that at times the state can demand that individuals give up some of their rights when the common good demands that. Thus it was concluded that the state because of economic and social difficulties, which were thought to be of great proportion, could have lawfully required the slaves of the day to give up their liberty. This would seem to be only a temporary measure. The common good seemed to demand more.

As far as the slave is concerned he has a right to personal liberty. Seeing that man's end and purpose in life concerns only himself and his Creator, and that in personal dignity all men are equal, there is no reason in the nature of things why one man should have the right to interfere with another's freedom of action. Each has natural rights to order his life in his own way as long as he observes God's laws and does not violate the rights of others.[221] By the State permitting slavery this right of several millions was restricted.

Moreover by the laws of slavery applying in most slave states such basic things as the right to marriage and a family were denied or made difficult to protect. These rights under no circumstances could be taken from the slave. By slavery he was kept in a rather miserable existence as was seen. But since the Negro contributed his brain, blood and brawn to the progress of civilization, as civilization offers a higher standard of living economically or culturally, so he naturally expects a share in that progress to which he has contributed. The basis and measure of the right to more goods than the minimum are the peculiar needs, capacities and abilities of the individual. The denial of these rights to progress and opportunity renders men bitter and destroys the contentment which is necessary for

[221] Cahill, *The Framework of a Christian State*, pp. 311 f.

a reasonable human life.[222] By slavery the Negro was kept in ignorance and was refused education.

Moreover, just as the essential rights of individuals, according to Christian ethics are equal, so are the rights of the various groups that make up society equal.[223] Slavery seemed to lower the Negro race in the eyes of the white man causing it to be considered an inferior race. It paved the way for race prejudice by making the differences between the two races more pronounced.

Now, race prejudice produces serious effects both upon those who practice it and upon those who are its victims.[224] Hence, it would seem that for the common good—the good of the blacks as well as the whites—the State should have taken means to put a stop to this system that was forcing the roots of race prejudice deeper and deeper.

But race prejudice is not the only evil coming to the white race from slavery. Many writers of the day pointed to the personal harm coming to the whites. It tended to cause them to become despots. It engendered in them a love for power, made them look upon themselves as having a superior destiny, and made them become more and more insensible to justice and kindness.[225] It also brought idleness and at times was the occasion of sensualities.[226] Jefferson said that only a prodigy could retain morals and manners undepraved in such circumstances. In a warm climate

[222] John LaFarge, *The Race Question and the Negro* (New York, Toronto: Longsmans, Green and Co., 1945), p. 91.

[223] *Ibid.*, p. 83.

[224] *Ibid.*, p. 182.

[225] Sunderland, *Anti-Slavery Manual*, pp. 30-32; *Report on Slavery to the Congregationalist Ministers*, p. 86; Polfrey, *Slave Power*, p. 62.

[226] *The Report to Congregationalist Ministers on Slavery*, p. 84.

The Irish Immigrant Society of New York, which was established in 1817 decided that the immigrants should be settled in a non-slaveholding region. The reason given was that they would, in a region where there were slaves, lay claims to idleness, as the white man's badge to superiority; and they would be too proud to stoop to the labors of the field, which are usually performed by Negroes. Cf. Nuesse, *The Social Thought of American Catholics*, pp. 163 f.

no one will work for himself who can make another work for him. He said that he trembled when he thought of the fact that God's justice could not sleep forever while men trample on liberties.[227]

Hence, it would seem that for the good of the nation some measures should have been taken by the competent government to rid the country of the conditions of slavery.

If it was feared that social and economic chaos would have resulted from immediate emancipation, then a scheme should have been planned whereby they would have been prepared for this step gradually. The government might have begun recognizing at least their inalienable rights, such as the right to marriage. Then their family life might have been improved. All the while they should have been educated so that they could be ready to live a happy social life as free men. If these things had been done then the fears presented in the social argument against abolition would have vanished to a great extent.[228]

Economically, gradual abolition would have had very little objection. If they would have been educated then they would have been equipped to make their own living after emancipation. Moreover, if they had been gradually freed the masters would not have lost all their laborers suddenly, but by degrees, and in this way they could have been more easily replaced, presuming that the Negroes would all leave immediately. It must be remembered that there were 400,000 immigrants coming each year, who would go to the South if there were work there.[229] Yet, there existed the problem of economic loss to the master, if the slaves would be immedaitely freed. What about compensation for the masters, who would lose their slave property? Brownson often spoke of this point. He reasoned that slavery existed

[227] Polfrey, *Slave Power*, p. 5.

[228] Bishop Dupanloupe said: "You refuse to set slaves free because you say they are incapable of liberty, and I tell you that the incapacity is kept alive by servitude, if not created by it, and that it causes the slave to stagnate under it." *RACHS*, 25 (1914), 24.

[229] Cochin, *The Results of Slavery*, p. 111.

by law, thus was sanctioned by the American people in
their highest legislative capacity. If the law was unjust the
injustice was on the side of the law-making power. Before
the law the master justly had slaves. The people, then,
who authorized him to have slaves could not burden the
slave-holder with their wrongs. If they sinned and wished
to repent they would have to indemnify the masters.[230]

Cochin went further. He thought that compensation was
due to the slaves for their gratuitous labor, especially to
the old and to the invalids; a subsidy, he thought, was
owed to the families who had been precluded by slavery
from saving. He held that in justice no indemnity was
due to the masters, but considering their good faith he
thought that it was due in equity. Then, too, he reasoned that the good of the country was involved, especially
if the masters would be financially ruined by having their
slaves emancipated. He suggested that this money for indemnity be raised partly by taxes and partly by the slaves
being required to labor for a certain number of days.[231]

Rufus King argued that further extension of slavery
would be unfair to the free States and fatal to their welfare. In his plan of abolition he proposed applying the
proceeds of the sale of public lands towards the emancipation of the Negro, and toward their removal to some
territory outside our national borders.[232]

The Congregational Ministers in their report on slavery,
argued that if abolition would be followed by great loss and
general distress in that part of the country where the in-

[230] Brownson, *Works*, 17: 21, 41; After the war had begun he felt
that this was no longer the case, "the slave-holders by their rebellion
have forfeited whatever right the law secured for them as loyal
citizens."

[231] Cochin, *op. cit.*, p. 110.

[232] Claude M. Fuess, "Rufus King," *Dictionary of American Bibli-
ography*, 10: 399. Cf. *The Life and Works of Rufus King*, edited
by his grandson, Charles King (6 vols., New York: G. P. Putnam's
Son, 1894-1900).

stitution was established, the Gospel would demand that the other half of the country share their burden.

Some Proposed Plans for Gradual Emancipation. Several plans for gradual emancipation were offered. Only a few samples will be given here. It seems that in 1701 Chief Justice Sewall of Massachusetts, while he was mostly concerned with the right of men to liberty and the abolition of the slave-trade, advised that a period be set beyond which Negroes would no longer be slaves although he had a natural antipathy for the Negro.[233] Frequently, beginning in 1714, ideas of emancipating the Negroes and sending them to some land outside the Colonies were proposed.[234] One of the earliest to suggest a concrete plan was Anthony Benezet in 1763. He proposed to have a law declare slaves purchased after a certain date declared free after a period of work. If the work was neglected the period could be prolonged. The freed slaves would be under an inspector or overseer of the poor, the children were to be instructed, and the family if possible was to be given a small tract of land and the members of the family required to work on it unless employed elsewhere.[235]

Three plans were suggested in the legislature of Virginia in the winter of 1831 and 1832. (1) That the entire black population be deported. Two objections were raised, namely: that the slaves made up one-third of the wealth of the State, and above this loss would be the actual cost of deportation. (2) Colonization of 6,000 Negroes a year. It was rejected because this would have cost the State $1,380,000 a year while the domestic slave-trade removed the surplus Negroes without any cost to the government. (3) That the masters keep the slaves until they came of age, at which time they were to be hired out to pay for their deportation. The objection here was that it would

[233] Locke, *Anti-Slavery in America*, pp. 17 f.

[234] Henry Noble Sherwood, "The Formation of the American Colonization Society" *JNH*, 2 (1917), pp. 209-228.

[235] Locke, *op. cit.*, pp. 31 f.

be too great a burden on the slave-holders, and that it violated property rights, and further since it was proposed that it go into effect only in 1840, in the interim many slave holders would move to other States.[236]

Brownson advised that it be done gradually by the authority that has the right in that regard. That first the moral rights of the slaves as persons, his marriage rights, therefore the right of family and domicile be secured. This would convert the slave into a serf and in time he would be converted into a free peasant.[237]

Marshall Hall, an Englishman who had traveled extensively in this country, advised that the slaves be prepared by education and discipline for civil rights. Then the slaves should be given credit for their work, from which they would have to pay for their maintenance. If there were a balance, it was to be kept by the state in trust for the slave. The State likewise was to set a just price on each slave, and when he had accumulated enough to buy himself the State would pay the owner, and the slave would be free. Further, when free, the slaves were to be retained in their former jobs, if they so desired, receiving a just wage.[238]

Another advised that strong expression of public opinion be created that would demand that the individual States emancipate. This movement should be started, it was thought, in the border States of Maryland, Virginia and New Jersey, and if successful there the other States would follow.[239]

---

[236] Locke, *op. cit.*, pp. 109 f.

[237] Brownson, *Works*, 17: 343.

[238] Marshall Hall, *The Two-fold Slavery in the United States with a Project of Emancipation* (London: Adam Scott, 1854), p. 7. Cf. Olmsted, *Seaboard States*, p. 446, who has a very similar plan. Professor Dew claimed that this scheme of wages was tried and failed. Cf. *Pro-Slavery Argument*, pp. 426-428.

[239] John Greeleaf Whittier, *Justice and Expediency* (Haverhill: C. P. Thayer and Co., 1833), p. 18; cf. Peabody, *Slavery in the United States*, p. 15 *et passim*. This author advises about the same scheme but adds to it colonization.

Another advised that the process should be started by beginning to educate the slaves. Then he hoped that philanthropic persons would buy a tract of land, where the ex-slaves could live a happy life together. Then the slaves should be bought by the government with money raised from duties placed on exported products made by slave-labor. The slaves were to be left for a time with their present owners under a civil guardianship until it was thought that they were ready to exercise the rights of freedom by themselves. By redeeming the present slaves there would be no necessity to purchase their dependents.[240]

President Lincoln on March 6, 1862 sent the following resolution to Congress asking them to pass upon it:

> Resolved, That the United States, ought to cooperate with any State which may adopt gradual abolishment of slavery, giving to such State pecuniary aid, to be used by such State, in its discretion to compensate for the inconveniences, public and private, produced by such change of system.[241]

In this regard it might be interesting to note that when an act of Congress of April 26, 1862 freed the slaves in the District of Columbia compensation of about three hundred dollars a head was given to the masters.[242]

Thus in conclusion it would seem that the common good, as well as justice, demanded that slavery come to an end. For it was detrimental to both the colored and the white inhabitants. If it had been done gradually, instructing the Negroes, and compensating the masters, it seems that there would have been very little force left to the arguments proposed by the pro-slavery element.

[240] Jesse Torey, *Portraiture of Domestic Slavery in the United States* (Phila.: John Bioren, 1817), pp. 21-25, 29, 61.

[241] James D. Richardson, *A compilation of the Messages and Papers of the Presidents, 1789-1897* (Washington, D.C.: Government Printing Office, 1897), 6: 68.

[242] Hart, *EA*, 27: 397.

CHAPTER V

KENRICK'S TEACHING CONCERNING THE OBLIGA-
TION OF MASTERS IN RELIGIOUS MATTERS
TOWARD THEIR SLAVES

Justice would not be done to Kenrick unless a chapter were added to give his moral teachings concerning the slaves in religious matters. Slavery must have borne heavily upon Kenrick's mind since, as will be shown, he considered slaves in discussing each of the sacraments and several of the commandments.

I. INSTRUCTION OF SLAVES

Kenrick's teaching. Regarding the right of the slave to be educated, Kenrick[1] merely said that it is to be regretted that there are so many slaves who are forbidden by law to be educated. These laws also greatly impede the practice of religion in some places, he said. On the other hand, in discussing the special obligations of masters and slaves, he noted in passing that if slaves neglect to learn the truths of faith, or to practice the duties of religion when given an opportunity, they are obviously guilty of sin. But, in practice, the obligation reduced itself into one binding the master, without whose permission and favor the education of the slave could hardly be effected.[2]

Kenrick treated this point under "special obligations." In the later edition he inserted a small paragraph to the effect that masters must solicitously provide for the Christian instruction of their slaves, seeing to it that they are instructed and encouraging them to embrace the faith. He thought, however, that no force is to be used beyond moder-

---

[1] Kenrick, *Theologia moralis*, tr. V, cap. V, no. 39.
[2] *Ibid.*, tr. VIII, cap. V, no. 104.

ate penalties used for the lazy and stubborn because of their temperament.[3]

Continuing the same line of thought he said that masters must provide for the salvation of the slaves, whose condition deprives them of the opportunity of seeking help to salvation. These helps the masters must supply, seeing to it that the slaves are instructed in the rudiments of religion and have the services of priests for the reception of the sacraments. Furthermore, he warned that masters sin gravely if they are so intent on their own gains that they neglect to instruct the slaves, or do not provide them with the opportunity of receiving the sacraments, or fail to safeguard their morals. Masters sin most gravely, he said, if they place obstacles in the way of the slaves practicing their religion, or if they encourage bad morals by example or wicked solicitations.[4]

For example, the master is obliged to guard against concubinage, which is often occasioned when many people of both sexes are grouped together in cramped quarters. Masters, however, could be excused for overlooking sins, if greater evils were feared. Thus, if it were feared that if a young man were expelled by force because he had come to violate a young girl, he would set fire to the place, the master would be excused for tolerating the condition. Or, if it were feared that by whipping a girl, who had misbehaved, the child whom she was carrying would be lost, he could ignore the crime. But, on the other hand, if a master favored the fornication of a slave girl because he would be enriched by the offspring resulting, or if he would refuse to consent to her marriage, without having a grave reason for so doing, he would be considered guilty of sin.[5]

It would seem that the slave did have a right to education for it seems to be a natural right, implied in the claim of every man to a right and reasonable life. Man is more

[3] *Ibid.*, tr. XIII, cap. IV, no. 101.
[4] *Ibid.*, no. 102.
[5] *Ibid.*

than an animal, for he has a spiritual soul with its power to reason and to will. The sensual in man must be subordinated to the spiritual. Ability to read is a great help to develop the mind. Even in Kenrick's day education was looked upon as being a necessity.

In the preceding chapter, an explanation of Kenrick's opinion justifying the state in continuing slavery for the sake of the common good, as a temporary measure, was given. Consistently with this view the state would be justified in keeping from the slaves the fiery material of the abolitionists, for no one has the right to be educated contrary to the good of the state. But, while the state might not be obliged to educate the slaves, it would appear an infringement of their natural rights to prevent the slaves from educating themselves.

Likewise, it seems that the common good was injured by preventing their education insofar as lack of education tended to accentuate the difference between the whites and blacks, which paved the way for prejudice and discrimination.

The Congregational ministers, in their report, have this to say:

> And if existing laws in the slave-holding States are incompatible with the intellectual advancement of and the general progress of the slaves according to their ability in those varied attainments, which exalt man in the scale of being, and enable him the more eminently to glorify God, can these laws be consistent with the Gospel?[6]

The Attitude toward instruction and education of slaves in the United States. It would seem that many planters gave very little thought to have their slaves instructed in the tenets of Christianity. In fact, they concerned themselves as little as possible with the personal and domestic habits of their servants. Once the slaves had finished their work, their morals and manners were in their own hands.

---

[6] *Report on Slavery to the Congregational Ministers*, p. 41.

The master's only concern was that his servants live peacefully.[7]

At the close of the Revolutionary War John Carroll sent a report to the Sacred Congregation for the Propagation of the Faith. The letter addressed to Cardinal Antonelli was dated February 27, 1785. He noted the "general lack of care" in instructing slaves in their religion, declaring further that "these people are kept constantly at work, so that they rarely hear any instructions from the priest, unless they spend a short time with one; and most of them are consequently very dull in faith and depraved in morals. It can scarcely be believed how much trouble and care they give the pastors of souls."[8]

However, the idea of the need of general education for the Negro underwent changes. In the earlier period it was thought necessary for the religious welfare of the Negro that he learn to read.[9] The proponents of education for the Negro in this early period were: (1) the masters, who thought to increase the efficiency of their labor supply thereby; (2) sympathetic persons, who wished to help the oppressed; (3) zealous missionaries.[10]

Later this attitude was changed, and it was then felt that it was a disadvantage for the Negro to be educated. While this attitude had begun in the eighteenth century, still it only gained real prominence after 1835.[11] At this time the industrial revolution changed slavery from a patriarchal to an economic institution, which needed a larger number of Negroes. On the other hand, some intelligent Negroes, encouraged by the abolitionists and their propaganda, as well as by their association with the refugees from Haiti, who settled at Baltimore, Norfolk, Charleston, and New

[7] Phillips, *Life and Labor in the Old South*, p. 204.

[8] Letters in the Archives of the Prop. Fide. *Scritture riferite Am. Centrale*, 21: ff 312, translated by Guilday, *Carroll*, I: 225-227.

[9] Joseph Butsch, "Negro Catholics in the United States," *CHR*, 3 (1917), 36 f.

[10] Woodson, *The Education of the Negro*, p. 2.

[11] Butsch, *CHR*, 3 (1917), 37.

Orleans, organized servile insurrections. Most whites of
the South took the attitude that it was impossible to cultivate the minds of the Negroes, without arousing self-
assertion.[12] As a result, public and private teachers were
prohibited from assisting the Negro to acquire knowledge.[13]

Instruction among the French and the Spanish was facilitated by a liberal attitude toward their slaves. The *Code
Noir* made it obligatory on the master to instruct his slaves,
to have been baptized and to permit them to worship on
Sundays.[14] But in the States of our nation that did not come
under this influence, religious assemblies of slaves were discouraged and often definitely outlawed in the nineteenth
century. At times these assemblies were permitted with
certain qualifications, for example, that discreet white persons be present, that the group be small in number, or that
it be held before dark, and the like. Any justice of the
peace, on his own knowledge, or the word of another, could
engage as many men as were thought necessary to disperse
the assembly. Any slaves found at such gatherings were
to be whipped on the bare back, without trial.[15]

Prohibitive legislation extended over a period of more
than a century beginning with the Act of South Carolina
in 1740. But, excepting South Carolina and Georgia, the
important measures which actually proscribed the teaching
of Negroes, were enacted during the first four decades of
the nineteenth century. The States attacked the problem
in various ways. Colored people beyond a certain number
were not allowed to assemble for social or religious purposes, except in the presence of certain "discreet white
men"; slaves were deprived of the helpful contact with free
persons of color because the latter were driven out of some

[12] Woodson, *Education of the Negro*, pp. 2-9.

[13] Butsch, *CHR* (1917), 37; Woodson, *Education of the Negro*,
p. 11.

[14] Butsch, *CHR*, 3 (1917), 37; Woodson, *Education of the Negro*,
pp. 21, 23.

[15] Stroud, *A Sketch of Laws Relating to Slavery*, pp. 63 ff; Goodell,
American Slave Code, pp. 326 ff.

of the southern States; masters who had employed favorite blacks in positions which required a knowledge of book-keeping, printing, etc., were compelled by law to discontinue the custom; public and private teachers were prohibited from assisting the Negro to acquire knowledge in any manner whatsoever.[16]

Kent sums up the legal situation in the following words:

> In Georgia, by an act of 1829, no person is permitted to teach a slave, negro, or free person of color, to read or write. So, in Virginia, by statute in 1830, meetings of free negroes, to learn reading or writing, are unlawful, and subjects them to corporal punishment; and it is unlawful for white persons to assemble with free negroes or slaves, to teach them to read or write. The prohibitory act of the legislature of Alabama, passed in the session of 1831-2, relative to instruction to be given to the slave, or free colored population, or exhortation, or preaching to them, or any mischievous influence attempted to exert over them, is sufficiently penal. Laws of similar import are presumed to exist in the other slave-holding states; but in Louisiana the law on this subject is armed with tenfold severity. It not only forbids any person teaching slaves to read or write but it declares that any person using language, in any public discourse, from the bar, beach, stage, or pulpit, or any other place, or in any private conversation, or making use of any signs or actions, having a tendency to produce discontent among the free colored population, or insubordination among the slaves, or who shall be knowingly instrumental in bringing into the state any paper, book or pamphlet having the like tendency, shall on conviction, be punished with imprisonment or death, at the discretion of the court.[17]

Stroud pointed out that at times the various ordinances extended even beyond the laws of the States.[18]

[16] Woodson, *The Education of the Negro*, pp. 9, 151-178.

[17] James Kent's *Commentaries on American Law* (4 vols.; 11th ed. Boston: Brown & Co.), pp. 133 ff; Hart, *Slavery and Abolition*, p. 94.

[18] Stroud, *op. cit.*, pp. 62 f.

Catholic education for Negroes was begun in a small
way by the English colonists in Maryland and the French
in Louisiana. Through religious devotion, certain rudiments of education were imparted to the Negro, before any
formal attempts at schooling were made. Father LaFarge
pictures the scene that took place in Old Maryland where-
in were gathered together

> ... the entire personnel of the plantations, slaves,
> and all, on Lenten evenings in the manor house,
> there to be relentlessly catechized by the mistress
> or the daughter of the household. So thorough
> was this instruction that practically to this day
> old people are found in whose memories are im-
> bedded the catechism lessons learned orally in
> former years. The duty of giving these instruc-
> tions particularly to the Negroes, and slaves, was
> one of the staple topics for the sermons of the
> eighteenth century and was particularly inculcated
> by such men as Father George Hunter.[19]

Likewise in Maryland, it seems that the benefit of the
Catholic ministry was confined to no one condition or race.
The Negroes were an integral part of the ecclesiastical life.
They had every opportunity to hear Mass, receive the sacraments and be visited by the priest in times of illness. There
were no separate churches in Maryland. "The church was
the Father's house, where all knelt before the same altar
and partook of the same Bread of Life." While there was
separate seating, there was little practical difference in
comfort or convenience.[20] Archbishop Carroll, despite the
fact that he might have guests, would gracefully depart
at the appointed hour to retire with the colored servants
and others of his household for the evening service.[21]

The Catholic interest in the Negro, however, was regarded by the Protestants as a possible preparation for
revolt. Governor Bladen of Maryland wrote to a Catholic

[19] LaFarge, *CHR*, 21 (1935), 11.
[20] *Ibid.*, p. 14.
[21] Miriam Murphy, "Catholic Missionary Work Among the Colored
People of the United States, 1776-1866," *RACHS* 35 (1924), 117.

leader in 1745 that Catholic religious duties should be fulfilled without such large gatherings that would give suspicions of designs other than religious. "Nothing could
give greater alarm to good subjects of King George than
such frequent meeting of whites and Negroes under pretense of divine worship."[22]

Thus the priests had to use tact in dealing with the masters and the slaves. The masters feared the loss of valuable
property. For example, a letter of Father John Souge to
Archbishop Carroll in March of 1801 reported hostility
among the parishioners. He was accused of being "entire-
ment contre l'esclavage," and was accused of inciting the
Negroes against the whites. He once taught them to sing
without the consent of their master. The Bishop, feeling
that this priest was no longer useful there, transferred
him.[23]

Hence, Rouse concluded that a study of the educational
activities indicates that "Catholic concern for the Negro's
welfare was restricted in the case of slaves to oral instructions, to secure just treatment for them, and to provide for
the spiritual aids of the Church."[24]

Over and above the external difficulties there were internal troubles, too. On May 20, 1833, Bishop England
presented to Pope Gregory XVI two long memorials on the
Indian and Negro situation in the United States. He
stressed the problem which was particularly pressing in
Charleston. He could do very little because he feared that
Archbishop Whitfield and those opposed to him would

[22] John Gillard, *The Catholic Church and the American Negro*
(Baltimore, 1929), p. 14.

[23] Rice, *American Catholic Opinion in the Slavery Controversy*,
p. 28.

[24] Michael Francis (Bro. Bede, C.F.X.) Rouse, *A Study of the
Development of Negro Education under Catholic Auspices in Mary-
land and the District of Columbia* (Johns Hopkins University Studies
in Education, no. 22 (Baltimore: Johns Hopkins Press, 1938), p. 28;
Woodson, *Education of the Negro*, Chap. VIII, "Religion without
Letters," pp. 179 ff.

cripple his efforts. He hoped that the Indians and Negroes
would be placed under a bishop especially devoted to their
spiritual welfare. He believed that the Pope should insist
on a Provincial Council at Baltimore to care for these
urgent problems.[25]

Among the examples of concentrated and effective work
done among the Negroes, the work done by the Sulpicians
in and around Baltimore should be mentioned. This was
especially true concerning the French speaking Catholics,
who came to Baltimore from Santo Domingo.[26] A Tobias
Society for colored women was established in this city for
the purpose of helping to bury the dead, visit the sick, receive Holy Communion in a group monthly and the like.[27]
From the earliest days the Jesuits cared for the Negroes
and the Indians in Louisiana territory.[28] In New Orleans
a Christian Doctrine Society for colored men, and later
on one for women, was established. The purpose of this
society was to promote the spiritual and temporal welfare
of the Negro. The first efforts were limited to those undertaken by pastoral initiative, but by 1818 at least one separate school for Negroes was established and in 1828 provisions were made for a definite organization.[29] Likewise,
one must not forget the work done in Kentucky by Bishop
Flaget, and Fathers Nerinkx, Badin, and Byrne.[30]

But generally speaking, what was done for the Catholic
Negro in a parochial way was not begun in earnest until
after the establishment of the colony of Liberia. After
that, the bishops really began to make provisions for the
spiritual wants of the would-be emigrants. True, the
Synod of 1791, did direct that the Negroes be instructed
before marriage, but this was a general directive, applicable

[25] Guilday, *Life of England*, 2: 275.
[26] Miriam Murphy, "Catholic Missionary Work among the Colored
People of the United States 1776-1866," *RACHS*, 35 (1924), 111.
[27] Nuesse, *The Social Thought of American Catholics*, p. 265.
[28] Murphy, *RACHS*, 35: (1924), 113.
[29] Nuesse, *op. cit.*, p. 265.
[30] Miriam Murphy, *RACHS*, 35 (1924), 114 f.

as well to others.[31] After the establishment of Liberia, the prevalent opinion was that the slave should not be manumitted, save on the condition that he be sent to Africa. The Bishops were mindful of the needs of the Catholic Negroes transported to Liberia, for the second Provincial Council of Baltimore held in 1833 provided for missionaries to be sent to a colony, as has been shown. The work among the Negroes was entrusted to the Jesuits, with the approval of the Propaganda.

Moreover, besides the work done by the white sisters in instructing the Negroes, at a very early date communities of colored sisters were founded with this work in mind. Josephine Alicot established a school for Negroes in 1825, and a few years later became co-foundress of the Sisters of the Holy Family, a colored community. The Oblate Sisters of Providence had their origin in Washington, D.C. Their rule was approved by Archbishop Whitfield in 1829, and by Pope Gregory XVI in 1831.[32]

The main purpose of the foundation of the above mentioned sisterhoods was the establishment of schools for the education of the Negro.[33] In the summer of 1835 Bishop England opened a school for the free Negroes in Charleston. "No action of his career was considered more imprudent by his friends in the city. The anti-slavery riots of 1834 had stirred the public consideration of the Abolition Movements to a white heat."[34]

The Charleston *Southern Patriot* announced, on January 29, 1836, that thousands of anti-slavery tracts had

[31] Theobold, *RACHS*, 35 (1924), 331.

[32] Cf. Grace H. Sherwood, *The Oblates One Hundred and One Years* (New York: Macmillan Co., 1931); George Casmir O'Connor, *Catholic Education and the Work among the Negroes* (Unpublished Master's thesis, The Catholic University of America, Washington, D.C., 1926); Raymond Hill, *Social Works of the Colored Sisterhoods, an Historical Study* (Unpublished Master's thesis, The Catholic University of America, Washington, D.C., 1932); Letter of Bishop England to the Propaganda, Guilday, *Life of England* 1: 528.

[33] Miriam Murphy, *RACHS*, 35 (1924), 120-124.

[34] Guilday, *Life of England*, 2: 151.

arrived in the Post Office. A mob organized, raided the
Post Office and burned the tracts. While the mob was there,
parishioners came to the seminary, where England lived,
to tell him that mobs would come there to apply the lynch
law. Guards were organized by the Bishop for resistance.
The ill-will was occasioned by the school for free Negroes
which England had established after realizing that, in his
fifteen years of work in the diocese, many of the Catholic
Negroes had lost the Faith through attendance at sectarian
schools. Enrollment had increased rapidly in his school
because of the superior instruction given there. About that
same time Bishop England had been selected by the Holy
See as its legate to Haiti. This action was looked upon as
an indication that the Holy See favored abolition in the
South. England had also written a letter to Daniel O'Connell, in which he took the *Liberator* to task for interferring
in a domestic problem, such as slavery in the south. Moreover, rumor was spread about that the Bishop had received
one of the mischievous anti-slavery tracts, but he denied
this is an open letter on July 30, 1835. Because of these
agitations, the school for free Negroes was eventually closed
when England was assured that all other schools of like
nature had been closed.[35]

The noble attempts to conduct Catholic Schools just
mentioned refer principally to schools for the free Negro.
But, when one realizes how almost impossible it was to
conduct these, then he will realize the difficulties encountered in educating the Negro slave.

II. Baptism of Slaves

Discussing the disposition necessary for those who are
to be baptized, Kenrick taught that slaves, incapable of
fuller instruction, may be baptized provided they truly believe in God and detest their sins. But generally, a fuller
instruction is demanded, especially concerning the contro-
verted doctrines, lest by trickery of the heretics, the slaves

[35] Guilday, *Life of England*, 2: 151-156.

be later turned from the faith. But where their faith seems to be sincere, they may be admitted into the fold of the Church, he held, and later more accurately instructed. Man is disposed, said Kenrick, to receive the grace of justification in Baptism by the fear of the divine judgments, by hope and confidence in God because of past sins committed, with the purpose of leading a new life, loving God as the principle of all justice.[36]

He noted that ordinarily the regular formula of abjuration is to be recited by those entering the Church, who have previously professed another religion. But, by epikeia, this formula could be omitted in the case of "persons of color and other ignorant persons, who would not be able to recite it or understand it."[37]

Furthermore, he taught that slaves are to be admitted to Baptism, even if the masters are unwilling, for they are not subject to the masters in things that are of divine law. Even should there be danger of venegance on the part of the master when he would learn that his slaves were baptized without his consent, or against his will, it would not be permitted to deny the sacrament to the servant desiring to care for his salvation, but all caution must be taken that the baptism not become known.[38]

In his treatment of "special obligations," Kenrick added a paragraph in the later edition to the effect that the Catholic master is bound to take care that the children of his slaves are baptized, when either of the parents is Catholic. But, if neither is Catholic, the rights that he has over them demands that at least he see to it that those whose lives are in danger, be baptized and instructed in the faith. If the parents are unwilling, the will of the master in those things that are of divine law ought to prevail.[39]

In the tract on Baptism, this teaching is explained a bit

36 Kenrick, *Theologia moralis*, tr. XV, cap. VI, no. 32.
37 *Ibid.*, no. 35.
38 *Ibid.*, no. 25.
39 Kenrick, *op. cit.*, tr. VIII, cap. IV, no. 100.

more thoroughly. He taught that the children of slaves are
to be baptized, if the masters are willing, even if the parents oppose, for the power of the master over them is complete, and can be used to their advantage by caring for their
salvation. He cited Antoine as holding the masters obliged
at least by charity to present these children for Baptism.[40]
But on the other hand, he taught if neither the parents
nor the masters are willing that the children be baptized,
they may not be baptized except in danger of death. For,
since the children are in their hands there would be little
chance of their being instructed, hence there would be a
danger of the profanation of the sacrament, and the one
baptized would be exposed to the danger of apostasy. But
in the case where the parents are willing that the child be
baptized, but the master opposes it, the child can be baptized, for the will of the parents should prevail in that
which is *juris divini*. In such a case, the parents are to
be encouraged to instruct the child in a Christian manner.
If only one of the parents, or the wife of the master, wishes
the Baptism of the child, the child should be baptized, for
the just will should prevail over the unjust will.[41]

In practice, the earliest difficulty was caused by a law
of the established Church of England as well as the non-
conformists, to the effect that no Christian could be a
slave.[42] According to this ancient law, then, a baptized slave
became free.[43] Accordingly, planters fearing to lose the
services of their slaves, opposed their baptism.[44] As a result "the large number of pagans continued to be pagans

[40] Paul Gabriel Antoine, *Theologia moralis universa* (Avenione:
Typis Francisci Seguin, 1818), De Bap. Qu. XIII, resp. 3, tom. V,
p. 53.

[41] Kenrick, *op. cit.*, tr. XV, cap. V, no. 26.

[42] Miriam Murphy, *RACHS*, 35 (1924), 104.

[43] Lord Baltimore in private decision declared that Baptism would
not free the slaves. This greatly encouraged Baptisms. Cf. Miriam
Murphy, *RACHS*, 35 (1924), 105.

[44] H. J. Catterall, *Judicial Cases Concerning American Slavery and
the Negro*, I: 55.

in a Christian land."[45] This law was later abrogated by the Bishop of London in 1678, and provincial statutes that Baptism did not constitute grounds for manumission. This greatly facilitated the baptizing of the slaves.[46] Catholic Church registers, however, show that many slaves were baptized during these days of dispute.[47] The *Code Noir*, as stated before, under which Louisiana was governed, made it obligatory to instruct and baptize the slaves.[48]

III. HOLY COMMUNION

In his chapter on the obligation of receiving Holy Communion, Kenrick taught that especially in danger of death, there is a very strict obligation of receiving the Eucharist. This precept of the divine law particularly obliges those who have never received or who have neglected their Easter Communion. Thus, those who have been recently received into the Church, are not to be sent from this life without the help of this necessary spiritual aid on the pretext that they are not sufficiently instructed. For if they have the faith necessary to be baptized and some knowledge of this sacrament, they are to be given It. But, on the other hand, if they were baptized without sufficient instructions, or only doubtfully disposed, then it would be lawful to refrain from giving them this sacrament. Then he concluded that persons of low intelligence and a lower condition of life, such as the slaves, are not to be sent from life without Viaticum provided they have the necessary dispositions, since they are obliged by the divine law and their salvation is helped by receiving it.[49]

---

[45] Hart, *EA*, 27: 393.

[46] Nuesse, *The Social Thought of American Catholics*, pp. 41 f; Catterall, *op. cit.*, I: 57; Woodson, *The Education of the Negro prior to 1861*, pp. 3-6; Stroud, *A Sketch of Laws on Slavery*, p. 152.

[47] Rice, *American Catholic Opinion in the Slavery Controversy*, p. 54.

[48] Joseph Butsch, "Negro Catholics in the United States," *CHR*, 3 (1917), 37.

[49] Kenrick, *op. cit.*, tr. XVII, cap. IV, no. 41.

Again, in speaking of those who are to be anointed, Kenrick said that the custom of giving Extreme Unction without Viaticum to those in danger of death, who are mentally dull, and have grown old in their vices, such as slaves, cannot be reconciled with the custom of the Church and law of Christ about receiving the Eucharist. They are to be instructed and prepared in the best way possible, that they may be fortified by both sacraments and thus not lack the necessary Viaticum. [50]

IV. ABSOLUTION OF SLAVES AND MASTERS

In his treatment of the sacrament of Penance, Kenrick[51] referred to the slaves when speaking of absolving people who are in a necessary occasion of sin. He said that he who finds himself in a physically necessary occasion of sin, is to be absolved, whenever there are signs that the penitent has contrition and purpose of amendment. But, he added, that outside of the danger of death, absolution is to be deferred sometimes, so that the person will be more solicitous about using means to avoid the sin, and may proceed to Holy Communion with better morals. In such a manner, he said, a confessor should handle slave girls who are accustomed to sin with their masters or with their sons. In another paragraph, still speaking of a necessary occasion of sin, he used the example of a slave whom the

---

[50] Kenrick, *op. cit.*, tr. XIX, cap. unicum, no. 18. The Code of Canon Law is in agreement with this opinion of Kenrick. Canon 854 decrees that Holy Communion is not to be administered to children, who, because of age have not proper recognition of the Eucharist, but in danger of death, for the Holy Eucharist to be administered to them, it is sufficient that they be able to distinguish the Body of Christ from common bread and reverently adore it.

Canon 864 says that in danger of death the faithful are bound by precept to receive Holy Communion and they are urged to receive It even if they have already received that same day.

Canon 865 warns those who have the care of souls that Holy Viaticum must be given to the sick while they are in possession of their senses.

[51] Kenrick, *op. cit.*, tr. XVIII, cap. IX, no. 190.

master abuses in his lust, as being in a necessary occasion of sin from which he or she is not able to flee.[52]

In treating of the virtue of faith, Kenrick taught that while heretics are praying, whether publicly or privately, it would not seem to be a denial of faith for the Catholic slaves who attend them to kneel, when understood to be done *causa humanitatis;* nevertheless, this custom is to be rejected, for it seems to favor heresy and contains the danger of perversion and bad example. Catholic slaves, may, however, drive their masters to heretical churches and accompany the daughters and wives of the masters for the sake of protection, without taking part in their heretical rites. They may also carry infants, who are to be baptized by an heretical minister, for all these things pertain to their work as servants and do not savor of partaking in worship. He noted that many, although not all, think that Eliseus permitted Naaman to accompany the king to adore the idols and to hold his garment while he offered incense.[53]

Kenrick noted that sometimes it happens that a man sins, not from affection toward a certain woman, but from an insane lust that he desires to satisfy with any woman. In such a way, masters are generally affected toward slaves. Such an occasion can hardly be removed, for vehement suspicions would then be aroused on the part of the wife, if one slave were replaced by another. In such conditions, the masters would not seem to be forced to remove the servant, who is hardly the occasion of the sin, although the object and associate of it. But opportune remedies are to be applied for allaying the lust, before the master is admitted to the Sacraments.[54]

V. MARRIAGE

The right of slaves to marry. Under special obligations,

[52] *Ibid.,* no. 185.

[53] Kenrick, *op. cit.,* tr. XIII, cap. III, no. 33; cf. 4 Kings, 5: 19; Diana, *op. cit.,* VII, tr. 8, resol. 52, p. 305.

[54] Kenrick, *op. cit.,* tr. XVIII, cap. IX, no. 188.

Kenrick[55] clearly taught that slaves retain their liberty to enter matrimony, preserving also the right of the master to their services. Thus, they many not lawfully marry contrary to the just will of their master under conditions in which they would be taken from the work owed to him, but, on the other hand, if the master unjustly refuses to permit them to marry, they may use the right that nature itself gives to them and makes the contract for life between themselves, even without the assistance of a priest.[56]

Again, in his treatment of the impediments of marriage, Kenrick taught that slaves may enter marriage between themselves even if the master be unwilling, for this right pertains to the natural law, namely, that they may decide for themselves in this matter. Thus, since there is neither slave nor free man in Jesus Christ neither should be refused the sacraments. Should slaves contract marriage against the opposition of their masters, the marriage contract cannot be dissolved for this reason alone.[57]

Indeed, in those states in which slavery existed the civil laws generally forbade slaves to enter marriage without the consent of their masters and prescribed very grave penalties for those who dared to marry them without this consent. Therefore, Kenrick advised that they make sure that they had this consent. If the master absolutely re-

---

[55] Kenrick, *Theologia moralis*, tr. VIII, cap. IV, no. 96.

[56] Canon 1098 of the present code is in agreement with this opinion of Kenrick, stating that in cases where persons wishing to contract marriage cannot appear before the priest in accord with canons 1095, 1096, without grave inconvenience, and that this condition will perdure for a month they may validly and licitly contract marriage before two witnesses. The Sacred Congregation on the Sacraments in a private decision, given 24 April, 1935, decreed that if a priest cannot assist at a marriage because of the civil law, the parties can use Canon 1098, Lincoln T. Bouscaren, *The Canon Law Digest* (Milwaukee: The Bruce Publishing Co., 1943), 2: 336. It should be pointed out, however, that at the time Kenrick wrote his text the presence of the priest was not necessary for validity of marriage in most of the territory of the United States.

[57] Kenrick, *op. cit.*, tr. XXI, cap. V, no. 140.

fused to give his consent then they were advised to marry without the assistance of the priest as shall be seen later.[58]

Kenrick does not consider the alternate of wedlock, namely, the right of a slave to observe virginity. Yet this might have been a problem, where, as mentioned earlier, many masters, desirous of having offspring generated, practically forced even very young girls to take a mate.

To marry or to practice virginity is a decision that dominates every activity of one's whole life, and is closely bound up with one's most intimate personal interests. Hence, freedom of choice in such a matter is the individual's inalienable right.[59]

On the contrary, in the average southern State the marriage of slaves was without legal recognition whatsoever.[60] There is a decision to the effect that the marriage of slaves has its civil effect only at his emancipation and not before.[61] But in the case of a marriage where only one of the parties is a slave the marriage is legal, and if the mother

[58] *Ibid.* This doctrine of Kenrick is in perfect accord with the theologians, who maintain that man has a right to marry, for the sake of propagating the human race, as a help to salvation, and as a remedy for concupiscence. This right comes from the natural law, which is above the law of nations and all civil law. The master may let it be known that a marriage may displease him, but no more. He would sin grievously by punishing a slave for contracting marrigae. Cf. St. Thomas, *Summa*, Suppl. Qu. 52, art. 2; Molina, *De justitia et jure*, I, tr. 2, disp. 38, no. 5; De Lugo, *De justitia et jure*, Disp. 3, sec. 2; Sanchez *De mat.*, II, lib. 7, disp. 21, no. 5-7; Diana, *De justitia et jure*, VII, resol. 57, p. 307.

[59] Leo XIII "Rerum novarum," *Acta Leonis XIII*, 11: 104. E. Cahill, *The Framework of a Christian State* (Dublin: M. H. Gill & Son, 1932), p. 312.

[60] Phillips, *American Negro Slavery*, p. 500; That the relation of husband and wife cannot exist between slaves. Cf. (Ala. 1854), *Malinda* v. *Gardner*, 24 Ala. 719; (D. C. 1867), *Brown* v. *Beckett*, 6 D. C. 253; (Mo. 1870) *Johnson* v. *Johnson*, 45, Mo. 595; (Tex. 1867) *Timmins* v. *Lacy* 30 Tex. 115; (Ky. 1870) *Ewing* v. *Bebb*, 70 Ky. 654.

[61] *Girod* v. *Lewis* (May Term, 1819), 5 Martin La. Rep. 559, Wheeler, *A Practical Treatise on the Laws of Slavery*, p. 199.

is free, the children will follow the condition of the mother.[62]

Marriage of Whites and Negroes. In treating of the impediments of marriage, Kenrick noted that although in some States marriage between whites and Negroes was forbidden and was considered invalid, the Church considers them valid as long as there is no impediment resulting from the servile condition. Thus he concluded that if persons enter such a union they cannot be refused the sacraments simply because the civil law or public opinion forbids such a marriage; for they use their natural right. But, he judged that it is not fitting that a priest assist at a marriage of this type. This point will be discussed more fully later.[63]

In the civil law, marriage between Negroes and whites was forbidden in some of the States where slavery did not exist and was prohibited in all the slave-holding States. In some States, attempted marriages of this type were held to be void. The laws further determined what degree of Negro ancestry brought persons under this prohibition, in cases where the person concerned was of mixed races. Moreover, penalties were attached for those who attempted these marriages contrary to the civil law.[64]

The celebration of matrimony. In his text, Kenrick presupposed that Catholic slaves, since they are human beings and members of the Mystical Body, would be married according to the rites and ceremonies prescribed by the Church. Thus, he presupposed that a priest will be there to perform the ceremonies attached to the wedding.

He advised the priest, however, not to be present for the ceremony where danger may arise, viz., where custom, the master or the State law forbids the marriage. Thus, in the case where a Negro marries a white person contrary to

---

[62] *Overseers of Marbletown* v. *Overseers of Kingston*, 20 **Johns** Rep. 1 (May Term, 1822), Wheeler, *op. cit.*, p. 199.

[63] Kenrick, *op. cit.*, tr. XXI, cap. V, no. 142.

[64] Kent, *Commentaries*, 2: no. 258, p. 285, no. A.

the state law he said that it is not fitting in such a case
that the priest take part in the ceremony, even though he
maintained that they have a right to enter such a marriage
validly in the eyes of the Church.[65]

Again, when speaking of the right of slaves to marry,
even if the master forbids such a marriage, he mentioned
that in many states the civil law forbidding slaves to enter
marriage without the consent of the masters, threatens
severe penalties to those who dare to join them in wedlock.
Therefore, the priest should attempt to get the consent of
the master, but if he unjustly refuses to grant it, and the
occasion warrants it, the slaves may be permitted to make
their consent between themselves, so that they may not be
placed in the occasion of sin, and so that the priest may
not be liable to grave inconveniences by assisting at their
nuptials. He noted that in the State of Mississippi the law
concerning slaves and Negroes does not give any instructions concerning marriages. Thus it would seem that they
could be celebrated without any special permission, but
that the masters usually use their powers over the slaves
to permit or prohibit them according to their good pleasure.
Hence, a priest could not perform a marriage without very
grave danger to himself, unless he had the permission of
the master.[66]

In his tract on the sacraments in general, in the chapter
dealing with the administration of the sacraments, Kenrick urged those priests, who assist at marriages, to take
care that the persons to be married are well instructed.
But regarding slaves and others of low intelligence, this
same discipline is not to be required. Because in our country, he added, there is constant danger that those who are

[65] Kenrick, *op. cit.*, tr. XXI, cap. V, no. 142.

[66] Kenrick, *op. cit.*, tr. XXI, cap. V, no. 140. From what Kenrick
has said, it is made sufficiently clear that before marriages could take
place, by custom the permission of the master had to be obtained.
Frequently marriages were not permitted between Negroes who
belonged to different masters. Cf. Phillips, *American Negro Slavery*,
p. 81. *The Negro in Virginia*, p. 81.

not so well instructed may go before a heretical minister,
they are not to be easily refused especially since necessity
demands that Catholics by dispensation marry heretics.[67]

In practice there was usually no period of betrothment
among the slaves. As soon as it was convenient after the
consent of the master had been obtained, the "ceremony"
took place.[68]

In Virginia, the simple ceremony took place on Saturday
or Sunday, in the home of the bride. All would walk in,
the bride and groom being in the center. Very solemnly
someone, usually the mid-wife, would lay a broom-stick
across the middle of the floor. Arm in arm the two would
step across it. This sufficed, unless someone present could
read a passage from the Bible.[69]

However, other slave-owners carefully supervised slave
marriages, insisting that consent be requested beforehand.
Some deemed it a matter of conscience to provide regular
marriage ceremonies for their slaves. House servants, close
to the master, were occasionally favored with marriage in
the "big house."[70]

[67] Kenrick, *op. cit.*, tr. XIV, cap. IV, no. 35.

[68] *The Negro in Virginia*, p. 82.

[69] Thus ninety-six-year-old Charles Grandy, Civil War veteran,
thrice married, declared:

> Marsa used to sometimes pick our wives fo' us. If he didn't
> have on his place enough women for the men, he would wait
> on de side of the road till a big wagon loaded with slaves
> came by. De Marsa would stop de ole nigger-trader and buy
> you a woman. Wasn't no use trying to pick one, cause
> Marsa wasn't gonna pay but so much for her. All he wanted
> was a young healthy one, who looked like she could have
> children, whether she was purty or ugly as sin. Den he
> would lead you an' de woman over to one of de cabins and
> stan' you on de porch. He wouldn't go in. No sir, he'd stan'
> right dere at the do' an' open de Bible ad de first things he
> came to an' read somepin real fast out of it. Den he close
> up de Bible and finish up wid dis verse:
>> Dat yo' wife
>> Dat yo' husban'
>> I'se yo' marsa
>> She yo' missus
>> You married.

The Negro in Virginia, pp. 81-84.

[70] *Ibid.*, pp. 81- 83.

There seems to be conflicting information concerning the attention given to marriage of slaves on Catholic plantations. On author quotes a Catholic bishop in 1860 as saying:

> Marriage is scarcely known among them (the (slaves) ; the masters attach no importance to it. We can judge of the disorders which must result from a state of things in a race greatly addicted to the pleasures of the senses.[71]

Another author, speaking of the Maryland plantation says that much attention was given on Catholic plantations to the matrimonial status of slaves but, it was an object of horrible abuse by other planters and traders, and often ignored by many well-intentioned but less religious people. He says that the zeal displayed by the missionaries in safeguarding marriages, despite the difficulties of contrary custom and law, did much to preserve Catholicism among the Negroes and was the source of good example to the white population.[72]

Father Augustus Thebaud said that the civil law prohibited the giving of the nuptial blessing to slaves, but on the large plantations, the Sacrament of Matrimony was often administered properly, yet he knew of no priest ever being convicted for so doing. Because the authorities of the State were aware that the Catholic Church would not consent to obey such State Laws they therefore refrained from enforcing them. It should also be noted that many non-Catholic planters who allowed the Negroes to marry were not molested by the State.[73] Many church registers show that slaves were married according to the laws of the Church, even though their marriages had no legal status.[74]

[71] Stephen L. Theobold, "Catholic Missionary Work among the Colored People in the United States (1776-1866)," *RACHS*, 35 (1924), 341.

[72] John LaFarge, *CHR*, 21: (1935-1936), 15, 18 f.

[73] Miriam Murphy, *RACHS*, 35 (1924), 124.

[74] Rice, *American Catholic Opinion in the Slavery Controversy*, p. 54.

Separation of husband and wife. In his treatise on the
special obligations of masters and slaves, Kenrick stated
that as far as is possible, masters should see to it that married couples live together, having the opportunity of being
with each other, have their children with them and be allowed to live the type of domestic life called for by legitimate marriage. Hence, he concluded that masters sin, who
rashly separate married couples from each other especially
where the "bond of necessity" is entirely broken and they
are exposed to the danger of concubinage. Thus, those
who send slaves outside of the State, while their marriage
partners remain behind, sin, unless they are led to the sale
by grave reason. But on the other hand, if a slave is wicked,
and the master has tried in vain to bring him to terms,
Kenrick would not condemn the master who, fearing
death or harm to his home from the slave, sends him far
away. At times, he said, masters sell slaves because of
thefts, attempted flight, or other crimes, in this manner
inflicting punishment. Such a master should not be condemned who, for grave reasons of this type, sells those
whom he could scarcely keep without peril to his life.[75]

The theologians make many distinctions in considering
the question whether or not the master may lawfully send
or sell his slave into a distant land where he will be separated from his marriage partner. In brief, these may be
summarized as follows: most all agree that if the master
consented to the marriage, he may not send the slave away
afterwards permanently separating him from his wife;
however, even here some theologians give some exceptions.
If he opposed the marriage, some say that he may send
him away without serious sin, while others say he may
never do so; others make a distinction to the effect that,
if the master is pressed by necessity which cannot be relieved except by the sale of the slave to a distant region—

[75] Kenrick, *op. cit.*, tr. VIII, cap. IV, no. 96. The last two sentences
are not found in the earlier edition.

because he could find no buyer at home then he could lawfully do so.[76]

Slavery as an impediment to marriage. In speaking of the impediments to marriage, Kenrick explained that error regarding the person, renders a marriage invalid, for in such a case, since true consent is lacking there would be no marriage. Hence, if a person marries a slave not knowing of the condition of slavery, the marriage would be invalid.[77]

The foundation for Kenrick's teaching that if a free man marries a slave not knowing that she is a slave, but afterwards when he discovers this fact treats her with marital affection, he is considered to consent to the marriage, is found in the Decretals of Gregory IX. This decree is taken from a decision given by Pope Alexander III.[78]

[76] Cf. Diana, *De justitia et jure*, VII, tr. 8, resol. 53, p. 307; Sanchez, *De Mat.* II, lib. 7, disp. 22, discusses the matter very thoroughly and attempts to favor the rights of the slaves; De Lugo, *op. cit.*, disp. 3, sec. 2, likewise discusses the matter thoroughly. He tends to take a more strict view, favoring the rights of the master. He attempts to refute some of the teachings of Sanchez.

[77] Kenrick, *op. cit.*, tr. XXI, cap. V, no. 139. Kenrick applied the genral norm on the validation of marriages to the impediment of servitude saying that if a free man, who had married a slave, not knowing that she was a slave would later learn of this impediment, but subsequently have carnal relations with her, he was compelled to retain her. Cf. Kenrick, *op. cit.*, tract XXI, cap. VI, no. 227.

[78] c. 2, X, *de conjugium servorum*, IV, 9.

The basis for this doctrine was laid in the Council of Vermia, held in the year 753. Cf. Mansi 17: B, 165. Chapter six of this council was incorporated in the decree of Gratian.

C. 4, C. XXIX, q. 2: "Si quis ingenuus homo ancillam uxorem alterius acceperit, et existimat, quod ingenua sit, si ipsa femina fuerit postea in servitute dectecta, si eam a servitute redimere potest faciat; si non potest, si voluerit, aliam accipiat. Si autem ancillam eam acceperat et collaudaverat, postea ut legitimam habeat. Similiter et mulier ingenua de servo alterius facere debet."

This decree has found its way into the present Code of Canon Law.

Can. 1083, 2, 2°: "Error circa qualitatem personae, etsi det causam contractui, matrimonium irritat tantum; ... si persona libera matri-

All theologians admit the principle involved. It will be
sufficient to note that St. Thomas devotes an article to the
matter, concluding that, since in marriage one party is
obliged to freely give the *debitum,* and since the condition
of slavery takes away the opportunity for freely rendering
the *debitum,* the condition of slavery necessarily voids
marriage if it is unknown.[79]

Validity of the marriage of slaves. In treating of the
impediments to marriage, Kenrick said that it is often difficult to judge the validity of marriage of slaves. Often slaves
enter into domestic relations without the intention to marry,
or call themselves husband and wife, as long as each properly conducts himself, or until the master separates them. At
times they seem to have wished to enter a permanent union;
but whether they are free from the former union can hardly be known. Hence, if it is evident that they seriously
entered marriage with the intention of binding themselves
permanently, the marriage is to be held as valid, and they
cannot enter another union until the former partner has
died. But generally their contract does not have the binding force of marriage, since the intention of permanently
binding themselves is wanting, and a condition was attached
to the consent. Therefore, those who are converted to the
Catholic faith, or return to a good life, are not to be forced
to immediately leave the one whom they then look upon as
their spouse, although others with whom they lived are
still living, or their death is not certain.[80]

monium contrahat cum persona quam liberam putat, cum contra sit
serva, servitute proprie dicta."

[79] *Summa theol.,* Supp, qu. 52, art. I; Antoine, *De Mat.,* tom. VI,
cap. III, qu. 3, p. 40. Sanchez used the same principle and applied
it in the different possiblities that might occur. Cf. Sanchez, *De Mat.,*
II, lib. 7, disp. 19, no. 3.

[80] Kenrick, *op. cit.,* tr. XXI, cap. V, no. 141. In the later edition he
has the following sentence which is not found in the early edition:
"but the matter is to be diligently investigated." In the early edition
he simply said: "but care must be taken that he enter a true marriage with her." Cf. Kenrick, *op. cit.,* (ed. of 1841), tr. XXII, cap. V,
no. 141.

In discussing the nature of marriage he spoke of various conditions that are placed. If these conditions are against the substance of the marriage, they invalidate it. He mentioned that the error of non-Catholics thinking that marriage can be dissolved, by the authority of the state, because of adultery, or other causes, does not affect the validity of the marriage, since the intention of contracting marriage according to the law of nature and Christ is the stronger. The marriages of slaves are invalid if they place a condition such as "as long as you conduct yourself properly."[81]

He also devoted a chapter to the doubtful contract. Here, he said, that if there is a probable impediment of the natural law one would not be permitted to enter a marriage because the validity of the sacrament would be endangered, since the Church is not able to remove the impediment if it exists. Hence, if it is doubted whether a certain marriage were valid, and there are probable reasons on both sides, the person is not permitted to enter a new marriage. Such a case can easily happen among slaves, he said, who sometimes have entered into several marriages, and it is not evident that any of them were valid contracts. He noted that St. Alphonsus said that in a matter of this kind, only the Supreme Pontiff can interpret the Divine Law. Pope Urban VIII made such a decision concerning marriages contracted in infidelity of persons who dwelt in Paraguay.[82]

In the passage to which Kenrick referred, St. Alphonsus said that, *per se*, it is not licit to administer the sacrament of matrimony with only a probable opinion that it will be valid. He based his opinion on one of the propositions condemned by Innocent XI.[83] But he insisted on the words

[81] *Ibid.*, tr. XXI, cap. II, no. 40. This opinion is not found in the early edition.

[82] Kenrick, *op. cit.*, tr. XXI, cap. II, no. 51.

[83] 1. "Non est illicitum, in sacramentis conferendis sequi opinionem probabilem de valore sacramenti, relicta tutiore, nisi id vetet lex, conventio aut periculum gravis damni incurrendi. Hinc sententia proba-

"per se loquendo" for, if there is a most grave reason matrimony could be contracted, provided there was a declaration to that effect by the Supreme Pontiff, who is the sole interpreter of the divine law. Then he mentions that Cardenas[84] related that Urban VIII once made such a declaration. John De Lugo, he said, brought to the Pontiff the doubt as to whether the marriages of infidel Indians living in the region of Paraguay were valid and whether after Baptism they were obliged to take the first wife, from among those whom they had or whether they could choose the one that they preferred. The Pontiff, having consulted De Lugo, said that since the opinions of both sides were probable he would follow those opinions, that were more favorable to the condition of the places and the people.[85]

Kenrick advised that Negro converts should not be forced to leave their present consorts, even though they had been married recently, since there was a probability that the former marriages were invalid.[86]

bili tantum utendum non est in collatione baptismi, ordinis sacerdotalis aut episcopalis." Denz., 1151.

[84] Joannis de Cardenas, *Crisis theologica* (Venice, Nicolas Pezzana, 1696), Dissertatio II, cap. 8, art. 5, no. 551-555. This author gives the letter sent by De Lugo to Pope Urban VIII explaining the case, and gives the substance of the reply of the letters as given by St. Alphonsus. He then posed the question as to how tsis action could be reconciled with the condemned proposition mentioned above. He answered by saying that when the custom of entering a marriage or of judging of its validity according to an opinion that is truly probable and commonly accepted as such, this custom has the force of law, hence, such a custom has the force of rendering the validity of the marriage certain.

[85] Alphonsus di Liguori, St., *Theologia moralis*, lib. VI, no. 902. It should be pointed out that the fact rested on the reasons that De Lugo offered to show that these unions were not real marriages, for they seem to have had no intention of a permanent union and no consent was manifested externally. Yet the most he could prove was that they were probably invalid.

[86] Kenrick, *op. cit.*, tr. XXI, cap. V, no. 141. In the case of a doubtful impediment of the divine or natural law, the Holy See recently allowed the parties to remain in their presumed marriage. Cf. G.

It would seem that slave marriages were often unstable. Since the Negroes did not feel a strong sense of obligation to their spouses, they frequently deserted one another.[87] When Negro men obtained their liberty they would then attempt to buy their wives and families. Unless the latter were the legally emancipated they would remain slaves. Some husbands were not anxious to liberate their wives immediately. They considered it advisable to put them on probation for a few years, and then, if they did not find them satisfactory, they would sell them as other slaveholders did.[88]

VI. Observance of Church Laws

Kenrick taught that slaves who do not care to oppose the command of the master, when commanded to work on Sunday are excused and may work lawfully. Moreover, they may repair their clothes on Sundays if they do not have the opportunity to do so on other days. But, he said, that it can be doubted whether or not they can on Sundays cultivate gardens permitted them by their masters, to acquire a *peculium*.[89] Kenrick is inclined to deny them this one opportunity of having a *peculium*. This opinion is given in his treatment of the third commandment.[90]

Discussing the point whether or not it is lawful for masters to make their slaves work on Sunday, Kenrick pointed out that, in some southern States, slaves were accustomed to work on Sunday. This was done, he said, because it was feared that idleness would be the occasion of uprisings and slaughters. This, he said, could be considered a most grave reason for permitting work on Sunday. About the fact

Payen, *De Matrimonio in Missionibus ac potissimum in Sinis Tractatus Practicus et Casus* (2nd ed., 3 vols., Ze-ka-wei': Typographia T'ou-se'-we, 1935-1936), I: 1058-1059.

[87] Hart, *Slavery and Abolition*, p. 103.

[88] *JNH*, 9 (1924), 11.

[89] Peculium is a small sum of money allowed the slaves, to be disposed of according to their own wishes.

[90] Kenrick, *op. cit.*, tr. III, cap. VII, no. 90.

that slaves easily get into small fights when having nothing to do, he preferred to remain silent. To add weight to his point, he quoted Ecclesiasticus: "The yoke and the thong bend a stiff neck; and continual labours bow a slave. Torture and fetters are for a malicious slave: send him to work, that he be not idle. For idleness has taught much evil."[91] But he called that a miserable condition where every opportunity to care for their salvation is denied to the slaves, on the presumption that the master's safety may be endangered otherwise. If there is danger in a very great crowd of slaves being gathered together in the one place, certainly the ecclesiastical law ceases to bind. In such a case other means are to be devised to provide for the slaves' spiritual welfare. Thus, they are to be taught privately and trained to works of piety in order to give to God what is due Him. Slaves should reverence their masters for His sake and should be given an opportunity to receive the sacraments. Masters who neglect this duty are not to be exused from sin.[92]

He posed the question as to whether a Catholic would sin who worked non-baptized persons on Sundays. He answered that it is a disputed point. Some theologians hold that it seems to detract from divine worship and cite in support of their view the fact that the Jews were not allowed to permit their servants to work on the Sabbath. The more common opinion, however, he said, holds that the whole of the Sunday obligation depends on the ecclesiastical law, which does not bind infidels. Thus, Catholics would not sin who would make their employees work on Sunday, nor would they sin if they gave them meat to eat on days of abstinence.[93]

In practice generally the master could determine the

---

[91] Ecclesiasticus, 33: 27-29; Kenrick, *op. cit.*, tr. III, cap. VII, no. 77.

[92] Kenrick, *op. cit.*, tr. III, cap. VII, no. 71.

[93] Kenrick, *op. cit.*, tr. III, cap. VII, no. 76; cf. Diana, *op. cit.*, VII, tr. 8, resol. 49, p. 304 with whom Kenrick is in agreement.

kind, degree and time of labor to which the slave would be subjected. Only Louisiana, Georgia, South Carolina and Mississippi had laws on this point.[94] Thus, for example, in Georgia, by the act of May 10, 1770, a master who worked his slaves on Sunday could be fined ten shillings for each slave.[95] In Mississippi by the act of June 13, 1832, the penalty was placed at two dollars per slave.[96] Olmsted says that the law was not well observed in Louisiana. The neighbors could scarcely afford to report the infraction because they would then incur the enmity of the person concerned and all his relatives.[97]

In his teaching about ecclesiastical law, Kenrick said that slaves are generally excused from the law of abstinence. Slaves are hardly given anything but pork meat and Indian corn. The masters are not required to buy fish and eggs for their slaves, since the expense would be very great and such food is little suited to them, especially when there are many of them who are occupied with hard work.[98] It is evident from what was said about ecclesiastical law binding only the baptized, there would be no doubt about the lawfulness of serving meat to infidel slaves on Friday.[99]

[94] Stroud, *op. cit.*, p. 40.
[95] 2 *Cobb's Digest*, p. 981.
[96] *Miss. Revised Code*, p. 317.
[97] Olmsted, *Seaboard States*, p. 651.
[98] Kenrick, *op. cit.*, tr. IV, cap. IV, no. 60.
[99] Kenrick, *op. cit.*, tr. III, cap. VII. no. 76; cf. Diana, *op. cit.*, VII, tr. 8, resol. 48, p. 304.

CHAPTER VI

KENRICK'S TEACHING CONCERNING THE OBLIGATIONS OF SLAVES TOWARD THEIR MASTERS

Thus far, consideration has been given to the right of the masters to hold slaves and the obligations that masters have to the slaves they hold. Kenrick being the thorough scholar that he was, also considered the obligations of slaves toward their masters. These obligations will be treated in this chapter.

I. OBEDIENCE OF SLAVES

Kenrick[1] in his tract on special obligations besides treating of the obligations of masters toward slaves also treated of the duties of slaves toward their masters. He pointed out, in the first place, that the slave should obey the master as the Apostle taught.[2] They were to obey for the sake of Christ and were to adore the divine will in the condition by which they were subject to another, remembering the heavenly reward proposed to pious and faithful servants. He again quoted St. Paul.[3] Therefore, the masters are to be honored, he said, and services are not to be withdrawn under the appearance of religion, lest by violating the order of society, an occasion be given to the non-believers to

[1] Kenrick, *Theologia moralis*, tr. VIII, cap. V, no. 103.

[2] Eph. 6: 5: "Servants be obedient to them that are your lords according to the flesh, with fear and trembling, and in the simplicity of your heart, as to Christ."

[3] I Tim. 6: 1. "Whosoever are servants under the yoke, let them count their masters worthy of all honor; lest the name of the Lord and his doctrine be blaspemed. But they that have believing masters, let them not despise them because they are brothers, but rather do them service because they are faithful and beloved, who are partakers of the benefit."

speak contumeliously of Christ. The necessary duties of slavery are to be done with that love which unites all Christians as brothers, so that they may be more pleasing to God. Peter forbade slaves to withdraw service from wicked masters, who cruelly treat their slaves. "Servants, be subject to your masters with all fear, not only to the good and gentle, but also to the froward."[4] But in safeguarding life and members he added the slaves is not under the master but *sui juris*.

Thus slaves sin, he taught,[5] if they neglect work assigned to them, or neglect things committed to their care, but they do not violate justice, but rather obedience. He agreed with Lessius.[6]

Other Catholic theologians while urging the slaves to obey their masters, place limits on that obedience. Thus proposing the question as to whether subjects are obliged to obey in all things. Thomas[7] said that they are not, in two cases. First, if there is a precept of a higher law to the contrary; secondly, if the master commands something in which the inferior is not subject to him. Man remains *sui juris*. Hence, man is obliged to obey in those things which exteriorly are done by the body but in those things that pertain to the very nature of the body man is not subject to man but only to God, because all men are equal; for example, man is not subject to man in those things that pertain to the substance of the body or the generating of children. Thus a servant does not have to obey a master regarding the contracting of marriage or the

---

[4] *I Pet.* 2: 18.

[5] Kenrick, *Theologia moralis*, tr. VIII, cap. V, no. 103. Here as frequently, Kenrick fails to hold a relationship between slave and master based on justice.

[6] Lessius, *De justitia et jure*, sec. II, cap. 8, dub. III, no. 20; "Non enim actiones servi sunt debitae domino lege justitiae, sicut mercenarii, qui pretium pro illis accipit: nec cogitur in foro conscientiae compensare, esti negligentius laboraverit."

[7] 2a, 2ae, qu. 104, art. 4.

preserving of chastity.[8] As a result, masters sin gravely by ordering slaves to do what they cannot do without mortal sin.[9]

Even those ministers who favored abolition of slavery, considered it unlawful and inexpedient to teach slaves to disobey. They observed that it was neither lawful nor expedient for Paul or the apostles to teach that slaves ought not to obey their masters and that if the masters would not set them free they would be justified in running away. It would not only have aggravated the evils of slavery in a thousand ways, but the minister would have been allowed by the civil authorities to live only long enough to be tried and condemned.[10]

Since it is obvious from what has been said regarding punishment, that slaves were obliged by law and even more by custom to obey, no further explanation of that point is needed.

II. Flight of Slaves

The view of Kenrick and the Theologians. In his treatment of slavery under the general title of *Jus Gentium*, Kenrick[11] asked the question: What is to be thought of slaves who flee? He answered by reminding his readers that the Apostle Paul sent the slave back to Philemon and that the council of Gangra quite severely forbade that any one on the pretext of religion take away slaves from their masters.[12] If a slave of his own accord escaped to a free state according to federal law, he could be brought

---

[8] Cf. Diana, *Resolutiones morales*, tom. VII, tr. 8, resol. 51, p. 305.

[9] Diana, *op. cit.*, VII, tr. 8, resol. 42, p. 303.

[10] *Report on Slavery to the Congregational Ministers*, (1849), p. 50.

[11] Kenrick, *Theologia moralis*, tr. V, cap. VI, no. 4.

[12] C. Si. quis servum, 37, c. 17, qu. 4: "Si quis servum alienum, occasione religionis, docet dominum suum contemnere, et ejus ministerium destituere, et non potius docuerit eum domino bona fide ac cum omni honorificentia deservire; anathema sit."

back.[13] But if a fugitive slave would hide and come to confession he should not be refused absolution because of his intention of not returning; for the fear of penalty was so great that no one would force him to return to his former condition with such danger to himself. Besides he suffered loss of liberty only by necessity, since he lost it by no fault of his own but only because of the misfortune of his ancestors.[14]

Roman law, he added, gave great privileges to slaves of war, who fled to their original home, and to Christian slaves, who had Jewish, pagan, or heretic masters, and to those who embraced the Christian Faith. But here by federal law the bond of slavery remained if the slave were brought back or detected in another state.[15]

The theologians treat the matter of slaves escaping in somewhat greater detail, giving many distinctions. They all agree that slaves may flee if they are not justly taken into slavery, and may repel those impeding them and take compensation for injury suffered and work done.[16] They also agree that if the master solicits a slave to sin and having been warned he refuses to desist, such a slave may flee and need not return until the danger ceases and the master is disposed not to punish or harm him.[17] Lessius[18] says that this is evident from the fact that no one is obliged to serve a master with danger to his soul. Likewise, they agree that if a slave is inhumanly treated, viz., left hungry or thirsty, exposed to the cold or beaten without cause, he

[13] In his footnote he alluded only to the case of *Prigg* v. *Pennsylvania* which will be explained later. This whole paragraph on fugitive slaves does not appear in the early edition, yet in the edition of 1860 he does not refer to the famous Fugitive Slave Law of 1850.

[14] Kenrick, *op. cit.*, tr. V, cap. VI, no. 4.

[15] *Ibid.*

[16] Lessius, *De justitia et jure*, sec. I. cap. V, dub. V; Migne, *TCC*, 15: 507; Molina, *De justitia et jure*, I, tr. 2, disp. 37; De Lugo, *De justitia et jure*, disp. VI, sec. III, no. 20, and disp. III, sec. II, no. 2.

[17] Molina, *op. cit.*, disp. 38; Diana, *Resolutiones morales*, tom. 7, tr. 8, resol. 17, p. 296; De Lugo, *De justitia et jure*, disp. III, sec. II.

[18] Lessius, *op. cit.*, sec. I, cap. V, dub. V, Migne, *TCC*, 15: 507.

may run away.[19] For a master thus treating a slave does
a great injury to him, from which he can withdraw by
flight if there is no other escape. After the danger passes
and unless there is danger in the future, and unless the
injury was by chance so great that rightly it is compen-
sated by liberty, the slave is bound to return.[20]

These theologians then discuss the morality of the escape
of those held by the various titles.

Those who sell themselves, or are sold by their parents
by contract, cannot flee from their masters excepting in the
cases noted above. For a contract has been made that must
be fulfilled.[21] But if they are treated unjustly they may
do so, for if the contract is broken on one side it can *ipso
facto* be broken on the other side.[22] But if they flee without reason then they deprive the master of that to which
he has a right in justice and they must then make restitution for themselves and the loss of service that he suffers.[23]

Those enslaved for crime may not escape, for the guilty
are held to undergo the just sentence. This is called by them
the common opinion. But they admit that an exception
would be made in the case where the condition of slavery
was very miserable, for to hold the contrary would be too
severe.[24]

There is some discussion concerning those enslaved by
war. Some say that in virtue of the *jus postliminii* of

[19] *Ibid.;* De Lugo, *op. cit.,* dub. III, sec. II.

[20] Lessius, *op. cit.,* sec. I, cap. V, dub. 5: Diana, *op. cit.,* tom. 7,
tr. 8, resol. 17, p. 296; De Lugo, *op. cit.,* disp. III, sec. III.

[21] Diana, *op. cit.,* tom. 7, tr. 8, resol. 11, p. 293; Carrière, *De justitia et jure,* no. 46, p. 36; Lessius, *op. cit.,* sec. I, cap. V, dub. V.

[22] Lyonnet, *De justitia et jure,* Appendix I, Pars I, De Jure et
Prin. Gen., Migne, *TCC,* 15: 845; De Lugo, *op. cit.,* disp. III, sec. II,
no. 21.

[23] Molina, *op. cit.,* I, tr. 2, disp. 37.

[24] Lessius, *op. cit.,* sec. I, cap. V, dub. V; Diana, *op. cit.,* tr. 8,
resol. 15, p. 295; Carrière, *op. cit.,* no. 46, p. 36. Molina, *op. cit.,*
I, tr. 2, disp. 37; De Lugo, *op. cit.,* disp. VI, sec. III, no. 28; Lyonnet,
op. cit., Migne, *TCC,* 15: 845.

Roman law slaves may lawfully escape to their original homes.[25] Molina, on the other hand, thinks that such slaves cannot lawfully escape.[26]

Those held by the title of nativity follow the condition of the mother and thus if she could have escaped so could they, but if she could not, then they cannot.[27]

From what has been said it follows that if one could escape from his first master lawfully then he can always escape regardless of how many times he has since been sold, for his condition is determined from the title under which he was first enslaved. Moreover, if one could lawfully escape, then others can lawfully assist him to escape.[28] However, De Lugo[29] points out that in such a case the one assisting cannot do all the things that the slave escaping can do, such as breaking down doors, etc.[30]

Laws and Practices concerning Fugitives. The earliest regulations concerning fugitive slaves is found in 1629 among "Freedom and Exemptions Granted by the West Indies Company to all Patrons, Masters or Private Persons, who would agree to settle in the Netherlands." The officials proposed to do all in their power to return the slaves to their masters.[31] A little later there were several inter-colonial regulations made on this subject.[32] It was also

[25] Lessius, *op. cit.*, sec. I, cap. V, dub. V; Lyonnet, *op. cit.*, Migne, *TCC*, 15: par. 845; De Lugo, *op. cit.*, sec. III; Diana, *op. cit.*, VII, tr. 8, resol. 12-15; pp. 294-295; Carrière, *op. cit.*, I: no. 46, p. 36.

[26] Molina, *op. cit.*, I, tr. 2, disp. 37.

[27] Diana, *op. cit.*, tom. 7, tr. 8, resol. 11, p. 293; Lyonnet, *op. cit.*, Migne, *TCC*, par. 845.

[28] Diana, *op. cit.*, tom. 7, tr. 8, resol. 12, p. 294.

[29] De Lugo, *De justitia et jure*, disp. VI, sec. III.

[30] Kenrick held that the ancestors of the slaves of his day were unjustly enslaved. Cf. *Supra*, p. 183. Hence, it would seem to follow that the descendants could escape.

[31] Marion Gleason McDogall, *The Underground Railroad* (Boston: Ginn & Co., 1891), p. 2.

[32] *Ibid.*, pp. 7-9.

found necessary to seek cooperation with the French, Spanish, and Dutch settlements.[33]

Later, in discussing the constitution, some of the states of the South refused to enter the union unless slavery became the basis of legislation.[34] In order to placate them the following article was inserted in the Constitution in order to enable owners to claim their fugitive slaves.

> No Person held to Service or Labour in one State under the laws thereof, escaping into another, shall in Consequence of any Law or Regulation therein, be discharged from such Service or Labour but shall be delivered up, on Claim of the Party to whom such Service or Labour may be due.[35]

Despite this provision, northerners began to protect the fugitives. As a result, the southern statesmen demanded a provision for carrying the article into effect. The act of 1793 was the result. The act in substance is as follows:

In case of the escape out of any state or territory of any person held to service or labor under the law thereof, the person to whom such labor was due, his agent, or attorney, might seize the fugitive, and carry him before any United States judge, or before any magistrate of the city, town or country, in which the arrest was made, and such judge or magistrate, on proof to his satisfaction either oral or by affidavit before any magistrate, that the person seized was a really a fugitive, and did owe labor as alleged, was to grant a certificate to serve as sufficient warrant for the removal of the fugitive to the state whence he had fled. Any person obstructing such seizure or removal, or harboring or concealing any fugitive after notice, was liable to a

---

[33] *Ibid.*, pp. 9-15; C. W. A. David, "The Fugitive Slave Law of 1793 and its Antecedents." *JNH*, 9 (1924), 19.

[34] Henry Wilson, *History of the Rise and Fall of Slave Power in America* (Boston: Houghton, Mifflin & Co., 1872-1875), 1: 54.

[35] Art. 4, sec. 2.

penalty of five hundred dollars to be recovered by the claimant.[36]

The States of the North badly defied the Act of 1793 by passing laws protecting any person within their borders from being taken back into slavery.[37] These laws were called "personal liberty laws" and their real purpose was to defeat the national Fugitive Slave Law. Their ostensible purpose was to protect the free Negroes from kidnapping, and to this end they secured for alleged fugitives the writ of habeas corpus, and trial by jury. But at times their frankly avowed aim was to interfere with the United States Statutes.[38] These bills dating from the passing of the Fugitive Slave Act of 1793 show the dissatisfaction of the North as fundamental, not as confined to merely a few in the van of the Anti-slavery movement. Practically all the northern states had them. Many of the abolitionists held the national law to be unconstitutional and at the same time so morally unjust and repugnant that it ought never to be executed.[39]

The effect of these personal liberty laws was that the national and state legislative bodies were brought into conflict.[40]

The question of the right of a State to make a law contrary to the Federal Constitution was settled in 1824 by the United States Supreme Court in its decision in the case of *Prigg* vs. *Pennsylvania*.

Edward Prigg was a citizen of Maryland. He was indicted by Pennsylvania for kidnapping a Negro woman

[36] Fugitive Slave Act of Feb. 12, 1793, *U.S. Statutes at Large*, I: 302-305; Cf. McDougall, *op. cit.*, pp. 18-19. William Renwick Riddell, "Fugitive Slave Law of 1793 and its Antecedents," *JNH*, 9 (1924), 18 ff.

[37] David, *JNH*, 9 (1924), 23.

[38] McDougall, *op. cit.*, p. 65.

[39] *Ibid.*, pp. 65-70; Cf. Commanger, *Documents of American History*, p. 355, where the Mass. Personal Liberty Act of May 21, 1855 is given.

[40] Wilbur Henry Seibert, *The Underground Railroad from Slavery to Freedom* (New York: Macmillan, 1898), p. 245.

in York County in Pennsylvania and returning her to Maryland as a fugitive slave, contrary to the Pennsylvania law
of 1826, providing for a fine of three thousand dollars and
from seven to twenty-one years imprisonment. He was
tried and convicted in the local court and the sentence was
confirmed by the Supreme Court of Pennsylvania. It was
then taken before the Supreme Court of the United States.
Prigg proved to the High Court that he had served a warrant, issued by a magistrate, for the woman but that the
magistrate refused to take further congnizance of the case,
thus making Prigg helpless to execute the law of 1793 which
depended on state functionaries. Thus he apprehended the
woman and returned her to her mistress in Maryland. The
Supreme Court decided that if Congress has constitutional
powers to regulate a particular subject, then the state legislatures have no right to interfere. The Act of 1793 was
a constitutional exercise of power to protect the slave-
holding states in the enjoyment of their rights. Hence,
every state law that interfered with a person when peace-
ably removing a servant bound to service was unconstitutional and void.[41]

It was quite generally held that the Constitution did not
compel the officers of a State to assist in capturing fugitive
slaves.[42] Justice Story in giving the verdict on Prigg said
that State magistrates could not be forced into action. All
the while there was a growing indisposition on the part of
the States to cooperate with the law.[43]

As a result of the decision of *Prigg* v. *Pennsylvania* there
was greater activity among the slave hunters. This activ-

[41] Commanger, *Documents of American History*, pp. 292-294, no.
158. Cf. Davis, *JNH*, 9 (1924), 24; Richard Peters, *Report of the
Case of Edward Prigg against the Commonwealth of Pennsylvania*
(Philadelphia: stereotyped by L. Johnson, 1842.)

[42] McDougall, *op. cit.*, p. 17.

[43] Commanger, *Documents of American History*, p. 293; cf. Wilson,
History of Rise and Fall of Slave Power in America, I: 469 ff;
McDougall, *op. cit.*, p. 28.

ity promoted the growth of the Underground Railroad.[44]

One of the earliest mentions of conspiracy to aid fugitives is found in a letter written by George Washington in 1786 concerning the case of a resident of Alexandria, whose slave a society of Quakers in Philadelphia attempted to liberate.[45] The Quakers are also responsible for the first attempts to organize for the protection of runaways.[46]

From time to time, as the number of runaways increased, new agencies constantly were established until there was a perfect chain of stations arranged—from the slave States to Canada—with not more than one day's journey apart.[47] The underground railroad was a mysterious organization which made it a business to rescue, forward, conceal and protect fugitives.[48] The term arose when those pursuing fugitives reached an abyss beyond which they could not see, said there must be an underground railroad somewhere.[49]

Formal organization of the Underground Railroad came in 1838 when Robert Purvis was made president.[50] Both colored and white agents worked in the system.[51] Great secrecy was observed, only two or three persons at the station having knowledge of the workings of the system.[52] The fugitives themselves were very careful not to reveal the method of their escape.[53]

[44] David, *JNH*, 9 (1924), 25.

[45] *The Negro in Virginia*, p. 128.

[46] Robert C. Smedley, *History of the Underground Railroad in Chester and Neighboring Counties in Pennsylvania* (Lancaster, Pa.: Office of the Journal, 1883), p. 25 ff.

[47] Siebert, *The Underground Railroad from Slavery to Freedom* chap. 2; cf. Henrietta Henkle, *Let My People Go* (New York: Harper & Bros. 1841).

[48] McDougall, *Fugitive Slaves*, p. 60.

[49] Smedley, *op. cit.*, pp. 34 f.

[50] *Ibid.*, p. 35.

[51] Siebert, *op. cit.*, p. 69.

[52] McDougall, *op. cit.*, p. 63.

[53] Frederick Douglass, *My Bondage and Freedom* (New York: Miller, Orton & Mulligan, 1855), p. 362.

Great courage and calmness was needed to conduct the fugitives.[54] In this they were so successful that one discouraged slave-hunter once said it was "as easy to find a needle in a hay mow as a Negro among the Quakers."[55]

After being smuggled across the borders the fugitives would arrive half-fed and half-clothed. They were fed and dressed in a disguise quite often that of a Quaker.[56] They were then sent to the next station usually on foot with a piece of paper containing a word or two which would be recognized at the next station.[57] Sometimes the slaves would borrow the protection papers from a free man, as was done by Frederick Douglass. Other times the fugitives, if they were of light complexion, would disguise themselves as whites.[58]

This system was the means of relieving the South of many of its despairing citizens. As soon as a leader arose, who would not be able to bear the yoke of slavery, he went to the North. Had they not done so, there might have been many dire scenes in the South.[59] On the other hand, the South lost millions of dollars in slave property. It is difficult to give figures for they vary considerably. But, along Ohio's southern boundary where there was an initial start of twelve routes it is estimated that between 1830 and 1860 not less than 40,000 were assisted.[60]

[54] Smedley, *op. cit.*, p. 34.

[55] Smedley, *op. cit.*, p. 146.

[56] Siebert, *op. cit.*, p. 64. Cf. Levi Coffin, *Reminiscences* (Western Tract Society: Cincinnati, 1876); this work contains reminiscences of Levi Coffin, an important leader of the Underground Railroad. It is a brief history of the labors of a lifetime in behalf of slaves, with stories of numerous fugitives who gained their freedom through his instrumentality.

[57] Smedley, *op. cit.*, pp. 64, 138; Siebert, *op. cit.*, p. 62.

[58] McDougall, *op. cit.*, pp. 58-60.

[59] Siebert, *op. cit.*, p. 340; cf. George W. Williams, *History of the Negro Race in America, from 1619-1880.* (2 vols. New York: G. P. Putnam's Son, 1883), 2: 58 f.

[60] Siebert, *op. cit.*, p. 341; William Siebert, "The Light on the Underground Railroad," *AHR*, 1 (1895-1896), 462 f.

The tremendous controversy over fugitives was one of the important causes which eventually led to the Civil War.

Turning the discussion towards the slaves themselves, one finds that as long as the families stayed together love acted as a stronghold to bind them together. But after the sale or separation of the members of the family there was no tie to hold them to the South.[61] Some escaped simply because of their thirst to gain liberty, even though they had kind masters.[62] But the most frequent reason given by the slaves was cruelty, which they claimed was excessive.[63] A third general reason was fear of being sold to the deep South under merciless masters in the rice swamps and the cotton fields.[64]

The continued activity of the abolitionists and the improved facilities of the Underground Railroad, resulted in bitter speeches by southern representatives demanding the protection of their property by the northern states. One of the famous cases that led to the new fugitive slave bill of 1850 was that of George Latimer. In 1842 a Virginia sheriff seized in Boston Latimer, who belonged to James Gray of Norfolk. Four thousand people gathered around the hall where he was being held to protest his being returned to slavery. The Bostonians took an oath that Latimer would never return and make James Gray seek police guard. Four hundred dollars was raised by popular subscription and forced on Gray as a payment for Latimer.[65]

[61] William Still, *The Underground Railroad* (Philadelphia: Porter and Coates, 1872), p. 443. This work contained a record of facts narratives, letters, etc., telling of the hardships, hairbreath escapes, and death struggles of the slaves in their effort for freedom, as related by themselves and others, and witnessed by the author; together with sketches of some of the largest stockholders and advisors of the railroad.

[62] McDougall, *Fugitive Slaves*, p. 54.

[63] Still, *op. cit., passim.* Cf. Anna L. Curtis, *Stories of the Underground Railroad* (New York: The Island Workshop Press co-op, Inc., 1941).

[64] Still, *op. cit., passim.*

[65] *The Negro in Virginia,* p. 130.

This brought on new agitation in Congress for a more stringent law. Such a bill was passed and was signed by President Fillmore on September 18, 1850.[66]

The new law was based on the Act of 1793 but contained some new regulations. Commissioners were to be chosen by the circuit courts of the United States and superior courts of the territories to act with the judges of these courts in fugitive slave cases. Such commissioners could be fined one thousand dollars for refusing to serve a writ, and were liable for the value of any slave escaping from them. The testimony required for rendition of the fugitive was an official declaration of the fact of escape of the slave by two witnesses, and establishment of his identity by oath. The testimony of the accused could not be admitted. The right of trial by jury was not admitted, and therefore practically denied. The sheriff might call on any bystander for help, and the penalty for harboring or aiding in a rescue was increased from five hundred to one thousand dollars, and imprisonment of not more than six months. Should the slaves escape, damages to the same amount were to be paid to the claimant. If mob violence were feared, military force could be employed; the fee of the commissioner was to be increased from five to ten dollars when the case was decided in favor of the claimant.[67]

A test case of the law took place in Boston shortly after it was passed. It concerned a Negro from Virginia, called Shodrack, who was arrested in Boston on February 15, 1851 in the Cornhill Coffee House. He was rushed to the court house in a waiter's uniform. He shouted that he would not go back to Virginia while he had breath in his body. Five prominent lawyers obtained a delay so that they could prepare a defense. At the court's adjournment a crowd of sympathetic colored persons surrounded the prisoner and

[66] *U. S. Statutes at Large*, 9: 462-465.
[67] *U. S. Statutes at Large*, 9: 462-465. Cf. Wilson, *Slave Power*, 2: 302-329; McDougall, *op. cit.*, pp. 31-33.

fled with him.[68]

The law quite generally was very unpopular. Many formerly indifferent persons were aroused to the point that they considered the law unjust. The cases recorded show to what great extent the people could be aroused when a fugitive was captured. Sometimes these mobs were impromptu while sometimes they were premeditated plots to prevent the capture. The persons taking part in these attempts were often brought to court but usually the judge on some pretext failed to prosecute.[69] There were sermons and speeches made by the members of the abolition movement to the effect that the Fugitive Slave Law was immoral.[70]

Perhaps the attitude of Catholics can be gleaned from an article written by Orestes Brownson. He says:

> For us Catholics, the Fugitive Slave law presents no sort of difficulty. We are taught to respect and obey the government as the ordinance of God in all things not declared to be repugnant to the divine law.[71]

He pointed out in the article that the abolitionists held that the Fugitive Slave Law was contrary to the law of God and contended that they did not have to obey it. He agreed that any law contrary to the divine law is a violence rather than a law and consequently does not have to be observed. But he asked how this could be determined.

[68] *The Negro in Virginia*, p. 131; cf. *Ibid.*, for case of Anthony Burns.

[69] McDougall, *op. cit.*, pp. 43-52.

[70] Cf. Rev. Nathaniel Clover, *The Fugitive Slave Bill or God's Laws Paramount to the Laws of Men* (Boston: J. W. Hewes & Co., 1850). This sermon was preached on Sunday, Oct. 20, 1850, in the Tremont St. Baptist Church in Boston. Theodore Parker, "The Chief Sins of the People," sermon delivered in Boston on April 10, 1851; Lydia Maria Child, *The Duty of Disobedience to the Fugitive Slave Act* (Boston: American Anti-Slavery Society, 1860).

[71] Brownson, "The Higher Law," *Works*, 17: 114 ff. Cf. *Ibid.*, "The Fugitive Slave Law," 17-39; "Sumner on Fugitive Slaves," 39-53.

The Protestants answer, he said, "by private judgment," but the difficulty is that would place the individual above the state, and private judgment above law, and is thus wholly incompatible with the concept of civil government. Such would be anarchy. Catholics have a public authority, the Church, which, being inerrable, can never be oppressive, and which is an authority higher than the state.[72] But since the Church had never decreed that to return fugitives is *per se* contrary to the law of God, ". . . we are bound to obey the law and could not, without resisting the ordinance of God and purchasing to ourselves damnation, refuse to obey it. This settles the question for us."[73]

III. WAYS OF OBTAINING LIBERTY

The teaching of the theologians. Kenrick said very little about slaves obtaining their liberty. He merely noted that people are to be praised who, from a motive of humanity or religion give liberty to their slaves by manumitting them, when this can be done with their own utility and without detriment to the country.[74]

Many theologians go into the question more thoroughly. They note that slaves are liberated by manumissions,

[72] *Ibid.*, pp. 6-14.

[73] *Ibid.*, p. 15.

[74] Kenrick, *Theologia moralis*, tr. 5, cap. 6, no. 40. In the first edition he omitted the qualification about the utility of the slaves and the possible detriment to the country, but added that it is praiseworthy to manumit them when there is an opportunity to send them to Liberia in Africa. He further added that by order of the Apostolic See two priests from his diocese had already sailed there to give religious counsel to the members of this colony. Cf. 1840 ed., tr. 5, cap. 6, no. 39, p. 258.

Kenrick in his chapter on things that can be owned has a special paragraph on slaves. In a rather haphazard manner he throws together quotations from various laws. Amongst the various state laws of this country he rather unexpectedly says that the civil law gives the slaves action against their masters if they say that they have been redeemed by their own money and not manumitted according to promise. This, however, refers to Roman Law. Cf. Kenrick, *op. cit.*, tr. 10, cap. 4, no. 48.

whether given gratis or by price paid by the slaves themselves, or by a third party.[75] Once a slave has made a contract with his master to obtain his liberty on the payment
of a certain sum of money, the obligation of fulfilling the
contract is binding in conscience, even though it does not
bind in civil law. For, while the slave because of the condition of slavery has no civil rights, he *does* have natural
rights that must be respected.[76]

State laws concerning manumission. The States of
Kentucky, Missouri, Virginia and Maryland gave greater
facility for emancipating.[77] Some states imposed restrictions and penalties. In North Carolina, by the Act of 1777,
manumissions were permitted only for meritorious services,
the value of which was to be judged by the court of the
county. If the permission of the court were not obtained,
any free preson could arrest the manumitted slave and
bring him to the sheriff. The court would then order him
to be sold at auction, one-fifth of the sale price going to
the one apprehending the slave, and the remaining four-
fifths going to the county treasury.[78]

In Georgia,[79] Alabama[80] and South Carolina[81] an owner
could not emancipate his slaves except by the authority of
the legislature specifically granted. Penalties were inflicted
on those who attempted to emancipate their slaves without
the consent of the legislature. For example, in Georgia
there was a fine of two hundred dollars levied on the master, half of which went to the county and the other half

[75] Molina, *De justitia et jure*, I, tr. 2, disp. 38; Diana, *Resolutiones
morales*, VII, tr. 8, resol. 24, p. 278, resol. 26, p. 298.

[76] Diana, *op. cit.*, VII, tr. 8. resol. 61; Molina, *op. cit.*, I, tr. 2, disp.
38. The older theologians also noted many ways of obtaining freedom
granted by the existing law—Roman and Canonical—of the day. Cf.
Diana, *op. cit.*, VII, tr. 8, resol. 18-25; Molina, *op. cit.*, I, tr. 2, disp.
38; Sanchez, *Opus morale*, I, lib. 2, cap. 24, no. 9-23.

[77] Stroud, *A Sketch of Laws Pertaining to Slavery*, p. 98.

[78] *Haywood's Manual*, pp. 525, 529, and 537.

[79] Act of Dec. 5, 1801, *Prince's Digest*, p. 787.

[80] Act of July 20, 1805, *Toulmin's Digest*, p. 632.

[81] Act of 1820, *James' Digest*, p. 398.

to the informer, and the slave was held in slavery.[82] In
Mississippi, masters were forbidden by law to emancipate
their slaves by will.[83]

How Slaves were freed. While in some cases the Negroes preferred shelter and support to responsibility, the
whole trend of the slave codes rested on the belief that
the normal frame of mind of the slaves was a desire for
freedom. This is further substantiated by the testimony
of countless fugitives, who ran away just to be free.[84]

The majority of the free Negroes received that status
by manumission. The process was quite restricted. Usually
the owner had to give a preliminary bond to protect the
community against future support of the slave, and the
process had to follow legal form. In more than one-half of
the states the emancipated slave had to move from the
state. No master could free himself from debt or contract
obligation by freeing his slave. For the latter could then
be subjected to attachment by his creditors.[85]

Many slaves of the period bought themselves by money
they acquired by work or gift. But buying one's self was
subject to such accidents as death or the forgetfulness of
the master. There is a case recorded where a slave saved
enough money three times to buy himself and was sold regardless of agreement.[86]

To buy one's self was often a task of between eight and
ten years. Frequently the purpose of a slave hiring himself out was to earn money with which to buy his freedom.
Good-natured masters put a modest price on them or gave
them opportunities to earn extra money.[87] Gifts given to
the slaves were used for buying freedom likewise. Money
gifts were not uncommon especially at Christmas time, when

---

[82] *Prince's Digest*, p. 787.

[83] *Miss. Revised Statutes* (1848), p. 540.

[84] Hart, *Slavery and Abolition*, p. 135.

[85] Hurd, *Law of Freedom and Bondage*, chaps. 17-19, *passim*.

[86] Goodell, *Slave Code*, p. 247.

[87] Hart, *Slavery and Abolition*, p. 131; Olmsted, *Seaboard States*,
p. 155 f.

tobacco, clothing and molasses were liberally dealt out sometimes to the value of ten dollars per slave.[88] Likewise, slaves
earned considerable sums by working on Sunday. On some
plantations the Negroes were allowed to keep bees, or sell
small articles made. The right to keep truck-patches was
highly appreciated.[89] One of the favorite charities of the
period was to furnish money to fugitives for their purchase.[90]

The manumitted slave. The objection against liberating
slaves might be listed under two headings, namely, harm
to society and harm to the manumitted slaves.

As early as 1784 a petition was signed by forty-five persons of Accomoc County in Virginia listing four reasons
why slaves should not be manumitted. They are: 1) manumitted slaves had helped other slaves to join the British;
2) manumission would depreciate the value of slave property and thus lessen revenue; 3) manumissions should be
reserved as a means of rewarding slaves for good conduct;
4) free Negroes easily become charges on the public.[91]

As the influx of free Negroes increased, the whites became more and more apprehensive. The grounds for these
apprehensions were of several sorts, but the general idea
was that through vagrancy, vice and indolence the Negroes
would be an economic burden; that exclusion from white
circles would make them discontent; that their sense of
grievance would ally them with slaves in plots of upheaval;
if they were educated and free to travel they would become
effective conspirators. Thus the forced slavery of all Negroes had brought on the idea of the servility of the race.
They were looked upon as addicted to sexual crimes, ignorant and indolent, and hence not fit to take their place
beside the white man in American society.[92]

[88] Olmsted, *Seaboard Slave States*, pp. 101-103.
[89] Hart, *Slavery and Abolition*, pp. 104 f.
[90] *Ibid.*, p. 132.
[91] *The Negro in Virginia*, p. 114.
[92] Phillips, *American Negro Slavery*, p. 2; Hart, *Slavery and Abolition*, pp. 104-108.

On the other side, there was great danger that if the Negroes were emancipated they might be kidnapped. This
was especially dangerous since they had little redress
through law.[93]

As a result of this thinking, many considered manumission a doubtful blessing, namely, because of the economic difficulties, and because it was full of spiritual dangers for the Negroes. Kenrick in the early edition of his
Theologia moralis wrote that it is praiseworthy through
religious motives to free the slaves, provided there is opportunity for them to go to Liberia.[94]

Possibly some of the Negroes themselves agreed with
this reasoning, for Bishop England claimed that he knew
slaves who had refused their liberty.[95]

Actually, manumission brought to the Negro in the South
not freedom but a halfway status having many of the sor-
rowful incidents of slavery.[96] In four of the states, the free
Negro had to have official guardians; in eight states he
had to be registered; in general, his testimony was not
accepted against a white person. In some places he was
forbidden to sell drugs, in others, wheat and tobacco, in
others to peddle market produce or to own a boat; in
several, from entering from elsewhere; in others, if set
free he had to move from the State.[97]

A setback was given to the manumitted slave in 1857
by the Supreme Court of the United States. As a result
of the decision given in the Dred Scott case, no Negro could
become a citizen of the United States. The court held that
African Negroes had never been recognized in American
law and customs as persons. This overruled the decision
of the Circuit Court that Negro blood was no bar to citizen-

---

[93] Phillips, *American Negro Slavery*, p. 443; Olmsted, *Seaboard
States*, pp. 95 f.

[94] Kenrick, *op. cit.*, 1840 ed., tr. V, cap. VI, no. 39.

[95] *Works*, (Messmer) 5: 194.

[96] Hart, *Slavery and Abolition*, p. 84.

[97] Hurd, *Laws of Freedom and Bondage*, 2: chaps. 17-19.

ship. The Court claimed that Negroes were regarded in the Constitution as only chattel property; were not included in the word "people" or "citizen" in the Declaration of Independence, the Articles of Confederation, or the Constitution; they remained in this condition of civil nullity even when emancipated, had no rights except such as each State might choose to grant them within that State and could not become citizens capable of suing and being sued. The written decision was not publicized until March 6, 1857. This decision remained the law of the United States and acted as an irremovable barrier to granting civil rights to the colored race until after the passage of the fourteenth amendment.[98]

Moreover, even if the free Negro desired to support himself and his family respectably, he rarely had an opportunity to do so, for dislike and suspicion were against him everywhere, and the moment he ogt away from the place where he was known he found himself in danger of being kidnapped.[99]

It was frequently charged that free Negroes were criminals "the very drones and pests of society."[100]

By 1840 this trend toward regarding the free Negro as having a lower status had become prevalent even in the benevolent slave-holding states. Just before the Civil War,

[98] *Howard Rep.* 393-633. Cf. William T. Alexander, *History of the Colored Race in America* (New Orleans: Palmetto Pub. Co., 1887), pp. 213-229; *EA*, 9: 322 f. Samuel Tyler, *Memoir of Roger Brooks Taney* (Baltimore: John Murphy & Co., 1872), discusses the case and its political background. Cf. pp. 359-390, for the majority opinion issued by the Chief Justice as well as the supplement, which he issued on Sept. 1858, p. 518-608; E. S. Corwin, "The Dred Scott Decision in the Light of Contemporary Legal Documents," *AHR*, 17 (1911), 52-69; Brownson, *Works*, 17: 91-93, where he disagrees with the court ruling that members of the African race are not citizens; W. H. Smith, *A Political History of Slavery* (2 vols.; New York and London: Knickerbocker Press, 1903), I: 242 ff.

[99] Hart, *Slavery and Abolition*, p. 88.

[100] Dew, *Pro-slavery Argument*, p. 422.

practically no consideration in the South and very little in the North was given to him.[101]

It may be noted that a Negro acquiring freedom by manumission or purchase could hold slaves. Frequently after a person was liberated, he tried to buy his family. But after he bought them, unless he formally manumitted them they would be regarded as his slaves, by the law. Hence, there were cases recorded where children became liable for the debts of the father and were taken into bondage. However, quite often in such cases the legislature came to the rescue.[102] The census always listed as slaves the children of a manumitted slave who had bought them, if they were not legally manumitted.[103]

Benevolent Negroes purchased other slaves besides their own relatives to make their lot easier by granting them freedom for a nominal sum or permitting them to work it out on liberal terms. Even the Negro given to exploitation who held slaves would at times feel the sting of conscience and liberate his slaves.[104]

True, some Negro owners had a bad reputation of cruelty toward their own slaves, and some Negro slaveholders of the South competed with the whites in the number of slaves held. Most of these lived in Louisiana, South Carolina, Maryland, and Virginia. Excepting those who lived in Louisiana, most of these lived in urban areas.[105]

Freed slaves to Liberia. Many leaders quite early picturing a number of difficulties arising from the increasing

[101] Association for the Study of Negro life and History, "Free Negro Owners of Slaves in the United States in 1830," *JNH*, 9 (1924), 43.

[102] Hart, *Slavery and Abolition*, p. 77; Brackett, *The Negro in Maryland*, p. 168; Olmsted, *Seaboard States*, p. 126.

[103] Association for Study of Negro Life and History, *JNH*, 9 (1924), 41.

[104] *Ibid.*, p. 42.

[105] *JNH*, 9 (1924), 43. Carter G. Woodson, *Free Negro Heads of Families in the United States in 1830* (Washington: the Association for the Study of Negro Life and History, 1924), *passim.*

number of free Negroes, began to think of establishing a separate colony where the manumitted slaves could live in peace and happiness. Some even proposed the possibility of using some of the land in the West for this purpose, but so many objections were immediately raised that such a plan was hardly given any consideration. The thoughts then turned to Africa.

The first emigration of colored people from the United States to Africa was conducted by Paul Cuffee in 1815. There were forty persons in his party.[106] In 1816 the American Colonization Society was founded for the purpose of colonizing free people of color in the United States.[107]

By an Act of Congress of March 3, 1819, the President of the United States was authorized to restore Africans captured from American or foreign vessels attempting to introduce them into the United States contrary to the law. It provided for the setting up on the coast of Africa a suitable agency for giving comfort to these people until they could be restored to their homes. The American Colonization Society decided to make the station of the government the site of the colonial establishment.[108]

In February of the year 1820, the Reverend Samuel Bacon went to Africa as the principal agent of the United States. He was accompanied by John P. Bankson, as his assistant, and Dr. Samuel A. Crozer, the agent of the American Colonization Society and eighty-eight emigrants. Unfortunately, most of them died of fever. This only induced the society

[106] G. S. Stockwell, *The Republic of Liberia* (New York: Barnes & Co., 1868), p. 55.

[107] Early Lee Fox, *The American Colonization Society, 1817-1840.* Johns Hopkins University Studies in History and Political Sciences, Series 37, no. 3; (Baltimore: Johns Hopkins Univ. Press, 1919), p. 50.

[108] Stockwell, *op. cit.*, p. 57. Cf. John Hanson Thomas McPherson, *History of Liberia* (Baltimore: Johns Hopkins Press, 1891); William Innes, *Liberia*, (or the Early History and signal Preservation of the American Colony of Free Negroes on the Coast of Africa) (Edinburgh: Waugh and Innis, 1831) a work based on American documents.

to more determined action. In November of 1820, Dr. Ayres was instructed to go to Sierra Leone to look for a suitable place. Captain Stocton of the United States Schooner, Alligator, was ordered to Africa to assist. After much difficulty, they obtained a valuable tract of land which included Cape Montserado.[109]

When the emigrants arrived the natives wanted to change their minds about giving them the land. The tribes were inimical because they realized that the colony was inimical to the slave trade.[110] A colony was finally established on the west coast of Africa and called Liberia. Its habitable area is between ten and twelve miles wide along an indented shore of three hundred fifty miles. The entire area of the colony is about 9,700 square miles.[111]

Besides the struggles with the native tribes there were many internal struggles. Some difficulties were experienced from jealousies of the colonists and from their refusal to work.[112] Another setback was the constant change of leaders due to resignations caused by ill-health or disgust.[113]

Little by little more colonists arrived. For example, on February 13, 1824, a group of one hundred and five emigrants mostly from Petersburg Virginia reached the colony, and on March 13, 1825 there were sixty-six more.[114] Meanwhile the little colony suffered from sickness, lack of

[109] Stockwell, *op. cit.*, pp. 59 f.

[110] *Ibid.*

[111] Thomas Meehan, "Liberia," *CE* 9: 216 f.

[112] Carey, *Letter to Mercer*, pp. 9-12; Stockell, *op. cit.*, pp. 71-75; for a refutation of some of these charges cf. Wilson Armistead, *Calumny Refuted by Facts from Liberia* (New York: W. Harned, Anti-slavery Office, 1848), which contains extracts from statements of leaders of Liberia.

[113] George Washington William, *History of the Negro Race in America from 1619-1880* (New York: G. P. Putnam's Sons, 1883), where an account is given of the government of Sierra Leone and Liberia.

[114] Stockwell, *op. cit.*, pp. 75 and 79. Cf. *The Negro in Virginia*, p. 118 ff, for some scenes about Negroes leaving for Liberia.

medical supplies and improper diet. The death rate was high.[115]

Nevertheless, the colony attempted to develop a navy and militia, a government,[116] commerce and agriculture.[117] Liberia continued to be managed by the American Colonization Society until commercial needs forced it to make its declaration as a sovereign state on July 26, 1847.[118] Later, its independence was recognized by the various powers.[119]

Bishop England had hoped that the Provincial Council of 1829 would take cognizance of the work of the American Society for the Colonization of Free People of Color in the United States which established the State of Liberia.[120] Since a number of the first colonists were Catholics from Maryland and the adjoining localities, the attention of the Holy See was called to the needs of these people.[121] Shea refers to the correspondence between Cardinal Maio and Archbishop Whitfield concerning the condition of these people. This eventually led to the establishment of a mission there.[122]

This mission was established by the second Council of Baltimore which took place in 1833.[123] Bishop Hughes as-

[115] James Washington Lugenbeel, *Sketches of Liberia* (Washington, D.C.: C. Alexander, 1850), which is a brief account of the geography, climate, products and diseases of Liberia.

[116] Cf. Charles Henry Huberick, *The Political and Legislative History of Liberia,* (New York: Central Book Co., Inc. 1947).

[117] George William Brown, *The Economic History of Liberia,* (Washington: The Associated Publishers, Inc., 1941).

[118] Meehan, *CE*, 9: 217.

[119] *Treaties, Conventions Concluded between Liberia and the Foreign Powers, 1848-1892* (Monrovia: Published by the Department of State, 1906).

[120] Guilday, *England*, 2: 275.

[121] Meehan, *CE*, 9: 217.

[122] John Gilmary Shea, *History of the Catholic Church within the Limits of the United States from the First Attempted Colonization to the Present Time,* (4 vols.; New York: J. G. Shea, 1886-1892), 3: 432.

[123] Guilday, *England*, 2: 274-276. Decree VI of the Council of 1833

signed the Reverend J. Kelly of Albany, who had volunteered, to the work in Liberia. He was to accompany the Very Rev. Dr. Barron of Philadelphia.[124] It seems that Denis Pindar, a lay catechist of Baltimore also joined the mission.[125]

They sailed from Baltimore on December 2, 1841 and the first Mass was said at Cape Palmas on February 10, 1842. Not receiving more missionaries, Father Barron returned to the United States thence to Rome where on January 22, 1842, he was made vicar apostolic of the two Guineas and titular bishop of Constantia. Returning with seven priests of the Congregation of the Holy Spirit, he arrived at Cape Palmas on November 30, 1843. Three of the five died of fever, as also did the catechist a few months later.[126] The Letter of the Provincial Council of Baltimore of 1843 to the Pope mentioned as one of the signs of progress the mission undertaken in Liberia.[127]

Bishop Barron and Father Kelly held out for two years more, then wasted by fever they determined to return to the United States, feeling it impossible to withstand the climate any longer. The Holy Ghost Fathers took it over for two years, then the work there lapsed until 1884 when it was taken over for two years again. Then it lapsed from

asked that the colony of Liberia be placed under the care of the Jesuits. The Letter of Cardinal Pedicini written on July 26, 1834 approved the petition. Cf. *Concilia Provincialia Baltimori Habita*, p. 108. The Jesuits never took up the work of that mission.

[124] *The Catholic Advocate*, 6 (Nov. 6, 1841), 317.

[125] Meehan, *CE*, 9: 217.

[126] Meehan, *CE*, 9: 217.

[127] Shea, History of the Catholic Church, 3: 461; Guilday, *History of the Councils*, p. 140. Shea says further that after Father Barron was made a bishop the mission of Liberia was heartily seconded by Bishop Kenrick, and some of his priests volunteered for the work and collections were taken up for the cause. Cf. Shea, *op. cit.*, 3: 568. *RACHS*, 14 (1903), 89-91 gives several letters between Father Kelly and Bishop Kenrick, principally about finances; *Cath. Hist. Researches*, 7 (1890), 105; 11 (1894), 35.

1886 to 1906 when the Propaganda gave it over to the priests of the African Missions (Lyons).[128]

IV. Theft or Damnification to Masters

Kenrick and the theologians. Kenrick taught that slaves sin if they fail to do the work assigned to them or if they neglect things committed to their care. But they do not violate justice but obedience owed to their masters. He also pointed out that those slaves who spend the night running around to visit girls sin not only by impurity and by placing themselves in the occasion of other dangers, but also are guilty of wrong-doing to their masters in so far as they are unable to work properly the following day, having spent the night without sleep.[129]

This agrees with Lessius, who taught that actions of slaves are not owed to the master by the law of justice as hired servants who work for a salary, hence, they are not obliged in conscience to make restitution if they work negligently.[130]

While Diana did not treat this problem expressly he seems to have held that the relation of slave and master is on the basis of justice. For in claiming that a slave may gamble with money or property that he owns, and keeps what he gains, said that if by so doing the master is deprived of labor the slave is held to restore what it is estimated that the master lost by the labor and no more.[131]

Kenrick held that if slaves take things that are used in the house for their maintenance, the consent of the master is often presumed and thus they are not to be urged to make restitution. It would seem that here he referred to foods that they would take to eat later. But he also mentioned that slaves sin more easily by taking things from

[128] Meehan, *CE*, 9: 217.

[129] Kenrick, *Theologia moralis*, tr. 8, cap. 4, no. 104. Here again Kenrick, inconsistent with his definition, does not place the relationship between slave and master on justice.

[130] Lessius, *De justitia et jure*, sec. 2, cap. 8, dub. 3, no. 20.

[131] Diana, *Resolutiones morales.* VII, tr. 8, resol. 19, p. 299.

their master to waste upon their friends. But, he continued, since they very rarely had a *peculium,* it would seem to be restitution enough if they would work more diligently to advance the profits of their master.[132] In another tract, he said that slaves are hardly expected to make compensation for damages by theft from the *peculium* that they have, since their whole life is used for the utility of the master.[133]

De Lugo judged that there is no grave sin if the thefts are small so that the master would not be thought to be unwilling.[134] Diana held that as long as it is a matter of food and drink, even a large quantity would not be thought to be sinful for in this the master would be more displeased at the manner of taking than the taking itself. It would be presumed that he would give such things if he were asked. But, if such foods and drinks would be taken for purposes that they know the master would not allow and hence would not concede permission, such as drinking parties, gambling and the like, then they would be thefts. If the act is sinful then the quantity required for serious sin would be the same as for a stranger.[135] If, on the other hand, the thefts do not concern food and drink but other things, then the slaves can easily sin mortally and are bound to restitution.[136]

Moreover, Kenrick taught that if a slave causes damage to the goods of another, he may not take from his master in order to make restitution.[137] But it seems that the law, he said, forces masters to restore what the slaves have taken.[138]

---

[132] Kenrick, *op. cit.,* tr. 8, cap. 4, no. 104.

[133] Kenrick, *op. cit.,* tr. 10, cap. 4, no. 48.

[134] De Lugo, *De justitia et jure,* I, disp. 3, sec. 3, no. 66.

[135] Diana, *op. cit.,* VII, tr. 8, resol. 45, p. 304.

[136] Diana, *op. cit.,* VII, tr. 8, resol. 14.

[137] Kenrick, *op. cit.,* tr. 8, cap. 4, no. 104.

[138] Kenrick, *op. cit.,* tr. X, cap. IV, no. 48. As a sample he refers to the Mississippi Act of June 18, 1822, sec. 56: "The master, employer, or overseer of such slave, shall restore the goods and chattels so stolen to the owner."

It might be mentioned here that in treating of the obligations of masters to give their slaves sufficient food Kenrick pointed out that in many instances the master gave the slaves no meat, thus allowing an occasion for stealing to arise.[139]

Stealing in Practice. While all authors seem to agree that the slaves did steal, there seems to be considerable difference about the extent of it. The Negro author, Williams,[140] says that petty stealing and persistent prevarication were prompted by hunger and fear, not by the Negro's inherent inclination. He says that it was due to the demolition of the family altar by the slaveholder. But, many masters believed that "the Negroes were so addicted to lying and stealing that they were not to be trusted out of sight or hearing.[141] Again, there was a complaint that slaves were guilty of injustice because of their shiftlessness, waste of their master's property, neglect of animals, and the like, which they claimed was almost proverbial.[142] Yet Olmsted observed that slaves often showed themselves worthy of trust, when their masters were kind and considerate toward them.[143]

He further pointed out that many petty traders along the coast encouraged the Negroes to steal. Then at night they would buy things thus stolen and still under the cover of darkness sail away with it. Ferquently the Negroes immediately spent the money thus obtained for whiskey.[144]

By law the masters were obliged to make restitution for things stolen by their slaves from other persons,[145] and might be prosecuted criminally for damages by theft of their

---

[139] Kenrick, *op. cit.*, tr. 8, cap. 4, no. 93.

[140] George Washington Williams, *Negro Troops in the War of Rebellion* (New York: Harper Bros., 1888), p. 169.

[141] Harper, *Pro-Slavery Argument*, p. 46.

[142] *Ibid.*, pp. 38-41.

[143] Olmsted, Seaboard States, p. 447.

[144] *Ibid.*, p. 674; Hart, *Slavery and Abolition*, p. 118.

[145] Miss. Act of June 18, 1822, sec. 55.

slaves.[146] But a master was not liable for injuries caused
by the negligent conduct of the slave when such slave was
not acting in his employment and under his authority.[147]

V. PROPERTY OF SLAVES

Kenrick and the theologians. In a short section in his
tract on the various persons or groups holding dominium,
Kenrick treated of the dominium of slaves over property.[148]

Kenrick, as was often his custom, because of his great
reverence for Roman law, bases much of his discussion of
this point on Roman law and then lets this love for law
flow into American law. He noted that by Roman law the
slaves had no civil rights but not so with natural rights, for
when these latter are concerned, all men are equal. Originally the slaves owned nothing, and whatever they acquired, in any manner whatsoever, they acquired for their
master. But this rigor had become somewhat mitigated by
custom, and as a result slaves could have some *peculium*
by consent of their master. Hence, he judged that slaves
may acquire things for themselves in the following manners: 1) whatever they earn at night after their daily
labors are completed. He noted, however, that they are not
allowed to tire themselves out by such work so that they
are rendered unfit for their daily tasks; 2) under the system where slaves are permitted to hire themselves out, and
are required to give to their masters a certain sum of money
each month, they may keep whatever they earn by greater

[146] *Moffit* v. *Vion* (Mar. Term, 1833), 5 La. Rep. 346, Wheeler,
Practical Treatise in the Laws of Slavery, p. 234. *Caldwell* v. *Sacra*
(Spring Term) 6 Littell's Rep. 118, Wheeler, *op. cit.*, p. 235.

[147] *Cawthorn* v. *Deas* (June Term, 1835) 2 Porter's Rep. 276,
Wheeler, *op. cit.*, p. 236.

[148] Kenrick, *Theologia moralis*, tr. X, cap. III, no. 48.

[149] By yielding her body, the girl sins seriously but if money is
offered she may take it as a compensation for the inconvenience suffered. She may keep it because the master has no dominium over
her body.

industry or cleverness; 3) girls may keep money given for the illicit use of their bodies, for this does not lie under the power of the master;[149] 4) gifts given to slaves for their use by the will of the donors.[150]

The theologians are in perfect agreement with what Kenrick has said and in fact some even add other means whereby slaves could acquire property.

While all the theologians agree that slaves in certain cases may acquire dominium of some sort over things they do, they disagree as to what type of dominium this is. Some say that all slaves may acquire an absolute dominium in the certain cases given. As a result, the master cannot take such goods away without injustice to the slaves, and if they are thus fraudulently taken, the slaves may use occult compensation. Regarding the contrary regulation of Roman law, these had been, they judged, abrogated and mitigated by custom in the favor of the slaves.[151]

Perhaps the issue is made clearer by those who say that the principle that whatever is acquired is acquired for the master, is to be understood as whatever is acquired by works *owed* to the master goes to him, for the contrary custom has been mitigated.[152]

In the following matters, the slave can acquire dominium over material things, according to the theologians, whether this be perfect or imperfect. 1) Things given to him, which he is permitted to have by tacit or express consent of the master.[153] 2) That which is given to a slave by a legacy with the express condition that he alone possess it and that it should pertain to the master in no manner what-

---

[150] *Ibid.*

[151] Diana, *Resolutiones morales*, VII, tr. 8, resol. 31, p. 300; Molina, *De justitia et jure*, disp. 38; Lessius, *De justitia et jure*, sec. I, cap. IV, dub. IV, Migne, *TCC* 15: 480.

[152] Diana, *op. cit.*, VII, tr. 8, resol. 19, p. 299.

[153] Lessius, *op. cit.*, sec. I, cap. IV, dub. IV; Diana, *op. cit.*, VII, tr. 8, resol. 19, p. 299; Molina, *De justitia et jure*, I, tr. 2, disp. 38; Carrière, *De justitia et jure*, I: p. 122, no. 146.

soever.[154] 3) Goods left to a slave absolutely, without any condition being placed but with no reference to the master, e.g., for service rendered or on account of industry, or work done: this seems to be given not to the master but only to the slave.[155] 4) Something which is given as compensation or as solace for pain suffered by a slave, not that the master be enriched.[156] This compensation goes to him as a man and he has dominium over it.[157] 5) The slave may keep whatever he gains by the use of his *peculium* or other goods he has as his own. It is to be understood that such business transacted or any gambling done must be done in this case without prejudice to the master.[158] 6) The slave may keep what he retains of foods that could have been consumed by him without prejudice to this master. If the food is rationed then he may keep whatever he saves of the amount given if he does not thereby diminish his strength. If he may eat as much as he wishes, then he may take as much as would be required to satisfy his appetite. Some seem to think that in this matter the slave rarely sins mortally; however, they agree that it depends on how unwilling the master is.[159] 7) The slave may keep gains made by labors done after and beyond the works required by the master.[160] 8) The slave may retain money received as compensation for the illicit and sinful use of the boy or for illicitly working on Sunday contrary to the wishes of

[154] Thus Lessius, Molina, Diana, Carrière, *op. cit., loc. cit.;* De Lugo, *op. cit.,* I, disp. III, sec. III, no. 53-55.

[155] Lessius, *loc. cit.*

[156] Lessius, Diana, Carrière, *loc. cit.*

[157] Molina, *loc. cit.,* cf. De Lugo, *op. cit.,* I, disp. 3, sec. 3, no. 46 for opposite view.

[158] Diana, *op. cit.,* VII, tr. 8, resol. 28, pp. 299 f; Lessius, *op. cit.,* sec. I, cap. 4, dub. 4; Carrière, *op. cit.,* I, p. 122, no. 146; Molina, *op. cit.,* I, tr. 2, disp. 38; cf. De Lugo, *op. cit.,* I, disp. III, sec. 3, no. 50 for opposite view.

[159] Diana, *op. cit.,* VII, tr. 8, resol. 32, p. 300 and resol. 31, p. 300; De Lugo, *op. cit.,* disp. 3, sec. 3, no. 66; Lessius, *op. cit.,* sec. I, cap. 4, dub. 4.

[160] Lessius, *loc. cit.;* Diana, *op. cit.,* VII, tr. 8, resol. 31, 32 and 19.

the master.[161]

Diana, in explaining his view, said that gains must be made by work done over and above the work required by the master, and it must not notably weaken them. The principle that whatever is acquired is acquired for the master is to be understood concerning the time deputed to the services of the master. For slaves are not possessed by masters as fields and beasts, that they always bear fruit for their masters. Hence, whatever they thus acquire, they acquire for themselves in conscience regardless of what they may be in the external forum, provided they do not thereby defraud the masters of services owed to them and do not thereby weaken their strength, which should be judged by the prudent confessor. Hence, they may retain and spend these things even if the master is unwilling and the master sins mortally by theft against the slaves, if he takes these things from them when they are unwilling. Such a view, he said, seems rational and probable.[162]

States' laws in the United States. By state laws, a slave was in absolute bondage. He had no civil rights, and could hold no property except at the will and pleasure of his master. His master was his guardian and protector, and all his rights and acquisitions were in the hands of his master. A slave was admitted to be a rational being endowed with volition and understanding like the rest of mankind, but whatever he lawfully acquired and gained possession of by finding or otherwise, was possessed by the master. A slave could not receive property by descent or purchase.[163]

Quite generally slaves could make no contracts. Note the law of South Carolina as a sample.

[161] Molina, *loc. cit.;* Diana, *op. cit.*, VII, tr. 8, resol. 31, p. 300. Cf. De Lugo, *op. cit.*, disp. 3, sec. 3, no. 47, who even in this case held the opposite view.

[162] Diana, *op. cit.*, VII, tr. 8, resol. 32, p. 300; cf. De Lugo, *op. cit.*, I, disp. 3, sec. 3 for opposite view.

[163] *Brandon et al* v. *Planters and Merchants Bank of Huntsville* (Jan. Term, 1828), I, Stewart's Rep., Wheeler, *op. cit.*, p. 5; cf. La. Act of 1806, *Revised Statutes (1852)*, p. 522.

It shall not be lawful for any slave to buy, sell,
trade, etc., any goods without license from the
owner, etc., nor shall any slave be permitted to
keep any boat, periauger or canoe, or raise or
breed, for the benefit of such slave, any horses,
mares, cattle, sheep or hogs, under pain of for-
feiting all the goods, etc., and it shall be lawful for any person whatsoever to seize and take
away from any slave all such goods, etc., and
to deliver the same into the hands of any justice of the peace, nearest to the place, where
the seizure shall be made and such justice shall
take the oath of the persons making such seizures concerning the master thereof: and if said
justice shall be satisfied such seizures was made
according to the law, he shall pronounce and declare the goods so seized to be forfeited and order
the same to be sold at public outcry, one-half of
the monies arising from such sale to go to the
state, and the other half to him or them that sue
for the same.[164]

Legislative enactments forbade slaves to hire themselves
out.[165] Yet in practice hiring out did exist and slaves did
cultivate gardens.

---

[164] Act of 1740, *James' Digest*, pp. 385 f; cf. (Ky.) *Littell and
Swigert's Digest*, p. 1151; (N. C.) *Haywood's Manual*, p. 525; *Miss.
Revised Code* (1848), p. 519.

[165] (S. C.) *James' Digest*, p. 385; (Ga.) *Prince's Digest*, p. 788;
(Ky.) *Littell and Swigert's Digest*, p. 1151; (N. C.) *Haywood's Manual*, p. 526.

VII. SUMMARY AND CONCLUSIONS

I. SUMMARY

Briefly, the background of slavery was considered in chapter two. The slave-trade was summarized, then the slavery controversy was considered. The arguments for abolition given by its proponents were indicated along with the pro-slavery arugments. The reasons why Catholics tried to keep aloof from the slavery controversy were indicated.

In the following chapter the definition of slavery given by Kenrick and the theologians was compared with laws and customs concerning slavery in the United States. It became evident that two completely different things were meant when the word slavery was used. To the theologian, the slave was a human being, made to the image and likeness of God. He consequently had definite rights. By the laws of the day in the United States and even more so sometimes in practice, the slave was a mere chattel, a piece of property, an animal, who had no rights. What laws there were, were made more for the protection of the master. At times, some feeble attempts were made to make laws that seem to be for the protection of the slave, but these were always made ineffectual by some legal escape. One of the biggest difficulties, was the fact that a slave could never be a witness in court.

According to the theologians, the master, in accepting the work of the slave, had an obligation to support him.[1] Some authors further distinguish between slaves condemned

[1] It should be pointed out here that although Kenrick in his definition of slavery seemed to indicate that the relationship of the master to the slave was based on justice, cf. *supra*, p. 55, yet in speaking of the obligation of the master to feed, etc., his slaves, he seemed to consider it only an obligation based on charity. Cf. *supra*, p. 65.

to servitude because of crime and those enslaved by contract. The former could be given plain or coarse foods, while the latter should be treated more benignly. Kenrick held that the slave of his day or his ancestors were unjustly taken by force from Africa. Yet from what has been seen, it would appear that slaves were, with the possible exception of house servants who ate in the "big house," given food that merely kept them alive, but was hardly appealing or satisfying. One really wonders why Kenrick, if he actually knew what slaves were generally fed, and how they were maintained in general, would issue the warning that it is not fitting to give them things too delicate. Yet, he indicated that he did know this, for he mentioned that they were usually given only Indian corn and sometimes pork meat.

While all the theologians, including Kenrick, cringe at the very idea of selling slaves, they admitted that it was intrinsically lawful to do so. But the sale that they only reproachfully admitted as lawful, differs greatly from the frequent sales practiced in the nineteenth century in the United States. Slaves seem to have been bred solely for sale in the internal slave-trade. The only reason for sale in many cases was pecuniary gain. One wonders how this is sufficient motive for the indiscriminate selling of human beings, separating them from their families. One considers the possibility of the words of Pope Gregory XVI on the slave-trade applying to this internal trade. He forbade as unworthy of the name of the Christian, the practice of reducing the Indian or Negroes to slavery and the "inhuman trade by which Negroes, as if they were not men, but mere animals, howsoever reduced to slavery, are without any distinction, contrary to the laws of justice and humanity, bought, sold and doomed, sometimes to the most severe and exhausting labors."[2]

---

[2] "... admonemus et obtestamur in Domino vehementer, ne quis audent in posterum vexare aut spoliare huic bonis, aut in servitutem redigere, vel aliis talia in eos patrantibus auxilium aut favorem prae-

By slavery, the theologians admitted that the master has the right to the work of his slaves. Yet, it would seem to be implied, especially when they speak of men selling themselves into slavery by contract, that they would not be expected to do more work than they would, were they working for themselves. One can scarcely justify that condition of work where the overseer stood over the row of slaves lashing them time and again to force them to produce more. Then, too, Kenrick and the other American teachers of the day seemed to fail to take into consideration the fact that the European theologians looked upon the work of slaves from the standpoint of considerations of their day when the Church instituted many holy days for the sake of the weary slaves or serfs. These did not exist here in the United States.

The master could punish the slaves—if such were necessary to force them to fulfill their part of the contract—they maintained, but they referred to punishment which is fitting and just for a human being, made to the image of the Creator, and consequently their equal. Was such the case, however, in the American institution of slavery?

Thus one would conclude that the slavery about which the older theologians spoke and whose teaching Kenrick, England and the other American divines to a great extent adopted, was quite a different thing from the slavery which was practiced in this country. They were using terms in an entirely different manner from the writers of the day.

While Kenrick's general treatment of slavery is not very orderly, it does contain a summary of the points made by the leading theologians. He was in agreement with the theologians in maintaining that slavery as he defined it, is not contrary to the natural law. Like the others, he used

stare, seu exercere inhumanum illud commercium quo nigritae, tamquam si non homines sed plura putaque animantia forent, in servitutem utcumque redacti, sine ullo discrimine contra justitiae et humanitatis jura emuntur, vendiuntur, ac durissimis interdum laboribus exantlandis dovoventur..." Gregory XVI, "In supremo apostolatus," *Collectanea S. Cong. De Propaganda Fide,* I: no. 891, p. 505.

arguments from Holy Scripture, the Fathers, and the councils of the Church. Likewise, he gave the four titles generally accepted by the other theologians, namely, capture in war, sale, punishment for crime and nativity. He accepted the latter title without question. While this title was sanctioned by Roman Law and later adopted in the various states of the American Union, it seems that it requires the support of the civil law for validity as some of the theologians observed. To accept it on its own merits would seem to justify chattel slavery. Yet Kenrick rejected chattel slavery, teaching that slaves are human beings.

As was observed, it seems impossible to agree completely with Kenrick's opinion on domestic slavery. It seems to be impossible to accept his opinion that the lapse of a long time healed the defect in the title by which slaves were held. Besides the fact that the conditions required before prescription can be used, seem to have been lacking, there is the fact that canon law of the day decreed that prescription could not be used against liberty. It seems strange that Kenrick who is usually very respectful to all law, overlooked this fact.

One might agree with the opinion to which Kenrick hinted but did not develop—that because of the social and economic arguments vehemently proposed by the opponents of abolition, the state for the common good could have been justified in limiting the liberties of the slaves temporarily. In reality, the arguments against emancipation were not as valid as was claimed. The events that followed the Civil War demonstrate this.

However, it should be pointed out that many evils—social and economic—were suffered by the whites and by the Negroes as a result of emancipation. Further, it must be borne in mind that had the South not seceded, the lot of the emancipated slaves would have been much more difficult. For, as a result of the war, the Federal Government stepped in and in a great measure protected the newly emancipated slaves.

Some criticism may be given to the effect that Kenrick in giving this opinion placed no limits of time on the toleration of slavery. It would seem that he was content to allow slavery to become a permanent condition. It is impossible **to** approve of this. For in the state, the ultimate purpose is not the good, or seeming good of the body politic, but of the individual members that compose it. These latter being persons have a destiny of their own, and cannot be made mere instruments for promoting the good of any other persons in the created universe. The state is established wholly for the good of the individuals, not the members for the state.[3] As was pointed out, the good of the whites as well as of the Negroes seemed to demand gradual emancipation.

Yet Kenrick seemed to have been satisfied to let conditions remain in *statu quo.* He regretted that the slaves were held in a condition of ignorance and degradation yet he taught that since the laws were such, nothing should be attempted against the laws but that masters should be encouraged to treat their slaves kindly and slaves were to be encouraged to obey their masters thinking of their future reward.

It would seem that a progressive theologian should have thought of social improvement and should have given his pastoral advice accordingly. But a man is influenced greatly by the conditions of the time in which he lives.

Kenrick did not limit his considerations of slaves to the retention of the Negroes as slaves, but throughout his work made frequent reference to them in discussing the various problems. While he did allow the retention of slaves, he demonstrated his solicitude—and that of the Church—for these unfortunate creatures who should receive at least a minimum of spiritual care to make possible their salvation. He therefore specifically mentioned slaves in treating the various sacraments and the obligations of Christians. Kenrick strongly insisted that the God-given rights of

[3] Cahill, *The Framework of a Christian State*, p. 280.

slaves be assured to them. His was merely the century-old traditional teaching of the Catholic Church.

He pointed out, therefore, that since slaves had a right to be instructed, their masters had a corresponding obligation to see that it was done. Their right to Baptism was likewise indicated. Kenrick also warned priests that they had a duty to give the Bread of Life to slaves who had a right to it.

Slaves further had the right to marry. This right is so basic that they might do so even should the master oppose the marriage, and the civil law forbid it. They may marry the persons of their choice, even if that person be of a different race, notwithstanding the prohibition. In such cases, some practical observations were proposed by Kenrick for the celebration of marriage. In all these matters, involving slaves' rights, it follows that the master had an obligation of not impeding the exercise of that right.

Even in the case where custom sanctioned the practice of indiscriminate sale, and the law offered no opposition, Kenrick clearly taught that the master had a moral obligation not to separate married persons, unless there was a grave justifying cause.

Kenrick's knowledge of the real situation that existed is made manifest in his treating of such points as work on Sunday, eating meat on Friday, and the possibility that many marriages of infidel slaves were invalid. In all these matters he gave his opinion as to what should be done in practice, and his reasons for such an opinion.

Likewise, in speaking of the obligations of the slaves toward their masters, Kenrick held a just conservative view. He taught that slaves should obey their masters. This is only just if it is presupposed—as Kenrick did in treating of the obligations of the master toward the slave—that the masters justly provided for all the necessities of the slave. For if the master fulfills his part of the contract by providing for the slave, the slave should fulfill his part by doing the work assigned to him by the master. Moreover, the community life of the plantation called for certain rules and regulations that needed to be observed for the common good of all concerned. But it was pointed out that obedience did not oblige when a higher law intervened. Likewise it was shown that the slave was not required by Kenrick to obey if the master, by his command, invaded the natural rights of the slaves.

Then, too, considering the master and slave as being under a contract, the one to supply maintenance the other to give his services for life, it would normally be wrong for the slave to break the contract by running away. Kenrick did not give a very definite view in this matter. He merely noted that St. Paul sent back Onesimus to Philemon, etc. He held that those who had escaped could not be morally required to return to their masters because the ancestors of the slaves were unjustly enslaved and because the fear of punishment they would receive would be so great.[4] But he noted how impractical this would be because of the federal law to the contrary. He said that a fugitive, who would come to confession should not be refused absolution.

In the matter of slaves obtaining liberty, Kenrick took a sane conservative view, saying that the manumission of slaves is praiseworthy if it can be done with benefit to the slave and without harm to the country. He might have pointed out—as did some of the other theologians—that once a master enters a contract with a slave for self-purchase he must fulfill it for the slave retains his natural rights as a man even though he has no civil rights.

---

[4] "... eorum majores injuria videantur ex Africa huc traducti..." Kenrick *Theologia moralis*, tr. V, cap. VI, no. 40. "... Si autem lateat, et ad sacrum tribunal accedat peccata deponendi causa, non videtur repelli posse ab voluntate numquam revertendi ad herum; nam poenae metus adeo gravis, ut nemo teneatur cum tanto sui discrimine ad pristinam conditionem preterquam quod liberatis dispendium non nisi ex necessitate quicquam censeatur pati, praesertim quum nullo sui actu amiserit sed ex majorum suorum calamitate," Kenrick, *op. cit.*, tr. V, cap. VI, no. 41.

Kenrick was very definite in his condemnation of those who abduct free persons and reduce them to slavery. He also showed his knowledge of the current practices by expressly condemning those who forced or tricked Negroes to go from a free state into a slave state and called for their restitution to liberty.

In the matter of theft or damage to the property of the master or other persons Kenrick's teaching is again conservative. In a certain sense he was quite lenient to the slaves insofar as he taught that they would scarcely be required to make restitution from their *peculium*, for things taken from the master. On the other hand, when one realizes that the masters frequently did not live up to their part of the contract by supplying decent sustenance, one wonders if such thefts might not be considered occult compensation.

II. Conclusion

Hence, it can be concluded that Kenrick's treatment of the matter of slavery was a definite contribution insofar as he gave a definite theological opinion on a contemporary problem which vexed the people of his day, applying accepted basic principles to current situations. It was evident that Kenrick had American problems foremost in his mind as he wrote his entire text on Moral Theology. His opinion on slavery that was studied in this dissertation had to be gathered from various sections of his two volumes.

However, it must be pointed out that in one sense he failed insofar as he did not pointedly state that when he taught that slavery is not contrary to the natural law and when he permitted slavery to be continued for the sake of society he was not talking about slavery as it existed in practice in America, but slavery as defined by him and the theologians. Certainly no theologian could have permitted slavery as it frequently existed in practice in America. There was equivocal usage of the word slavery that should have been more clearly pointed out.

Then, too, it would seem that he should have more definitely pointed out the obligations of the state to work toward future emancipation. It would seem that for fear of being considered a protagonist of abolition, he avoided any mention of striving toward giving the slaves the liberty that he admitted had been unjustly taken from them. It would seem—possibly for the same reason—that at times his teachings concerning relationships of slaves and masters favored the side of the masters. The slavery controversy was a very heated one. Perhaps even the great mind of Francis Patrick Kenrick could not think completely objectively amidst such tension.

BIBLIOGRAPHY

A. SOURCES

American Colonization Society, *The African Repository*, vols. 1-67 (Mar. 1825-Jan. 1892) Washington, 1826-1892.

American Colonization Society, *Annual Report*, 1st-91st, (1818-1908). Washington, D.C., 1818-1910.

The American Digest. Century edition, 50 vols. St. Paul: West Publishing Co., 1897-1904.

Annals of Congress.

Annuario Pontificio per l'anno 1948. Citta' del Vaticano: Typographia Poliglotta Vaticana, 1948.

Bullarium Benedicti XIV, 4 vols. Prati: Typographia Aldena, 1845-1847.

Bullarium diplomatum et privilegiorum sanctorum romanorum pontificum, 24 vols., Taurensis Editio. Augustae Tanurinorum, 1857-1872.

The Catholic Encyclopedia. Edited by Charles G. Herberman, Edward A. Pace, Conde B. Pallen Thomas J. Shahan, John J. Wynne. 15 vols. New York: Robert Appleton Co., 1907-1912.

Cobb, Howell, (ed.), *Analysis of the statutes of Georgia in general use, with the form and precedents necessary to the practical operation, and an appendix*. New York: Edward O. Jenkins, 1846.

Code of Mississippi, compiled by A. Hutchinson. Jackson, Miss.: Price and Fall, State printers, 1848.

Code of Virginia Published Pursuant to an Act of the General Assembly of Virginia Passed on 15 August 1849. Richmond: William F. Richie, 1849.

Codex iuris canonici. Rome. 1917.

Collectanea S. Congregationis De Propaganda Fide, 2 vols. Rome: Typographia Polyglotta, 1907.

Commanger, Henry Steele (ed.), *Documents of American History*. 3rd ed. New York: F. S. Crofts & Co., 1943.

Concilia Provincialia Baltimori Habita ab anno 1829 usque ad annum 1849. 2nd ed. Baltimore: John Murphy & Co., 1851.

The consolidation and revision of the statutes of the State (Louisiana) *of general nature. Prepared by Levi Pierce, Miles Taylor, William W. King, Commissioners appointed by the State*. New Orleans: Bee Office, 1852.

Decretales D. Gregori IX suae integritate una cum glossis restitutae cum privilegio Gregori XIII et aliorum principum. Rome: In Aedibus Populi Romani, 1582.

Decretum Gratiani emendatum et observationibus illustratum una cum glossis Gregori XIII Pont. Max. jussi editum. Rome: In Aedibus Populi Romani, 1582.

Denzinger, Henricus, *Enchiridion symbolorum*, Edition 18-20, Freiburg: Herder & Co., 1932.

Ditcionaire apologetique de la foi catholique. Edited by A. D'Ales. 4 vols. Paris: Beauchesne, 1911-1922.

Dictionaire de theologie catholique. Edited by A. Vancant and E. Mangenot, 15 vols. Paris: Letouzey et Ane, 1903-1946.

Dictionary of American Biography. Edited by Allen Johnson. 20 vols. New York: Scribner's Sons, 1928-1936.

A Digest of the Laws of the State of Alabama. Compiled by Appointment and under the Authority of the General Assembly by Harry Toulmin. Cahawka: Ginn & Curtis, 1823.

A Digest of the Laws of the State of Georgia. Compiled by the appointment and under the authority of the General Assembly by Oliver H. Prince. Athens: Pub. by the compiler, 1837.

Digest of the Statute Laws of Kentucky. Compiled by William Littell and Jacob Swigart, printed under the patronage of the Legislature. Frankfort: Kendall and Russell, printers for the State, 1822.

A Digest of the Laws of the State of South Carolina, containing all such Acts, parts of Acts of a General and Permanent Nature, as are now in force, under proper heads. Compiled by Benjamin James. Columbia: D. & J. J. Faust, 1822.

The Encyclopedia Americana, 1943 ed. 30 vols. New York and Chicago: Americana Corporation, 1943.

Encyclopedia of Religion and Ethics. Edited by James Hastings. 12 vols. New York: Charles Scribner's Sons, 1908-1922.

Encyclopedia of the Social Sciences. Edwin A. A. Seligman, Editor-in-chief, 15 vols. New York: The Macmillan Co., 1930-1935.

Guilday, Peter K., (ed.), *The National Pastorals of The American Hierarchy* (1792-1919). Washington, D.C.: The National Catholic Welfare Council, 1923.

Haywood, John, *A manual of the laws of North Carolina, arranged under distinct heads and in alphabetical order.* Raleigh: J. Gales, printers to the State, 1801.

The Jewish Encyclopedia, Isidore Singer, managing editor. 12 vols. New York and London: Funk and Wagnalls, 1901-1905.

Kenrick, Francis Patrick, *Theologia moralis*, 3 vols. Philadelphia: Eugene Cummiskey, 1840-1843.

———, *Theologia moralis*, 2 vols. Mechlin & Baltimore: H. Dessain, 1860-1861.

Leonis XIII Pontificis Maximi Acta. 23 vols. Rome: Typographia 1881-1905.

Mansi, Joannis (ed.), *Sacrorum Conciliorum nova et amplissima collectio.* 53 vols. in 59. Paris: Arnhem, Leipzig, 1901-1927.

Migne, J. P. (ed.), *Patrologiae Cursus Completus.* Series Latina, 221 vols. Paris, 1844-1864.

Migne, J. P. (ed.), *Theologiae cursus completus.* Paris: J. P. Migne, 1845-1860.

Prince, Oliver, *A Digest of the Laws of the State of Georgia.* Compiled by the appointment and under the authority of the General Assembly. Athens: the author, 1837.

The Public Statutes at Large of the United States of America. 60 vols. edited by authority of Congress, 1845-present. Washington,D.C.: The Government Printing Office, 1946.

Richardson, James D. (ed.), *A Compilation of the Messages and Papers of the Presidents, 1789-1897.* Washington, D.C.: Government Printing Office, 1897.

Schroeder, Henry Joseph, O.P., *Disciplinary Decrees of the General Councils.* St. Louis, Mo. and London: B. Herder Book Co., 1937.

Treaties, Conventions, Concluded between Liberia and Foreign Powers 1848-1890. Monrovia, published by the Department of State, 1906.

Wheeler, Jacob D., *A Practical Treatise on the Laws of Slavery.* New York: Allan Pollock, Jr., 1856.

B. Books

Adams, Alice B., *The Neglected Period of Anti-slavery* (1808-1831). Boston and London: Ginn & Co., 1908.

Alexander, William T., *History of the Colored Race in America,* New Orleans: Palmetto Pub. Co., 1887.

Allard, Paul, *Les esclaves chretiens, deuis les premiers temps de l'eglise jusqu'a la fin de la domination romaine en accident.* 3rd ed. Paris: V. Lecoffre, 1900.

Allen, Gardner Wild, *The Trustees of Donations for Education in Liberia.* Boston: Thos. Todd Co., 1923.

Alphonsus di Ligori, St., *Theologia moralis,* 2 vols. Augustae Taurinorum: Ex typis Hyacinthi Marietti, 1879.

American Board of Commissioners for Foreign Missions, *Report of the Committee on Anti-Slavery Memorials.* Boston: Press of T. R. Marvin, 1845.

Antoine, Paul Gabriel, S.J., *Theologia moralis universa*. Avenione: Typis Francisci Seguin, 1818.

Aptheker, Herbert, *American Negro Slave Revolts*. New York: Columbia University Press, 1943.

Aquinas, St. Thomas, *Opera omnia*. Eds. E. Frette and P. Mare, 34 vols. Paris: L. Vives, 1871-1880.

Armistead, William, *Calumny Repudiated by Facts from Liberia*. New York: W. Harned, Anti-Slavery Office, 1848.

Austin, George Lowell, *The Life and Times of Wendell Phillips*. Boston: Lee and Shepherd, 1888.

Balmes, Rev. J., *European Civilization*. Baltimore and New York: John Murphy Co., 1850.

Barrow, M. A., *Slavery in the Roman Empire*. New York: Lincoln MacVeagh, 1928.

Bassett, John Spencer, *The Federalist System*. Vol. 11. A. B. Hart, editor, *The American Nation: A History*, 28 vols.; New York: Harper and Bros. 1904-1918.

Baudier, Roger, *The Catholic Church in Louisiana*. New Orleans: A. W. Hyatt Stationery Mfg. Co., Ltd., 1939.

Blake, William O., *The History of Slavery and the Slave-Trade*. Columbus, O.: H. Miller, 1860.

Bouscaren, Lincoln T., *The Canon Law Digest*, 2 vols. Milwaukee: The Bruce Publishing Co., 1943.

Bowditch, William, *The Anti-Slavery Reform*. Boston: Robert F. Wallcut, 1850.

The British and Foreign Anti-Slavery Society, *Slavery and the Internal Slave-Trade in the United States of North America*. London: Thomas Ward & Co., 1841.

Brown, George William, *The Economic History of Liberia*. Washington, D.C.: The Associated Publishers Co., 1941.

Brownson, Orestes A., *Works*, Edited by Henry Brownson, 20 vols. Detroit: Thorndike, Nours Pub., 1884.

Buckingham, James Silk, *The Slave States of America*. London, Paris: Fischer, Son & Co., 1842.

Buckland, W. W., The Roman Law of Slavery. Cambridge University Press, 1908.

Buxton, Sir Thomas F., *The Slave-Trade and Remedy*. London: John Murray, 1840.

Cahill, E., S.J., *The Framework of a Christian State*. Dublin: M. H. Gill & Son, 1932.

Cairnes, John Elliott, *The Slave Power*, London: Macmillan & Co., 1863.

Calhoun, John, *Speeches*, Edited by Richard K. Cralle, 6 vols. New York: D. Appleton & Co., 1856-1861.

Calhoun, John, *The Works of John C. Calhoun*, 6 vols. New York: D. Appleton & Co., 1854-1861.

Cardenas, Joannis de, *Crisis theologica*. Venice: Nicholas Pezzana, 1696.

Carey, Henry Charles, *The Slave-Trade Domestic and Foreign*. Phila.: A Hart, 1853.

Carey, Matthew, *Letters on the Colonization Society and its Probable Results Addressed to the Honorable C. F. Mercer, N. H. R. U. S.* Phila.: Stereotyped by L. Johnson, 1832.

Carrière, Joseph, *Praelectiones theologicae de justitia et jure*. 3 vols. Louvain: C. J. Fonteyn, 1845.

Castelein, A., S.J., *Institutiones philosophiae moralis et socialis*, 9th ed. Societe Belge de Librairie, 1899.

Cathrein, Victor, S.J., *Philosophia moralis*. Friburg: Herder & Co., 1927.

Catterall, Helen Honor (Tunnicliff), *Judicial Cases Concerning American Slavery and the Negro*. Washington, D.C.: Carnegie Institute of Washington, 1926-1936.

Channing, Edward, *The Jeffersonian System*. Vol. 12 of *The American Nation: A History*. Edited by A. B. Hart, 28 vols. New York: Harper & Bros., 1904-1918.

Channing, Edward, *A History of the United States*, 6 vols. New York: Macmillan Co., 1919-1936.

Child, Lydia Maria, *The Duty of Disobedience to the Fugitive Slave Act*. Boston: American Anti-slavery Society, 1860.

Church Anti-slavery Society, *Proceedings of the Convention met at Worcester, Mass, Mar. 1, 1859*. New York: F. Trow, 1859.

Clarke, James Freeman, *Theodore Parker and his Theology*. 2nd ed. Boston: Walker, Wise and Co., 1859.

Cochin, Austin, *The Results of Slavery*. Translated by Mary L. Booth. Boston: Walker, Wise & Co., 1863.

Coffin, Levi, *Reminiscences of Levi Coffin*. Cincinnati: Western Tract Society, 1876.

Collins, Winfield, Hazlitt, *The Domestic Slave Trade of the Southern States*. New York: Broadway Pub. Co., 1904.

Colver, Rev. Nathaniel, *The Fugitive Slave Bill or God's Law Paramount to the Laws of Men*. Boston: J. W. Hewes & Co., 1850.

Congregational Ministers. *Report of the Committee on Slavery to the Convention of the Congregational Ministers of Massachusetts, presented May 30, 1849*. Boston: T. R. Marvin, 1849.

Cromwell, John Wesley, *The Negro in American History*. Washington, D.C.: The American Negro Academy, 1914.

Cunningham, Andrew McLaughlin, *The Confederation and the Con-*

stitution. Vol. 10 of *The American Nation: A History.* New York and London: Harper Bros., 1905.

Davis, Henry, S.J., *Moral and Pastoral Theology,* 4 vols., 5th ed. New York: Sheed and Ward, 1946.

Diana, Antonius, *Resolutiones morales,* 7 tomae. Venice, 1728.

Douglass, Frederick, *My Bondage and Freedom,* New York: Miller, Orton and Mulligan, 1855.

DuBois, William Edward Burghardt, *The Suppression of the African Slave-Trade,* 1638-1870. New York: Longmans, Gree & Co., 1896.

DuBois, William Edward Burghardt, *Black Reconstruction.* New York: Harcourt, Brace & Co., 1935.

Elliott, Charles, *Sinfulness of American Slavery.* Cincinnati: L. Swormstedt & J. H. Power, 1850.

England, John, *Works.* Edited by the Most Rev. Sebastian G. Messmer. Cleveland, Ohio: The Arthur H. Clark Co., 1908.

Fox, Early Lee, *The American Colonization Society 1817-1840.* Johns Hopkins University Studies in History and Political Sciences, Series 37, No. 3. Baltimore: Johns Hopkins University Press, 1919.

Frobenius, Leo, *Im schatten des Kongostaates.* Berlin: G. Reiner, 1907.

———, *Der schwarze Dekameron.* Berlin: Vita deutches verlaghaus, 1910.

———, *Kulturgeschichte Africas.* Zurich: Phaedon-verlag, 1935.

Frothingham, Octavius Brooks, *Theodore Parker: A Biography.* Boston: J. R. Osgood & Co., 1874.

———, *Gerrit Smith: A Biography.* New York: G. P. Putnam's Sons, 1909.

Garrison, William Lloyd, *Selections from his Writings and Speeches.* Boston: R. F. Wallcut, 1852.

Gerdil, Giacinto Sigismondo, *Opere edite ed inedite,* 7 vols., Florence: Giuseppe Celli, 1844-1850.

Goodell, William, *Slavery and Anti-slavery.* New York: H. Harned, 1852.

Goodell, William, *Our National Charters.* New York: American Abolition Society, 1857.

Greenslet, Ferris, *James Russell Lowell.* Boston and New York: Houghton, Mifflin Co., 1912.

Gray. Thomas, *Sermon delivered in Boston before the African Society on the 14th day of July 1818: the Anniversary of the Abolition of Slave Trade.* Boston: Parmenter and Norton, 1818.

Grimke, Archibald Henry, *William Lloyd Garrison, the Abolitionist.* New York: Funk & Wagnalls, 1891.

Guilday, Peter K., *The Life and Times of John Carroll, Archbishop of Baltimore (1735-1815).* 2 vols. New York: The Encyco- pedia Press, 1922.

———, *The Life and Times of John England,* 2 vols. New York: The America Press, 1927.

———, *A History of the Councils of Baltimore 1791-1884.* New York: The Macmillan Co., 1932.

Hall, Marshall, *The Two-fold Slavery of the United States.* London: Adam Scott, 1854.

Hart, Albert, Buchnell, *Slavery and Abolition.* Vol. 16 of *The Amer- ican Nation: A History.* Edited by A. B. Hart, 2 vols. New York and London: Harper and Bros., 1904-1918.

Harvey, Rudolph John, *The Metaphysical Relation Between Person and Liberty.* Washington, D.C.: The Catholic University of American Press, 1942.

Hefele, Rev. Charles Joseph, *History of the Councils of the Church,* vol. 1. Translated by Henry Nutcombe Oxenham. Edinburgh: T. & T. Clark, 1876.

Helper, Hirton Rowan, *The Impending Crisis of the South: How to Meet It.* New York: Burdick Bros., 1857.

Helps, Sir Arthur, *The Conquerors of the New World and their Bondsmen,* 2 vols. London: W. Pickering, 1848-1852.

———, *The Spanish Conquest in America,* 4 vols. London: J. W. Parker & Son, 1855-1861.

Henkle, Henrietta, *Let my People Go.* New York and London: Harper & Bros., 1941.

Hopkins, John Henry, *A Scriptural, Ecclesiastical, and Historical View of Slavery, from the Days of the Patriarch Abraham to the Nineteenth Century.* New York: W. J. Pooley & Co., 1864.

Huberech, Charles Henry, *The Political and Legislative History of Liberia.* New York: Central Book Co., Inc., 1947.

Hughes, Most Rev. John, *Complete Works.* Edited by Lawrence Kehoe, 2 vols. New York: Lawrence Kehoe, 1865.

Hurd, John Godman, *The Law of Freedom and Bondage in the United States,* 2 vols. Boston: Little, Brown & Co., 1858.

Husslein, Joseph, S.J., *Social Wellsprings.* Milwaukee: Bruce Pub. Co., 1943.

Innes, William, *Liberia, or The Early History and Signal Preservation of the American Colony of Free Negroes on the Coast of Africa.* Edinburgh: Waugh and Innes, 1831.

Iorio, Thomas A., *Compendium theologiae moralis, juxta methodum*

Joannis Petri Gury, S.J. ad norman Codicis Iuris Canonici redactum, 5th ed. Naples: M. D'Auria, 1934.

Janet, P., *Histoire de la science politidans ses rapports avec la morale*. 2 vols. Paris: Felix Alcan, no date.

Jarrett, Bede, O.P., *Social Theories of the Middle Ages*. Westminster, Md.: Newman Book Shop, 1942.

Jenkins, William Sumner, *Pro-slavery Thought in the Old South*. Chapel Hill: University of North Carolina Press, 1935.

Jervey, T. D., *The Slave-Trade*. Columbia, S.C.: The State Co., 1925.

Johnson, Oliver, *William Lloyd Garrison and his Times*. Boston: B. B. Russell, 1880.

Kenrick, Francis Patrick, *Theologia moralis*, 3 vols. Philadelphia: Eugene Cummiskey, 1840-1843.

———, *Theologia moralis*, 2 vols. Mechlin & Baltimore: Dessain, 1860-1861.

———, *Diary and Visitation Record*. Lancaster, Pa.: Wickersham Printing Co., 1916.

The Kenrick Frenaye Correspondence, 1830-1863. Edited by F. E. Tourscher, Philadelphia: Wickersham Printing Co., 1920.

Kent, James, *Commentaries on American Law*. 4 vols. 11th ed. Edited by George F. Comstock. Boston: Little, Brown & Co., 1867.

King, Rufus, *The Life and Correspondence of Rufus King*. Edited by his grandson, Charles King. New York: P. G. Putnam's Son, 1894-1900.

Konings, A., C.SS.R., *Theologia moralis*, 2 vols, 2nd ed. St. Louis, New York: Benziger Bros., 1876.

La Farge, John, S.J., *The Race Question and the Negro*. New York: Longmans, Green and Co., 1845.

Lessius, Leonard, S.J., *De jure et justitia compendium*. Duaci: G. Peneman, 1634.

Livermore, George, *An Historical Research Respecting the Opinions of the Founders of the Republic on Negroes as Slaves, as Citizens, as Soldiers*. Boston: John Wilson & Son, 1862.

Lloyd, Arthur Young, *The Slavery Controversy, 1831-1860*. Chapel Hill, N.C.: The University of North Carolina Press, 1939.

Locke, Mary Stroughton, *Anti-slavery in America from the Introduction of African Slaves to the Prohibition of Slave Trade*. Boston: Ginn & Co., 1901.

Lowell, George, *The Life and Times of Wendell Phillips*. Boston: Lee & Shepard, 1888.

Lugenbeel, James Washington, *Sketches of Liberia*. Washington: C. Alexander, 1850.

De Lugo, Joannis, *Disputationes de justitia et jure.* Lugduni: Sump. Laurentii Arnaud et Petri Borde, 1670.

Lyonnet, D., *Appendix prima ad tractatum de justitia et jure.* Migne, *Theologiae cursus completus*, Tom. 15, 821-1007.

Manaricua, Andes E., *El matrimonio de los esclavos.* Rome: Gregorian University, 1940.

Maritain, J., *The Things that are Not Caesar's.* Translated by J. P. Scanlan, London: 1932.

Mathieson, William Low, *British Slave Emancipation, 1838-1849.* London, New York: Longmans, Green & Co., 1932.

Matlack, Lucius C., *The History of American Slavery and Methodism from 1780-1849.* New York: Lucius Mallack, 1849.

Mattingly, Mary Ramona, *The Catholic Church on the Kentucky Frontier* 1785-1812. Washington, D.C.: The Catholic University of America, 1936.

McDougall, Marian Gleason, *Fugitive Slaves.* Boston: Ginn & Co., 1891.

McKeen, Silas, *A Scriptural Argument in favor of withdrawing Fellowship from Churches and Ecclesiastical Bodies tolerating Slave-holding among them.* New York: American and Foreign Anti-Slavery Society, 1848.

McLaughlin, Andrew Cunningham, *The Confederation and the Constitution.* Vol. 10 of *The American Nation: A History.* New York: and London: Harper & Bros., 1904-1918.

McPherson, John Hanson, *History of Liberia*, Baltimore: Johns Hopkins Press, 1891.

Mellon, Matthew Taylor, *Early American Views on Negro Slavery.* Boston: Meador Pub. Co., 1934.

Merkelbach, Benedictus Henricus, O.P., *Summa theologiae moralis*, 3 vols. 3rd ed. Paris: Desclee, 1938.

Molina, Ludovicus, *De justitia et jure*, 6 tom. Fratres de Tournes: Coloniae Allobrogum, 1759.

Morce, Jedidah, D.D., *Discourse delivered at the American Meeting House in Boston, July 14, 1808.* Boston: Lincoln & Edwards, 1808.

The Negro in Virginia. Compiled by workers of the writer's program of the Works Projects Administration in the State of Virginia. New York: Hastings House, 1940.

Nolan, Hugh J., *The Most Reverend Francis Patrick Kenrick Third Bishop of Philadelphia 1830-1851.* Washington, D.C.: The Catholic University of America Press, 1948.

Noldin, H., S.J., *Summa theologiae moralis.* 3 vols. Innsbruck: F. Rauch, 1936.

Nott, Samuel, *Slavery and the Remedy.* New York: Appleton & Co., 1857.

Nott, Samuel, *The Present Crisis with a Reply and Appeal to European Advisors.* Boston: Crocker and Brewster, 1860.

Nuesse, Celestine Joseph, *The Social Thought of American Catholics, 1634-1829.* Washington, D.C.: Catholics University of America Press, 1945.

O'Brien, George, *An Essay on Medieval Economic Teaching.* New York: Longmans, Green and Co., 1920.

O'Connor, Charles, *Letter to a Committee of Merchants in New York,* Dec. 20, 1859. New York: New York Tribune, 1859.

O'Connor, Charles, *Negro Slavery not Unjust.* Speech delivered at the Union meeting at the Academy of Music, New York, Dec. 19, 1859. New York: Van Evrie, Horton & Co., 1859.

Olmsted, Frederick, *A Journey in the Seaboard Slave States with Remarks on their Economy.* New York: Dix & Edwards & Co., 1856.

————, *A Journey Through Texas.* New York: Dix, Edwards & Co., 1857.

O'Shea, John J., *The Two Kenricks,* Phila.: John J. McVey, 1904.

Paley, William, *The Principles of Moral and Political Philosophy.* 5th ed. London: F. Davis, 1788.

Parker, Theodore, *A Letter to the People of the United States Touching the Matter of Slavery.* Boston: J. Munroe & Co., 1848.

Payen, G., S.J., *De Matrimonio in missionibus ac potissimum in Sinis tractus et casus.* 2nd ed. 3 vols. Ze-ka-Wei': Typographia Y'ou-se'-we, 1935-1936.

Peabody, Ephraim, *Slavery in the United States.* Boston: C. C. Little & J. Bom, 1851.

Phillips, Ulrich B., *American Negro Slavery.* New York: D. Appleton and Co., 1918.

————, *Life and Labor in the Old South.* Boston: Little, Brown, reprint, 1941.

Phillips, Wendell, *The Philosophy of the Abolition Movement.* New York: American Anti-Slavery Society, 1869.

Polfrey, John G., *Papers on the Slave Power.* First published in "Boston Whig" in July, Aug., Sept. of 1846. Pamphlet, 2nd ed. Boston: Merrill, Cobb & Co., no date.

The Pope's Bull and the Words of Daniel O'Connell. New York: Joseph H. Ladd, no date.

Posada, Eduardo, *La ensclavitud en Colombia.* Bogota': Imprenta nacional, 1933.

Pro-slavery Argument. Essays on the subject of slavery by Chancellor Harper, Governor Hammond, Dr. Simms, and Professor Dew. Charleston, S.C.: Walker Richards & Co., 1852.

Reuter, Edward Byron, *The American Race Problem.* New York: Thomas Y. Crowell Co., 1938.

Rice, Madeline Hooke, *American Catholic Opinion in the Slavery Controversy.* New York: Columbia University Press, 1944.

Robinson, John, *The Testimony and Practice of the Presbyterian Church in Reference to American Slavery.* Cincinnati: J. D. Thorpe, 1852.

Ross, Rev. F. A., *Slavery Ordained of God.* Phila.: Lippincott & Co., 1857.

Rouse, Michael Francis (Bro. Bede, C.F.X.), *A Study of the Development of Negro Education under Catholic Auspices in Maryland and the District of Columbia.* No. 221 of the *Johns Hopkins Studies in Education.* Baltimore: Johns Hopkins Press, 1938.

Sanchez, Thomas, *Opuscula moralia,* 2 vols. Lugduni: Jacob Prost, 1635.

———, *De santo martrimonii sacramento disputationes,* 2 vols. Venice: N. Pezzane, 1712.

Seeber, Edward Derbyshire, *Anti-Slavery Opinion in France During the Second Half of the Eighteenth Century.* Baltimore: Johns Hopkins Press, 1937.

Shea, John Gilmary, *History of Catholic Church within the Limits of the U.S. from the First Attempted Colonization to the Present Time.* New York: J. G. Shea, 4 vols. 1886-1892.

Sherwood, Grace H., *The Oblates' Hundred and One Years.* New York: Macmillan Co., 1931.   . .

Siebert, Wilber Henry, *The Underground Railroad from Slavery to Freedom.* New York: Macmillan Co., 1898.

Smedley, Robert C., *History of the Underground Railroads in Chester and Neighboring Counties of Pennsylvania.* Lancaster, Pa., Office of the Journal, 1883.

Smith, Theodore Clarke, *Parties and Slavery,* 1850-1859. New York & London: Harper & Bros., 1906.

Smith, William Henry, *A Political History of Slavery.* 2 vols. New York and London: Knickerbocker Press, 1903.

Spears, John Randolf, *The American Slave Trade.* New York: C. Scribner's Son, 1900.

Starr, Eliza Allen, *The Life and Letters of Eliza Allen Starr.* Edited by Rev. James J. McGovern, D.D. Chicago: Lakeside Press, 1905.

Still, William, *The Underground Railroad.* Phila.: Porter & Coates, 1872.

Stockwell, G. S., *The Republic of Liberia*. New York: A. S. Barnes & Co., 1868.

Stroud, George M., *A Sketch of Laws Relating to Slavery in the Several States of the United States of America*, 2nd ed. Phila.: Kimbler and Sharpless, 1857.

Sunderland, La Roy, *Anti-Slavery Manual*, 2nd ed. New York: Peercy & Read, 1837.

Sweet, William Warren, *The Story of Religion in America*. New York & London: Harper & Bros., 1939.

Torey, Jesse, *A Portraiture of Domestic Slavery in the United States*. Phila.: John Bioren, 1817.

Turner, Lorenzo Dow, *Anti-Slavery Sentiment in American Literature prior to 1865*. Washington: The Association for the Study of Negro Life and History, Inc., 1929.

Tyler, Samuel, *Memoirs of Roger Brooke Taney*, LL. D. Baltimore: John Murphy & Co., 1872.

Underwood, Francis Henry, *James Russell Lowell*. Boston: J. R. Osgood & Co., 1882.

Van Evrie, John H., *Negroes and Negro Slavery*. New York: Van Evrie, Horton and Co., 1861.

Wade, G. Woosung, *Old Testament History*. New York, 1904.

Weatherford, W. D., *The Negro from Africa to America*. New York: George Doran Co., 1924.

Whittier, John Greenleaf, *Justice and Expediency*. Haverhill: C. P. Thayer & Co., 1833.

Williams, George W., *History of the Negro Race in America from 1619-1880*. 2 vols. New York: G. P. Putnam's Sons, 1883.

Williams, Geroge W., *A History of the Negro Troops in the War of Rebellion*. New York: Harper & Bros., 1888.

Wilson, Henry, *History of the Rise and Fall of Slave Power in America*, 3 vols. Boston: Houghton, Mifflin & Co., 1872-1875.

Woodson, Carter G., *The Education of the Negro Prior to 1861*. New York and London: The Knickerbocker Press, 1915.

——, *Free Negro Heads of Families in the United States in 1830*. Washington: The Association for the Study of Negro Life and History, 1924.

——, *The African Background Outlined*. Washington, D.C.: Association for the Study of Negro Life and History, Inc., 1936.

Wright, Benjamin Fletcher, Jr., *American Interpretation of the Natural Law*. Cambridge, Mass.: Harvard University Press, 1931.

C. ARTICLES

Association for the Study of Negro Life and History, "Free Negro Owners of Slaves in the United States in 1830" *JNH*, 9 (1924), 41-85.

Butsch, Joseph, S.S.J., "Catholics and the Negro," *JNH*, 2 (1917), 393-410.

Butsch, Joseph, S.S.J., "Negro Catholics in the United States," *CHR*, 3 (1917), 31-51.

Carroll, John, "Letter to Father John Thayer," *RACHS*, 20 (1909), 58-59.

————, "Will of Archbishop Carroll," *American Catholic Historical Soicety Researches*, 7: 52-55.

David, C. W. A., "The Fugitive Slave Law of 1793 and its Antecendents," *JNH*, 9 (1924), 19 ff.

Dowd, Jerome, "Slavery and the African Slave Trade," *JNH*, 2 (1917), 1-20.

Dupanloupe, Rt. Rev. Felix, Bishop of Orleans, "Reprint of the Pastoral Letter sent to his Clergy on the Subject of the Civil War in the United States, Apr. 6, 1862," *RACHS*, 25 (1914), 18-29.

Fisher, Henry P., "The Catholic Church in Liberia," *RACHS*, 30 (1929), 249-310.

Jackson, L. P., "Elizabethan Seamen and the African Slave Trade," *JNH*, 9, (1924), 1-17.

Kelly, Rev. J., "Letters to Bishop Kenrick," *RACHS*, 14 (1903), 89-91.

LaFarge, John, "The Survival of the Catholic Faith in Southern Maryland," *CHR*, 21 (1935), 1-20.

Lynch, Bishop P. N., "Letters to the Hon. J. P. Benjaman, Secretary of the State of the Confederate States," *American Catholic Historical Researches*, 22 (1905), 248-259.

Mecklin, John M., "Slave Status in the American Democracy," *JNH*, 2, (1917), 229-251.

Moran Michael, "The Writings of Francis Patrick Kenrick Archbishop of Baltimore (1797-1863)." *RACHS*, 41 (1930), 230-261.

Mosley, Joseph, S.J., "Letters of Fr. M. and Some Extracts from his Diary, 1757-1786." Edited by Edward I Devill. *RACHS*, 22 (1906), 299.

Murphy, Miriam, "Catholic Missionary Work among the Colored People of the United States, 1776-1866," *RACHS*, 35 (1924), 101-136.

Phillips, Ulrich B., "Slave Crime in Virginia," *AHR*, 22 (1914-1915), 336-340.

Riddell, William Renwick, "Fugitive Slave Law of 1793 and its Antecedents," *JNH*, 9 (1924), 18-33.

Sherwood, Henry Noble, "The Formation of the American Colonization Society," *JNH*, 2 (1917), 209-229.

Siebert, Wilbur H., "The Light on the Underground Railroad," *AHR*, 1 (1895-1896), 455-463.

Taylor, A. A., "The Negro in South Carolina," *JNH*, 9 (1924), 241-569.

Taylor, R. H., "Feeding Slaves," *JNH*, 9 (1924), 139-143.

Theobold, Stephen L., "Catholic Missionary Work among the Colored People in the United States (1776-1866)" *RACHS*, 35 (1924), 325-344.

Trunk, Joseph V., "The Philosophy of Civil Rights," *Proceedings of the American Catholic Philosophical Association.* Edited by Chas. Hart, vol. 25, Reprint: Baltimore: Wilkins Pub. Co., 1940.

Williams, Mary W., "The Treatment of Negro Slaves in the Brazilian Empire," *JNH*, 25 (1930), 315-336.

Woodson, Carter G., "The Negro from Africa to America," *JNH*, 9 (1924), 574-577.

D. Unpublished Materials

Alexander, Louise Paulette, "Anti-slavery Sentiment as Expressed through Newspapers and Periodicals 1820-1860." Unpublished Master's thesis, Howard University, Washington, D.C., 1934.

Banks, Melvin J., "The Coastwise-Slave-Trade." Unpublished Master's thesis, Howard University, Washington, D.C., 1927.

Brown, Avonia Aldora, "Anti-Slavery Societies in the South 1788-1835." Unpublished Master's thesis, Howard University, Washington, D.C., 1938.

Jones, Elsie Cabell, "Waterways of the Domestic Slave-Trade as shown by Ships Manifests, 1808-1860." Unpublished Master's thesis, Howard University, Washington, D.C., 1935.

Kelley, Walter Edward, "The Concept of the Common Good in St. Thomas." Unpublished Master's thesis, The Catholic University of America, Washington, D.C., 1938.

McConnell, Rowland Calhoun, "The Reopening of the African Slave-Trade to the United States of America, 1850-1860." Unpublished Master's thesis, Howard University, Washington, D.C., 1933.

O'Connor, George Casimir, "Catholic Education and Work Among the Negro." Unpublished Master's thesis, Catholic University of America, Washington, D.C., 1926.

ABBREVIATIONS

AAS—*Acta Apostolicae Sedis*
AHR—American Historical Review
CE—Catholic Encyclopedia
CHR—Catholic Historical Review
DAFC—*Dictionaire apologetique de la foi catholique*
DTC—*Dictionaire de theologie catholique*
EA—Encyclopedia Americana
ESS—Encyclopedia of the Social Sciences
JNH—Journal of Negro History
RACHS—Records of the American Catholic Historical Society
TCC—Migne, *Theologiae cursus completus*

VITA

Joseph Delfmann Brokhage was born in Vincennes, Indiana on October 4, 1913, the son of Louis A. Brokhage and Jessie M. Sertel Brokhage. He received his elementary education in St. Francis Xavier School at Vincennes, Indiana and his high school education at Gibault High School also in Vincennes, Indiana. He entered St. Mary's College, St. Mary, Kentucky in the Fall of 1934, where he took his junior college work. His Philosophical training was completed at St. Meinrad Seminary, St. Meinrad, Indiana. His training in theology was completed at the Gregorian University, Rome, Italy. He was ordained to the priesthood on March 19, 1939 in Rome, Italy. He received the Licentiate of Sacred Theology in July, 1939 from the Gregorian University. Subsequently he held parochial assignments as follows: St. Joan of Arc, Indianapolis, Indiana, September, 1939; Holy Rosary Church, Indianapolis, Indiana, September, 1940. Six years later he enrolled in the School of Theology of the Catholic University of America, where he studied for two years. In September, 1948 he was assigned to the Church of St. Tomas Aquinas, Indianapolis, Indiana. On May 29, 1951 he became pastor of the Church of St. Leonard of Port Maurice in West Terre Haute, Indiana and professor of philosophy at St. Mary-of-the-Woods College.

ALPHABETICAL INDEX

THE CATHOLIC UNIVERSITY OF AMERICA

STUDIES IN SACRED THEOLOGY

SECOND SERIES

1. The Right of Nations to Expand by Conquest. by Raymond De Martini, O.F.M. Pages x + 174. 1947. Price $2.00.
2. The Concept of Heresy according to Cardinal Hosius. by Francis J. Zdrodowski. Pages xiii + 83. 1947. Price $1.00.
3. A Study of the Metaphor of the Olive Tree in Romans XI. by Myles M. Bourke. Pages viii + 139. 1947. Price $1.50.
4. The Eucharistic Controversy of the Eleventh Century against the Background of Pre-scholastic Theology. by Charles E. Sheedy, C.S.C. Pages xi + 138. 1947. Price $1.50.
5. Ecce Agnus Dei! by Eric E. May, O.F.M. Cap. Pages xiv + 177. 1947. Price $2.00.
6. Sacramental Penance in the Twelfth and Thirteenth Centuries. by Joseph A. Spitzig. Pages xi + 196. 1947. Price $2.00.
7. The Nature of Sacramental Grace. by Lawrence P. Everett, C.SS.R. Pages ix + 151. 1948. Price $1.75.
8. Social Ideas in the Wisdom Literature of the Old Testament. by Joseph W. Gaspar, M.S.C. Pages xiv + 207. 1947. Price $2.25.
9. The Christology of Zeno of Verona. by Martin F. Stepanich, O.F.M. Pages xiv + 69. 1948. Price $1.00.
10. The Numerical Distinction of Sins According to the Franciscan School of the Seventeenth and Eighteenth Centuries. by Bonaventure A. Brown, O.F.M. Pages xvii + 114. 1948. Price $1.50.
11. The Measure of Responsibility in Persons Influenced by Emotion. by Virgil Patrick O'Brien, C.M. Pages ix + 81. 1948. Price $1.00.
12. A Study of Psalm 72 (71). by Roland E. Murphy, O.Carm. Pages vii + 144. 1948. Price $1.50.
13. The Offertory Rite in the Ordo Romanus Primus. by George J. Booth, S.P.M. Pages ix + 58. 1948. Price $1.00.
14. The Theophanies of the Old Testament in the Writings of St. Justin. by Benedict Kominiak, O.S.B. Pages x + 76. 1948. Price $1.00.
15. Artificial Insemination among Human Beings. by William Kevin Glover, S.M. Pages xii + 177. 1948. Price $2.00.
16. Catholic Teaching About the Morality of Falsehood. by Julius A. Dorszynski. Pages vii + 116. 1948. Price $1.50.
17. The History, Nature and Use of EPIKEIA in Moral Theology. by Lawrence Joseph Riley. Pages xi + 498. 1948. Price $5.00.
18. Charity the form of the Virtues according to Saint Thomas. by Anthony J. Falanga, C.M. Pages xvi + 265. 1948. Price $3.00.
19. The Elizabethan Puritan's Conception of the Nature and Destiny of Fallen Man. by Bart M. Reilly, S.S. Pages xvi + 59. 1948. Price $1.00.
20. The Use of Sacred Scripture in the Sermons of St. Anthony of Padua. by Louis F. Rohr, O.F.M. Pages x + 119. 1948. Price $1.50.
21. The Priesthood in the Writings of the French School: Berulle, De Condren, Olier. by Eugene A. Walsh, S.S. Pages xvii + 135. 1949. Price $1.75.
22. Catholic Teaching on the Morality of Euthanasia. by Joseph A. Sullivan. 1949. Pages xii + 85. Price $1.25.
23. The Scholastic Teaching on the Sacrament of Confirmation. by Michael Kevin O'Doherty. Pages xiii + 90. 1949. Price $1.25.
24. Angelology of the Old Testament. by William George Heidt, O.S.B. Pages vii + 119. 1949. Price $1.50.

25. **The Church and the Synagogue in St. Ambrose.** by Gregory Figueroa, S.A. Pages xxiv + 47. 1949. Price $1.00.
26. **The Dogmatic Theology on the Intention of the Minister in the Confection of the Sacraments.** by Raphael De Salvo, O.S.B. Pages xi + 115. 1949. Price $1.50.
27. **Moral Obligation of Fraternal Correction.** by Joseph A. Costello, S.M. Pages viii + 134. 1949. Price $1.50.
28. **Moral Aspects of Dishonesty in Public Office.** by William Joseph King. Pages xiii + 225. 1949. Price $2.50.
29. **The Spirit of God in the Didactic Books of the Old Testament.** by Alphonsus Benson, M.S.SS.T. Pages xvii + 96. 1949. Price $1.25.
30. **The Terminology of the Sacrament of Regeneration According to Clement of Alexandria.** by Harry A. Echle. Pages xi + 48. 1949. Price .75
31. **L'Institution Catechistique au Canada Francais.** by Fernand Porter, O.F.M. Pages xxxv + 332. 1949. Price $3.75.
32. **Moral Problems of Interracial Marriage.** by Joseph F. Doherty. Pages x + 168. 1949. Price $2.00.
33. **The Doctrine of the Effects of Extreme Unction in Its Historical Development.** by Henry S. Kryger, C.R. Pages viii + 107. 1949. Price $1.25.
34. **Orestes Brownson's Approach to the Problem of God.** by Bertin J. Farrell, C.P. Pages xiii + 140. 1950. Price $1.75.
35. **St. Gregory the Great's Concept of Papal Power.** by Neil Sharkey, C.P. Pages vii + 50. 1950. Price $.75.
36. **The Distinction between the Episcopate and the Presbyterate According to Thomistic Opinion.** by George E. Dolan, C.M. Pages vii + 173. 1950. Price $2.00.
37. **The Catholic Missions in China During the Middle Ages.** by Paul S. Hsiang. Pages xiii + 43. 1950. Price $.75.
38. **Anointing in the Old Testament.** by John J. Castelot, S.S. 1950. Price $1.25. (Microcard)
39. **Various concepts of the Essence of Original Sin Current in the Twelfth Century.** (Microcard). by William R. Murphy, S.S. 1950. Price $2.25.
40. **The Essential Structure of Marriage.** by James P. Lyons. pages vii + 51. 1950. Price $1.00.
41. **The Moral Principles Governing the Sin of Detraction and an Application of these Principles to Specific Cases.** by Kenneth B. Moore, O.Carm. Pages xii + 176. 1950. Price $2.00.
42. **De Concelebratione Eucharistica.** by Albinus Veszelovsky, O. Praem. 1950. (Microcard). Price $1.75.
43. **The Purposes of Christian Marriage.** by Francis W. Carney. pages ix + 275. 1950. Price $3.00.
44. **The Eucharistic Teaching of William Ockham.** by Gabriel N. Buesher, O.F.M. Pages xxvii + 175. 1950. Price $2.25.
45. **The Symbolism of the Baptismal Font in Early Christian Thought.** by Walter Maurice Bedard, O.F.M. Pages xv + 60. 1950. Price $1.00.
46. **State of Perfection and the Secular Priest.** by C. Harry Dukehart, S.S. 1950. (Microcard). Price $1.50.
47. **St. Augustine's 'De Fide et Operibus'.** by Gregory Lombardo, C.S.C. 1950. (Microcard). Price $1.00.
48. **Il concetto teologica de carita attraverso le maggiori interpretazioni patristiche e medievali di 1 ad Cor. XIII.** by Ruggero Balducelli, O.S.F.S. Pages xxxi + 225. 1950. Price $2.75.
49. **St. Ildephonse of Toledo LIBER DE COGNITIONE BAPTISMI.** by Method C. Billy, O.F.M. Conv. (Microcard). 1951. Price $1.50.
50. **The Theology of St. John Damascene's DE FIDE ORTHODOXA.** by Paul M. Baur. 1951 (Microcard). Price $1.00.
51. **The Apologetics of Martin John Spalding.** by Adam A. Micek. Pages xvii + 124. 1951. Price $1.50.

52. The Resurrection of the Body according to Tertullian. An analysis of DE CARNE CHRISTI and DE CARNIS RESURRECTIONE. by Firmin M. Schmidt, O.F.M.Cap. (Microcard). Price $1.50.
53. Tractatus de Spiritu Sancto Ioannis a Sancto Ioanne. by Peter Farre, O.S.B. (Microcard). 1951. Price $1.25.
54. Fear and Hope According to Saint Alphonsus Liguori. by Clayton Kramer, C.SS.R., Pages ix + 39. 1951. Price $.50.
55. Moral Theology of the Confessions of Saint Augustine. by John F. Harvey, O.S.F.S. Pages xxiv + 162. 1951. Price $2.00.
56. The DE MYSTERIIS and DE SACRAMENTIS of St. Ambrose. by Humberto Medeiros. 1951. (Microcard). Price $1.75.
57. The Nature of the Eucharistic Accidents. by Germain Williams, O.F.M. Conv. 1951. (Microcard), Price $2.00.
58. The Fruits of the Sacrifice of the Mass, according to the Council of Trent. (Microcard) by William F. Hill, S.S. 1951. Price $2.00.
59. The Concept of Charity in the Writings of St. Gregory the Great. (Microcard) by Vincent J. Nugent, C.M. 1951. Price $1.75.
60. La Doctrina Monastica de San Gregorio Magno y la "Regula Monachorum". by Olegario M. Porcel, O.S.B. 1951. Price $2.50.
61. Catholic Moral Teaching on the Distribution of Profits in the Modern Corporation. by George Francis Bardes. Pages ix + 180. 1951. Price $2.00.
62. An Historical Study of the Doctrine of the Omnipresence of God in Selected Writings between 1220-1270. by Adrian Fuerst, O.S.B. Pages ix + 259. 1951. Price $2.75.
63. St. Paul's Conception of the Priesthood of Melchisedech: an Historico-Exegetical Investigation. by Gerald Thomas Kennedy, O.M.I. 1951. pages x + 152. Price. $1.75.
64. Morality of Universal Military Conscription in Peacetime. by Robert Hammond Stafford. (Microcard) 1952. Price $1.25.
65. De Culpa Theologica in Problemata Restitutionis Damni. by F. Hubert Kostrzanski, S. O. Cist. (Microcard) 1952. Price $2.25.
66. Eternal Punishment in the Writings of Gregory the Great. by Ignatius Fonash, M.SS.SS.T. (Microcard). 1952. Price $.75.
67. The Divine Child. by Paul Bernardi, S.M.B. (Microcard) 1952. Price $1.25.
68. The Person and Work of the Holy Spirit according to the Theories of Denys Petau, S.J. Theodore de Regnon, S.J. and Matthias J. Sheeben. by Thomas William Sabrey. 1952. (Microcard). Price $1.75.
69. The Church in the Works of Leo the Great. by Eugene M. Burke, C.S.P.
70. The Moral Obligation of Voting by Titus Cranny, S.A. 1952. Pages x + 190. Price $2.00.
71. The Morality of Prizefighting. by George C. Bernard, C.S.C. 1952. pages xxvii + 152. Price $2.00.
72. St. Augustine and the Real Presence. by Augustine F. Donegan, T.O.R. 1952. (Microcard). Price $1.00.
73. The Right of the State to make Disease an Impediment to Marriage. by Joseph P. O'Brien 1952. pages vii + 150. Price $1.75.
74. Banking Profit. by William T. Cortelyou, C.M. 1952. pages xi + 221. Price $2.50.
75. Episcopal and Vatican Reaction to the Persecution of the Catholic Church in Czechoslovakia. by Ludvik Nemec. 1953. Price $1.25.
76. Catholic Ecumenism. by Edward Francis Hanahoe, S.A., 1953. viii + 182. Price $2.00.
77. The Necessity of Confession for the Sacrament of Penance. by Paul E. McKeever. 1953. pages xv + 216. Price $2.50.
78. The Moral Obligations of Catholic Civil Judges. by John Denis Davis. 1953. 231 pages. Price $2.50.
79. Catholic Moral Teaching on the Nature and Object of Conjugal Love. by Michael Francis McAuliffe. 1954. Pages xiv + 142. Price $1.75.

80. **Pere Lagrange and Bibilcal Inspiration.** by Francis J. Schroeder, S.S.J. 1954. Pages xii + 47. Price .75¢.
81. **The Recognition of the True Church according to John Henry Newman.** by J. Richard Quinn. 1954. Pages xi + 204. Price $2.50.
82. **Pneuma in the Gospels.** by Francis J. Crump, O.M.I. 1954. vii + 57 pages.
83. **Dionysius the Pseudo-Areopagite — The Ecclesiastical Hierarchy.** by Thomas Campbell, C.S.C.
84. **The Parental Obligation to Care for the Religious Education of Children within the Home with Special Attention to the Training of the pre-School Child.** by Donald M. Endebrock. 1955. 249 pages.
85. **Francis Patrick Kenrick's Opinion on Slavery.** by Joseph D. Brokhage. 1955. 259 pages.